CLEP
Analyzing and Interpreting Literature Exam

SECRETS

Study Guide
Your Key to Exam Success

DEAR FUTURE EXAM SUCCESS STORY

First of all, **THANK YOU** for purchasing Mometrix study materials!

Second, congratulations! You are one of the few determined test-takers who are committed to doing whatever it takes to excel on your exam. **You have come to the right place.** We developed these study materials with one goal in mind: to deliver you the information you need in a format that's concise and easy to use.

In addition to optimizing your guide for the content of the test, we've outlined our recommended steps for breaking down the preparation process into small, attainable goals so you can make sure you stay on track.

We've also analyzed the entire test-taking process, identifying the most common pitfalls and showing how you can overcome them and be ready for any curveball the test throws you.

Standardized testing is one of the biggest obstacles on your road to success, which only increases the importance of doing well in the high-pressure, high-stakes environment of test day. Your results on this test could have a significant impact on your future, and this guide provides the information and practical advice to help you achieve your full potential on test day.

Your success is our success

We would love to hear from you! If you would like to share the story of your exam success or if you have any questions or comments in regard to our products, please contact us at **800-673-8175** or **support@mometrix.com**.

Thanks again for your business and we wish you continued success!

Sincerely,
The Mometrix Test Preparation Team

> **Need more help? Check out our flashcards at:**
> **http://MometrixFlashcards.com/CLEP**

TABLE OF CONTENTS

INTRODUCTION _____ 1

SECRET KEY #1 – PLAN BIG, STUDY SMALL _____ 2

SECRET KEY #2 – MAKE YOUR STUDYING COUNT_____ 3

SECRET KEY #3 – PRACTICE THE RIGHT WAY _____ 4

SECRET KEY #4 – PACE YOURSELF _____ 6

SECRET KEY #5 – HAVE A PLAN FOR GUESSING _____ 7

TEST-TAKING STRATEGIES _____ 10

ANALYZING AND INTERPRETING LITERATURE ABILITIES _____ 15

ANALYZING AND INTERPRETING LITERATURE KNOWLEDGE _____ 34

CLEP PRACTICE TEST _____ 89

ANSWER KEY AND EXPLANATIONS _____ 113

HOW TO OVERCOME TEST ANXIETY _____ 125
    CAUSES OF TEST ANXIETY _____ 125
    ELEMENTS OF TEST ANXIETY_____ 126
    EFFECTS OF TEST ANXIETY _____ 126
    PHYSICAL STEPS FOR BEATING TEST ANXIETY _____ 127
    MENTAL STEPS FOR BEATING TEST ANXIETY _____ 128
    STUDY STRATEGY _____ 129
    TEST TIPS _____ 131
    IMPORTANT QUALIFICATION_____ 132

THANK YOU _____ 133

ADDITIONAL BONUS MATERIAL_____ 134

Introduction

Thank you for purchasing this resource! You have made the choice to prepare yourself for a test that could have a huge impact on your future, and this guide is designed to help you be fully ready for test day. Obviously, it's important to have a solid understanding of the test material, but you also need to be prepared for the unique environment and stressors of the test, so that you can perform to the best of your abilities.

For this purpose, the first section that appears in this guide is the **Secret Keys**. We've devoted countless hours to meticulously researching what works and what doesn't, and we've boiled down our findings to the five most impactful steps you can take to improve your performance on the test. We start at the beginning with study planning and move through the preparation process, all the way to the testing strategies that will help you get the most out of what you know when you're finally sitting in front of the test.

We recommend that you start preparing for your test as far in advance as possible. However, if you've bought this guide as a last-minute study resource and only have a few days before your test, we recommend that you skip over the first two Secret Keys since they address a long-term study plan.

If you struggle with **test anxiety**, we strongly encourage you to check out our recommendations for how you can overcome it. Test anxiety is a formidable foe, but it can be beaten, and we want to make sure you have the tools you need to defeat it.

Secret Key #1 – Plan Big, Study Small

There's a lot riding on your performance. If you want to ace this test, you're going to need to keep your skills sharp and the material fresh in your mind. You need a plan that lets you review everything you need to know while still fitting in your schedule. We'll break this strategy down into three categories.

Information Organization

Start with the information you already have: the official test outline. From this, you can make a complete list of all the concepts you need to cover before the test. Organize these concepts into groups that can be studied together, and create a list of any related vocabulary you need to learn so you can brush up on any difficult terms. You'll want to keep this vocabulary list handy once you actually start studying since you may need to add to it along the way.

Time Management

Once you have your set of study concepts, decide how to spread them out over the time you have left before the test. Break your study plan into small, clear goals so you have a manageable task for each day and know exactly what you're doing. Then just focus on one small step at a time. When you manage your time this way, you don't need to spend hours at a time studying. Studying a small block of content for a short period each day helps you retain information better and avoid stressing over how much you have left to do. You can relax knowing that you have a plan to cover everything in time. In order for this strategy to be effective though, you have to start studying early and stick to your schedule. Avoid the exhaustion and futility that comes from last-minute cramming!

Study Environment

The environment you study in has a big impact on your learning. Studying in a coffee shop, while probably more enjoyable, is not likely to be as fruitful as studying in a quiet room. It's important to keep distractions to a minimum. You're only planning to study for a short block of time, so make the most of it. Don't pause to check your phone or get up to find a snack. It's also important to **avoid multitasking**. Research has consistently shown that multitasking will make your studying dramatically less effective. Your study area should also be comfortable and well-lit so you don't have the distraction of straining your eyes or sitting on an uncomfortable chair.

The time of day you study is also important. You want to be rested and alert. Don't wait until just before bedtime. Study when you'll be most likely to comprehend and remember. Even better, if you know what time of day your test will be, set that time aside for study. That way your brain will be used to working on that subject at that specific time and you'll have a better chance of recalling information.

Finally, it can be helpful to team up with others who are studying for the same test. Your actual studying should be done in as isolated an environment as possible, but the work of organizing the information and setting up the study plan can be divided up. In between study sessions, you can discuss with your teammates the concepts that you're all studying and quiz each other on the details. Just be sure that your teammates are as serious about the test as you are. If you find that your study time is being replaced with social time, you might need to find a new team.

2

Secret Key #2 – Make Your Studying Count

You're devoting a lot of time and effort to preparing for this test, so you want to be absolutely certain it will pay off. This means doing more than just reading the content and hoping you can remember it on test day. It's important to make every minute of study count. There are two main areas you can focus on to make your studying count:

Retention

It doesn't matter how much time you study if you can't remember the material. You need to make sure you are retaining the concepts. To check your retention of the information you're learning, try recalling it at later times with minimal prompting. Try carrying around flashcards and glance at one or two from time to time or ask a friend who's also studying for the test to quiz you.

To enhance your retention, look for ways to put the information into practice so that you can apply it rather than simply recalling it. If you're using the information in practical ways, it will be much easier to remember. Similarly, it helps to solidify a concept in your mind if you're not only reading it to yourself but also explaining it to someone else. Ask a friend to let you teach them about a concept you're a little shaky on (or speak aloud to an imaginary audience if necessary). As you try to summarize, define, give examples, and answer your friend's questions, you'll understand the concepts better and they will stay with you longer. Finally, step back for a big picture view and ask yourself how each piece of information fits with the whole subject. When you link the different concepts together and see them working together as a whole, it's easier to remember the individual components.

Finally, practice showing your work on any multi-step problems, even if you're just studying. Writing out each step you take to solve a problem will help solidify the process in your mind, and you'll be more likely to remember it during the test.

Modality

Modality simply refers to the means or method by which you study. Choosing a study modality that fits your own individual learning style is crucial. No two people learn best in exactly the same way, so it's important to know your strengths and use them to your advantage.

For example, if you learn best by visualization, focus on visualizing a concept in your mind and draw an image or a diagram. Try color-coding your notes, illustrating them, or creating symbols that will trigger your mind to recall a learned concept. If you learn best by hearing or discussing information, find a study partner who learns the same way or read aloud to yourself. Think about how to put the information in your own words. Imagine that you are giving a lecture on the topic and record yourself so you can listen to it later.

For any learning style, flashcards can be helpful. Organize the information so you can take advantage of spare moments to review. Underline key words or phrases. Use different colors for different categories. Mnemonic devices (such as creating a short list in which every item starts with the same letter) can also help with retention. Find what works best for you and use it to store the information in your mind most effectively and easily.

Secret Key #3 – Practice the Right Way

Your success on test day depends not only on how many hours you put into preparing, but also on whether you prepared the right way. It's good to check along the way to see if your studying is paying off. One of the most effective ways to do this is by taking practice tests to evaluate your progress. Practice tests are useful because they show exactly where you need to improve. Every time you take a practice test, pay special attention to these three groups of questions:

- The questions you got wrong
- The questions you had to guess on, even if you guessed right
- The questions you found difficult or slow to work through

This will show you exactly what your weak areas are, and where you need to devote more study time. Ask yourself why each of these questions gave you trouble. Was it because you didn't understand the material? Was it because you didn't remember the vocabulary? Do you need more repetitions on this type of question to build speed and confidence? Dig into those questions and figure out how you can strengthen your weak areas as you go back to review the material.

Additionally, many practice tests have a section explaining the answer choices. It can be tempting to read the explanation and think that you now have a good understanding of the concept. However, an explanation likely only covers part of the question's broader context. Even if the explanation makes sense, **go back and investigate** every concept related to the question until you're positive you have a thorough understanding.

As you go along, keep in mind that the practice test is just that: practice. Memorizing these questions and answers will not be very helpful on the actual test because it is unlikely to have any of the same exact questions. If you only know the right answers to the sample questions, you won't be prepared for the real thing. **Study the concepts** until you understand them fully, and then you'll be able to answer any question that shows up on the test.

It's important to wait on the practice tests until you're ready. If you take a test on your first day of study, you may be overwhelmed by the amount of material covered and how much you need to learn. Work up to it gradually.

On test day, you'll need to be prepared for answering questions, managing your time, and using the test-taking strategies you've learned. It's a lot to balance, like a mental marathon that will have a big impact on your future. Like training for a marathon, you'll need to start slowly and work your way up. When test day arrives, you'll be ready.

Start with the strategies you've read in the first two Secret Keys—plan your course and study in the way that works best for you. If you have time, consider using multiple study resources to get different approaches to the same concepts. It can be helpful to see difficult concepts from more than one angle. Then find a good source for practice tests. Many times, the test website will suggest potential study resources or provide sample tests.

Practice Test Strategy

If you're able to find at least three practice tests, we recommend this strategy:

UNTIMED AND OPEN-BOOK PRACTICE

Take the first test with no time constraints and with your notes and study guide handy. Take your time and focus on applying the strategies you've learned.

TIMED AND OPEN-BOOK PRACTICE

Take the second practice test open-book as well, but set a timer and practice pacing yourself to finish in time.

TIMED AND CLOSED-BOOK PRACTICE

Take any other practice tests as if it were test day. Set a timer and put away your study materials. Sit at a table or desk in a quiet room, imagine yourself at the testing center, and answer questions as quickly and accurately as possible.

Keep repeating timed and closed-book tests on a regular basis until you run out of practice tests or it's time for the actual test. Your mind will be ready for the schedule and stress of test day, and you'll be able to focus on recalling the material you've learned.

Secret Key #4 – Pace Yourself

Once you're fully prepared for the material on the test, your biggest challenge on test day will be managing your time. Just knowing that the clock is ticking can make you panic even if you have plenty of time left. Work on pacing yourself so you can build confidence against the time constraints of the exam. Pacing is a difficult skill to master, especially in a high-pressure environment, so **practice is vital**.

Set time expectations for your pace based on how much time is available. For example, if a section has 60 questions and the time limit is 30 minutes, you know you have to average 30 seconds or less per question in order to answer them all. Although 30 seconds is the hard limit, set 25 seconds per question as your goal, so you reserve extra time to spend on harder questions. When you budget extra time for the harder questions, you no longer have any reason to stress when those questions take longer to answer.

Don't let this time expectation distract you from working through the test at a calm, steady pace, but keep it in mind so you don't spend too much time on any one question. Recognize that taking extra time on one question you don't understand may keep you from answering two that you do understand later in the test. If your time limit for a question is up and you're still not sure of the answer, mark it and move on, and come back to it later if the time and the test format allow. If the testing format doesn't allow you to return to earlier questions, just make an educated guess; then put it out of your mind and move on.

On the easier questions, be careful not to rush. It may seem wise to hurry through them so you have more time for the challenging ones, but it's not worth missing one if you know the concept and just didn't take the time to read the question fully. Work efficiently but make sure you understand the question and have looked at all of the answer choices, since more than one may seem right at first.

Even if you're paying attention to the time, you may find yourself a little behind at some point. You should speed up to get back on track, but do so wisely. Don't panic; just take a few seconds less on each question until you're caught up. Don't guess without thinking, but do look through the answer choices and eliminate any you know are wrong. If you can get down to two choices, it is often worthwhile to guess from those. Once you've chosen an answer, move on and don't dwell on any that you skipped or had to hurry through. If a question was taking too long, chances are it was one of the harder ones, so you weren't as likely to get it right anyway.

On the other hand, if you find yourself getting ahead of schedule, it may be beneficial to slow down a little. The more quickly you work, the more likely you are to make a careless mistake that will affect your score. You've budgeted time for each question, so don't be afraid to spend that time. Practice an efficient but careful pace to get the most out of the time you have.

Secret Key #5 – Have a Plan for Guessing

When you're taking the test, you may find yourself stuck on a question. Some of the answer choices seem better than others, but you don't see the one answer choice that is obviously correct. What do you do?

The scenario described above is very common, yet most test takers have not effectively prepared for it. Developing and practicing a plan for guessing may be one of the single most effective uses of your time as you get ready for the exam.

In developing your plan for guessing, there are three questions to address:

- When should you start the guessing process?
- How should you narrow down the choices?
- Which answer should you choose?

When to Start the Guessing Process

Unless your plan for guessing is to select C every time (which, despite its merits, is not what we recommend), you need to leave yourself enough time to apply your answer elimination strategies. Since you have a limited amount of time for each question, that means that if you're going to give yourself the best shot at guessing correctly, you have to decide quickly whether or not you will guess.

Of course, the best-case scenario is that you don't have to guess at all, so first, see if you can answer the question based on your knowledge of the subject and basic reasoning skills. Focus on the key words in the question and try to jog your memory of related topics. Give yourself a chance to bring the knowledge to mind, but once you realize that you don't have (or you can't access) the knowledge you need to answer the question, it's time to start the guessing process.

It's almost always better to start the guessing process too early than too late. It only takes a few seconds to remember something and answer the question from knowledge. Carefully eliminating wrong answer choices takes longer. Plus, going through the process of eliminating answer choices can actually help jog your memory.

Summary: Start the guessing process as soon as you decide that you can't answer the question based on your knowledge.

7

How to Narrow Down the Choices

The next chapter in this book (**Test-Taking Strategies**) includes a wide range of strategies for how to approach questions and how to look for answer choices to eliminate. You will definitely want to read those carefully, practice them, and figure out which ones work best for you. Here though, we're going to address a mindset rather than a particular strategy.

Your chances of guessing an answer correctly depend on how many options you are choosing from.

How many choices you have	How likely you are to guess correctly
5	20%
4	25%
3	33%
2	50%
1	100%

You can see from this chart just how valuable it is to be able to eliminate incorrect answers and make an educated guess, but there are two things that many test takers do that cause them to miss out on the benefits of guessing:

- Accidentally eliminating the correct answer
- Selecting an answer based on an impression

We'll look at the first one here, and the second one in the next section.

To avoid accidentally eliminating the correct answer, we recommend a thought exercise called **the $5 challenge**. In this challenge, you only eliminate an answer choice from contention if you are willing to bet $5 on it being wrong. Why $5? Five dollars is a small but not insignificant amount of money. It's an amount you could afford to lose but wouldn't want to throw away. And while losing $5 once might not hurt too much, doing it twenty times will set you back $100. In the same way, each small decision you make—eliminating a choice here, guessing on a question there—won't by itself impact your score very much, but when you put them all together, they can make a big difference. By holding each answer choice elimination decision to a higher standard, you can reduce the risk of accidentally eliminating the correct answer.

The $5 challenge can also be applied in a positive sense: If you are willing to bet $5 that an answer choice *is* correct, go ahead and mark it as correct.

Summary: Only eliminate an answer choice if you are willing to bet $5 that it is wrong.

Which Answer to Choose

You're taking the test. You've run into a hard question and decided you'll have to guess. You've eliminated all the answer choices you're willing to bet $5 on. Now you have to pick an answer. Why do we even need to talk about this? Why can't you just pick whichever one you feel like when the time comes?

The answer to these questions is that if you don't come into the test with a plan, you'll rely on your impression to select an answer choice, and if you do that, you risk falling into a trap. The test writers know that everyone who takes their test will be guessing on some of the questions, so they intentionally write wrong answer choices to seem plausible. You still have to pick an answer though, and if the wrong answer choices are designed to look right, how can you ever be sure that you're not falling for their trap? The best solution we've found to this dilemma is to take the decision out of your hands entirely. Here is the process we recommend:

Once you've eliminated any choices that you are confident (willing to bet $5) are wrong, select the first remaining choice as your answer.

Whether you choose to select the first remaining choice, the second, or the last, the important thing is that you use some preselected standard. Using this approach guarantees that you will not be enticed into selecting an answer choice that looks right, because you are not basing your decision on how the answer choices look.

This is not meant to make you question your knowledge. Instead, it is to help you recognize the difference between your knowledge and your impressions. There's a huge difference between thinking an answer is right because of what you know, and thinking an answer is right because it looks or sounds like it should be right.

Summary: To ensure that your selection is appropriately random, make a predetermined selection from among all answer choices you have not eliminated.

Test-Taking Strategies

This section contains a list of test-taking strategies that you may find helpful as you work through the test. By taking what you know and applying logical thought, you can maximize your chances of answering any question correctly!

It is very important to realize that every question is different and every person is different: no single strategy will work on every question, and no single strategy will work for every person. That's why we've included all of them here, so you can try them out and determine which ones work best for different types of questions and which ones work best for you.

Question Strategies

READ CAREFULLY

Read the question and answer choices carefully. Don't miss the question because you misread the terms. You have plenty of time to read each question thoroughly and make sure you understand what is being asked. Yet a happy medium must be attained, so don't waste too much time. You must read carefully, but efficiently.

CONTEXTUAL CLUES

Look for contextual clues. If the question includes a word you are not familiar with, look at the immediate context for some indication of what the word might mean. Contextual clues can often give you all the information you need to decipher the meaning of an unfamiliar word. Even if you can't determine the meaning, you may be able to narrow down the possibilities enough to make a solid guess at the answer to the question.

PREFIXES

If you're having trouble with a word in the question or answer choices, try dissecting it. Take advantage of every clue that the word might include. Prefixes and suffixes can be a huge help. Usually they allow you to determine a basic meaning. Pre- means before, post- means after, pro - is positive, de- is negative. From prefixes and suffixes, you can get an idea of the general meaning of the word and try to put it into context.

HEDGE WORDS

Watch out for critical hedge words, such as *likely, may, can, sometimes, often, almost, mostly, usually, generally, rarely,* and *sometimes*. Question writers insert these hedge phrases to cover every possibility. Often an answer choice will be wrong simply because it leaves no room for exception. Be on guard for answer choices that have definitive words such as *exactly* and *always*.

SWITCHBACK WORDS

Stay alert for *switchbacks*. These are the words and phrases frequently used to alert you to shifts in thought. The most common switchback words are *but, although,* and *however*. Others include *nevertheless, on the other hand, even though, while, in spite of, despite, regardless of*. Switchback words are important to catch because they can change the direction of the question or an answer choice.

FACE VALUE

When in doubt, use common sense. Accept the situation in the problem at face value. Don't read too much into it. These problems will not require you to make wild assumptions. If you have to go beyond creativity and warp time or space in order to have an answer choice fit the question, then you should move on and consider the other answer choices. These are normal problems rooted in reality. The applicable relationship or explanation may not be readily apparent, but it is there for you to figure out. Use your common sense to interpret anything that isn't clear.

Answer Choice Strategies

ANSWER SELECTION

The most thorough way to pick an answer choice is to identify and eliminate wrong answers until only one is left, then confirm it is the correct answer. Sometimes an answer choice may immediately seem right, but be careful. The test writers will usually put more than one reasonable answer choice on each question, so take a second to read all of them and make sure that the other choices are not equally obvious. As long as you have time left, it is better to read every answer choice than to pick the first one that looks right without checking the others.

ANSWER CHOICE FAMILIES

An answer choice family consists of two (in rare cases, three) answer choices that are very similar in construction and cannot all be true at the same time. If you see two answer choices that are direct opposites or parallels, one of them is usually the correct answer. For instance, if one answer choice says that quantity x increases and another either says that quantity x decreases (opposite) or says that quantity y increases (parallel), then those answer choices would fall into the same family. An answer choice that doesn't match the construction of the answer choice family is more likely to be incorrect. Most questions will not have answer choice families, but when they do appear, you should be prepared to recognize them.

ELIMINATE ANSWERS

Eliminate answer choices as soon as you realize they are wrong, but make sure you consider all possibilities. If you are eliminating answer choices and realize that the last one you are left with is also wrong, don't panic. Start over and consider each choice again. There may be something you missed the first time that you will realize on the second pass.

AVOID FACT TRAPS

Don't be distracted by an answer choice that is factually true but doesn't answer the question. You are looking for the choice that answers the question. Stay focused on what the question is asking for so you don't accidentally pick an answer that is true but incorrect. Always go back to the question and make sure the answer choice you've selected actually answers the question and is not merely a true statement.

EXTREME STATEMENTS

In general, you should avoid answers that put forth extreme actions as standard practice or proclaim controversial ideas as established fact. An answer choice that states the "process should be used in certain situations, if…" is much more likely to be correct than one that states the "process should be discontinued completely." The first is a calm rational statement and doesn't even make a definitive, uncompromising stance, using a hedge word *if* to provide wiggle room, whereas the second choice is a radical idea and far more extreme.

BENCHMARK

As you read through the answer choices and you come across one that seems to answer the question well, mentally select that answer choice. This is not your final answer, but it's the one that will help you evaluate the other answer choices. The one that you selected is your benchmark or standard for judging each of the other answer choices. Every other answer choice must be compared to your benchmark. That choice is correct until proven otherwise by another answer choice beating it. If you find a better answer, then that one becomes your new benchmark. Once you've decided that no other choice answers the question as well as your benchmark, you have your final answer.

PREDICT THE ANSWER

Before you even start looking at the answer choices, it is often best to try to predict the answer. When you come up with the answer on your own, it is easier to avoid distractions and traps because you will know exactly what to look for. The right answer choice is unlikely to be word-for-word what you came up with, but it should be a close match. Even if you are confident that you have the right answer, you should still take the time to read each option before moving on.

General Strategies

TOUGH QUESTIONS

If you are stumped on a problem or it appears too hard or too difficult, don't waste time. Move on! Remember though, if you can quickly check for obviously incorrect answer choices, your chances of guessing correctly are greatly improved. Before you completely give up, at least try to knock out a couple of possible answers. Eliminate what you can and then guess at the remaining answer choices before moving on.

CHECK YOUR WORK

Since you will probably not know every term listed and the answer to every question, it is important that you get credit for the ones that you do know. Don't miss any questions through careless mistakes. If at all possible, try to take a second to look back over your answer selection and make sure you've selected the correct answer choice and haven't made a costly careless mistake (such as marking an answer choice that you didn't mean to mark). This quick double check should more than pay for itself in caught mistakes for the time it costs.

PACE YOURSELF

It's easy to be overwhelmed when you're looking at a page full of questions; your mind is confused and full of random thoughts, and the clock is ticking down faster than you would like. Calm down and maintain the pace that you have set for yourself. Especially as you get down to the last few minutes of the test, don't let the small numbers on the clock make you panic. As long as you are on track by monitoring your pace, you are guaranteed to have time for each question.

DON'T RUSH

It is very easy to make errors when you are in a hurry. Maintaining a fast pace in answering questions is pointless if it makes you miss questions that you would have gotten right otherwise. Test writers like to include distracting information and wrong answers that seem right. Taking a little extra time to avoid careless mistakes can make all the difference in your test score. Find a pace that allows you to be confident in the answers that you select.

12

KEEP MOVING

Panicking will not help you pass the test, so do your best to stay calm and keep moving. Taking deep breaths and going through the answer elimination steps you practiced can help to break through a stress barrier and keep your pace.

Final Notes

The combination of a solid foundation of content knowledge and the confidence that comes from practicing your plan for applying that knowledge is the key to maximizing your performance on test day. As your foundation of content knowledge is built up and strengthened, you'll find that the strategies included in this chapter become more and more effective in helping you quickly sift through the distractions and traps of the test to isolate the correct answer.

Now it's time to move on to the test content chapters of this book, but be sure to keep your goal in mind. As you read, think about how you will be able to apply this information on the test. If you've already seen sample questions for the test and you have an idea of the question format and style, try to come up with questions of your own that you can answer based on what you're reading. This will give you valuable practice applying your knowledge in the same ways you can expect to on test day.

Good luck and good studying!

Analyzing and Interpreting Literature Abilities

EXPLANATIONS OF MEDIEVAL/RENAISSANCE CHRISTIAN ALLEGORY

The student should explain that in literature, authors of allegory use all of the literal plot elements of their writing as symbols to represent more abstract subjects. For example, in *The Divine Comedy*, Dante symbolizes the human soul's efforts to achieve moral beliefs and behaviors and become united with God by narrating his persona's literal adventures as he travels through the kingdoms of Hell, Purgatory, and Heaven (*Inferno, Purgatorio,* and *Paradiso*). What appear literal stories of fantasy experiences are allegorical references to the human spiritual quest. The student should provide textual evidence, for example, quoting the *Inferno*'s opening: "Midway on our life's journey, I found myself / In dark woods, the right road lost". The student could then explain that by the plural first-person possessive in "*our* life's journey", Dante connects his persona's story to all of humanity's universal experience, reinforcing this by referring to "the right road" of which he has lost track. The student should explain the "dark woods" as an allegorical symbol of a human being's sinful, unenlightened Earthly existence and the "right road" symbolizing the life of virtue that unites people with God.

EXAMPLE STUDENT EXPLANATION OF A POET USING A QUOTE FROM AN EARLIER POET'S WORK

In "The Love Song of J. Alfred Prufrock", Eliot's six-line epigraph is from Canto 27 of Dante's *Inferno*. Eliot quotes Dante's original Italian, spoken by Guido da Montefeltro: "*S'io credesse che mia risposta fosse / A persona che mai tornasse al mondo, / Questa fiamma staria senza piu scosse. /Ma perciocche giammai di questo fondo/Non torno vivo alcun, s'i'odo il vero, / Senza tema d'infamia ti rispondo.*" Eliot omits translation: "If I believed my answer would be to a person who could return to the world, this flame would stay without more motion; but because nobody has ever come back alive from this abyss, if what I hear is true, without fear of infamy I can reply." Guido, fearing worldly ill repute for evil Earthly deeds, believed he could confide these to Dante—also trapped in Hell, hence unable to repeat them. Guido's "flame" represents his disembodied form in Hell: if he believed Dante could return to Earth (which he ultimately did), he/it would move/speak no more. "Prufrock" echoes the hellish setting, depicting hypocrites pretending goodness. Prufrock's concern for his reputation echoes Guido's: *Prufrock*'s dramatic monologue is best safely addressed to nobody who would repeat it.

INTERPRETATION OF QUOTES AND REFERENCES IN FIRST SECTION OF T. S. ELIOT'S *THE WASTE LAND*

In *The Waste Land*'s first section, "The Burial of the Dead", Eliot refers to Chaucer's *Canterbury* Tales opening about April—but twisting it from Chaucer's happy depiction of its "sweet showers" to "...the cruelest month, breeding / Lilacs out of the dead land, mixing / memory and desire..." He quotes Wagner's opera *Tristan and Isolde* retelling the Arthurian story of adulterous lovers and the loss experienced through their actions. Eliot used his extensive knowledge of literature to reinforce his depiction of the fragmented, decayed "waste land" of post-World War I twentieth-century society. Two major influences Eliot took were *From Ritual to Romance* by Jessie Weston and *The Golden Bough* by Sir James Frazier—both British contemporaries of Eliot (born in America but resettled in England). Both authors described ancient fertility rites reflected Arthurian legend and modern religion and thought—prominently, the Fisher King legend. His wounds, causing impotence, made his country a "waste land." The land's fertility could be reclaimed by healing the

15

Fisher King. Eliot incorporates the Fisher King theme in *The Waste Land*—yet without healing potential, reinforcing the modern world's lack of mythological or religious narrative to unify it.

EXAMPLE STUDENT EXPLANATION OF EXTENDED METAPHOR OF MECHANICAL OBJECT AS AN ANIMAL

In her poem "I like to see it lap the Miles", Emily Dickinson describes a railroad train, a new invention during her time, via extended metaphor comparing it to a horse. She writes of seeing the train "lap the miles—/And lick the Valleys up—/And/...feed itself at Tanks..." She describes seeing it "...prodigious step / Around a Pile of Mountains...And then a Quarry pare / To fit its Ribs..." She describes the train's whistle as "...horrid—hooting stanza" and further characterizes it as a "neigh". She concludes the poem by describing how the train, like a horse, will "...punctual as a Star / Stop— docile and omnipotent / At its own stable door—", representing the train depot/station as a horse's "stable". Juxtaposing the opposites of docility and omnipotence, Dickinson alludes to the way horses are physically powerful, yet often gentle and obedient to much smaller, physically weaker humans. Through the extended metaphor, she moreover likens the train to a horse, for its great power harnessed and controlled by humans.

STUDENT INTERPRETATION OF IMAGERY

In Act I, Scene V of *Romeo and Juliet*, Shakespeare writes dialogue wherein Romeo describes how beautiful Juliet is using visual imagery: "O, she doth teach the torches to burn bright! / It seems she hangs upon the cheek of night / Like a rich jewel in an Ethiope's ear..." By saying she "teaches" torches to burn brightly, Shakespeare makes the point that Juliet's radiance surpasses that of the flames, contrasting it with the darkness of night. Then, he compares night's darkness to an Ethiopian's skin, and Juliet's contrasting brilliance to a gem's glow in an earring against the dark skin. In "Ode to Autumn", Keats uses auditory imagery to bring the season's "music" alive: "...in a wailful choir the small gnats mourn /...Or sinking as the light wind lives or dies; / And full-grown lambs loud bleat from hilly bourn; / Hedge-crickets sing; and now with treble soft / The redbreast whistles from a garden-croft, / And gathering swallows twitter in the skies." He appeals to readers' hearing, describing intermittent wind; gnats mourning in a "wailful choir"; lambs bleating; crickets singing; a robin's soft treble whistling; and swallows twittering.

RHETORICAL DEVICES VS. FIGURES OF SPEECH

Although figures of speech and rhetorical devices are very similar and overlap in many aspects of their definitions, one difference is that a figure of speech uses the effect of altering word meanings to express an idea more colorfully or vividly. For example, instead of saying a woman is strong-willed; free-spirited; feisty; attractive, yet unpredictable; and maybe dangerous, some people use the figure of speech, "She's a pistol." When the main purpose of a figure of speech becomes that of convincing or persuading the audience—the writer's readers or the speaker's listeners—of the writer's point or argument, then the figure of speech can be said to become a rhetorical device. One type of rhetorical device is anaphora: the repetition at regular intervals of the same word or phrase, used to create an effect. Walt Whitman used anaphora in his poems *Crossing Brooklyn Ferry*: "Flood-tide below me! I watch you, face to face; / Clouds of the west! sun there half an hour high! I see you also face to face." and *Song of Myself* (Part 51): "Do I contradict myself? / Very well then I contradict myself, / (I am large, I contain multitudes.)"

Both figures of speech and rhetorical devices are used to create calculated effects and communicate specific emphases. One main difference is that figures of speech change the meanings of words. For example, instead of writing, "She is brave", one writes "She is a tiger": this figure of speech employs a metaphor, conveying the same meaning but using a different word than the original. By contrast, one example of a rhetorical device is using repetition to create emphasis without changing word meanings: "I am never ever going to rob anyone for you and never, never ever give in to your sinful wish." In Book V of *Paradise Lost,* the great poet John Milton uses rhetoric: "...advise him of his happy state—/ Happiness in his power left free to will, / Left to his own free will, his will though free / Yet mutable..." Describing Adam, Milton emphasized humanity's free will by repeating the words "free" and "will". But he also created ambiguity by writing "though free / Yet mutable", i.e. free will was changeable: Adam could lose freedom by sinning/erring.

Review Video: Figure of Speech
Visit mometrix.com/academy and enter code: 111295

USE OF RHETORIC IN POETRY

In Holy Sonnet 10 – "Death, be not proud" – the great Metaphysical poet John Donne rhetorically berates Death. In the final sestet, Donne writes: "Thou art slave to fate, chance, kings, and desperate men, / And dost with poison, war, and sickness dwell, / And poppy or charms can make us sleep as well / And better than thy stroke; why swell'st thou then?" This illustrates the message stated in the first quatrain: "Death, be not proud, though some have called thee / Mighty and dreadful, for thou art not so; / For those whom thou think'st dost overthrow / Die not, poor Death, nor yet canst thou kill me." Donne opens denying Death is as powerful or horrible as some say, then adding that some whom Death thinks it kills do not die, and neither can Death kill him. He supports this argument by subsequently diminishing Death's reputed power, characterizing Death as a "slave"; associating it with the poor company of "poison, war, and sickness"; and ultimately asks the rhetorical question, "why swell'st thou then?" meaning Death has no reason to swell with pride—deflating Death's value and strength.

RHETORICAL DEVICES

ALLITERATION AND HYPERBOLE

Alliteration is both a literary and rhetorical device, using several words in sequence with the same initial sound. An example as literary device is in Wallace Stevens' (1922) poem "The Emperor of Ice Cream": "And bid him whip in kitchen cups concupiscent curds." Two examples of alliteration as rhetorical devices used by speakers for effect are Julius Caesar's "Veni, vidi, vici" ("I came, I saw, I conquered"), and John F. Kennedy's 1961 Inaugural Address: "Let us go forth to lead the land we love." Both repeated word-initial sounds to make their speeches more memorable. Hyperbole is extreme exaggeration for emphasis or effect. An example is in Andrew Marvell's famous (1650~1652) *carpe diem*-tradition poem "To His Coy Mistress": "My vegetable love should grow / Vaster than empires, and more slow; / An hundred years should go to praise / Thine eyes and on thine forehead gaze; / Two hundred to adore each breast, / But thirty thousand to the rest." Marvell exaggerates his love "Had we but world enough and time" as potentially growing longer than empires, hundreds and thousands of years.

IRONY AND OXYMORON

Irony is the literary and rhetorical device of expressing one meaning by stating it using words that have the opposite meaning. In everyday speech it is also called sarcasm. An example of irony in literature in Shakespeare's tragedy *Julius Caesar* is in Act 3, Scene 2, in Marc Antony's famous eulogy speech at Caesar's funeral: "He was my friend, faithful and just to me. / But Brutus says he was ambitious, / And Brutus is an honorable man." Antony is using irony when he calls Brutus "honorable" to mean he is not. Four lines earlier, he also says "For Brutus is an honorable man; / So are they all, all honorable men..." ironically and indirectly indicting the many dishonorable men involved. Oxymoron juxtaposes apparently contradictory words; some everyday speech examples include "jumbo shrimp", "deafening silence", "conspicuous absence", etc. A literary example is in

Shakespeare's *Hamlet,* Act 3, Scene 4: "I must be cruel only to be kind." Shakespeare's phrasing was so popular it has since been adopted into everyday expressions.

LITERARY IRONY

In literature, irony demonstrates the opposite of what is said or done. Three types are verbal irony, situational irony, and dramatic irony. Verbal irony uses words opposite to the meaning. Sarcasm may use verbal irony. An everyday example is describing something confusing as "clear as mud." In his 1986 movie *Hannah and Her Sisters,* author/director/actor Woody Allen says to his character's date, "I had a great evening; it was like the Nuremburg Trials." Notice these employ similes. In situational irony, what happens contrasts with what was expected. In dramatic irony, narrative informs audiences of more than its characters know. O. Henry's short story *The Gift of the Magi* uses situational irony: a husband and wife each sacrifice their most prized possession to buy each other a Christmas present. The irony is that she sells her long hair to buy him a watch fob, while he sells his heirloom pocket-watch to buy her the jeweled combs for her hair she had long wanted; in the end, neither of them can use their gifts.

LITERAL AND FIGURATIVE MEANING

When language is used literally, the words mean exactly what they say and nothing more. When language is used figuratively, the words mean something more and/or other than what they say. For example, "The weeping willow tree has long, trailing branches and leaves" is a literal description. But "The weeping willow tree looks as if it is bending over and crying" is a figurative description—specifically, a simile or stated comparison. Another figurative language form is metaphor, or an implied comparison. A good example is the metaphor of a city, state, or city-state as a ship, and its governance as sailing that ship. Ancient Greek lyrical poet Alcaeus is credited with first using this metaphor, and ancient Greek tragedian Aeschylus then used it in *Seven Against Thebes,* and then Plato used it in the *Republic.* Henry Wadsworth Longfellow later famously referred to it in his poem, "O Ship of State" (1850), which has an extended metaphor with numerous nautical references throughout.

DRAWING INFERENCES

Inferences about literary text are logical conclusions that readers make based on their observations and previous knowledge. By inferring, readers construct meanings from text relevant to them personally. By combining their own schemas or concepts and their background information pertinent to the text with what they read, readers interpret it according to both what the author has conveyed and their own unique perspectives. Authors do not always explicitly spell out every meaning in what they write; many meanings are implicit. Through inference, readers can comprehend implied meanings in the text, and also derive personal significance from it, making the text meaningful and memorable to them. Inference is a natural process in everyday life. When readers infer, they can draw conclusions about what the author is saying, predict what may reasonably follow, amend these predictions as they continue to read, interpret the import of themes, and analyze the characters' feelings and motivations through their actions, and much more.

TEXTUAL EVIDENCE TO ANALYZE LITERATURE

Knowing about the historical background and social context of a literary work, as well as the identity of that work's author, can help to inform the reader about the author's concerns and intended meanings. For example, George Orwell published his novel *1984* in the year 1949, soon after the end of World War II. At that time, following the defeat of the Nazis, the Cold War began between the Western Allied nations and the Eastern Soviet Communists. People were therefore concerned about the conflict between the freedoms afforded by Western democracies versus the oppression represented by Communism. Author Orwell had also previously fought in the Spanish

18

Civil War against a Spanish regime that he and his fellows viewed as oppressive. From this information, readers can infer that Orwell was concerned about oppression by totalitarian governments. This informs *1984*'s story of Winston Smith's rebellion against the oppressive "Big Brother" government of the fictional dictatorial state of Oceania and his capture, torture, and ultimate conversion by that government.

LITERARY THEME

When we read parables, their themes are the lessons they aim to teach. When we read fables, the moral of each story is its theme. When we read fictional works, the authors' perspectives regarding life and human behavior are their themes. Unlike in parables and fables, themes in literary fiction are not meant to preach or teach the readers a lesson. Hence themes in fiction are not as explicit as they are in parables or fables. Instead they are implicit, and the reader only infers them. By analyzing the fictional characters through thinking about their actions and behavior, and understanding the setting of the story and reflecting on how its plot develops, the reader comes to infer the main theme(s) of the work. When writers succeed, they communicate with their readers such that some common ground is established between author and audience. While a reader's individual experience may differ in its details from the author's written story, both may share universal underlying truths which allow author and audience to connect.

DETERMINING THEME

In well-crafted literature, theme, structure, and plot are interdependent and inextricable: each element informs and reflects the others. The structure of a work is how it is organized. The theme is the central idea or meaning found in it. The plot is what happens in the story. (Plots can be physical actions or mental processes—e.g., Marcel Proust.) Titles can also inform us of a work's theme. For instance, Edgar Allan Poe's title "The Tell-Tale Heart" informs us of its theme of guilt before we even read about the repeated heartbeat the protagonist begins hearing immediately before and constantly after committing and hiding a murder. Repetitive patterns of events or behaviors also give clues to themes. The same is true of symbols: in F. Scott Fitzgerald's *The Great Gatsby,* for Jay Gatsby the green light at the end of the dock symbolizes Daisy Buchanan and his own dreams for the future. More generally, it symbolizes the American Dream, and narrator Nick Carraway explicitly compares it to early settlers' sight of America rising from the ocean.

THEMATIC DEVELOPMENT

In *The Great Gatsby*, F. Scott Fitzgerald portrayed 1920s America as greedy, cynical, and rife with moral decay. Jay Gatsby's lavish weekly parties symbolize the reckless excesses of the Jazz Age. The growth of bootlegging and organized crime in reaction to Prohibition is symbolized by the character of Meyer Wolfsheim and by Gatsby's own ill-gotten wealth. Fitzgerald symbolized social divisions using geography: the "old money" aristocrats like the Buchanans lived on East Egg, while the "new money" bourgeois like Gatsby lived on West Egg. Fitzgerald also used weather, as many authors have, to reinforce narrative and emotional tones in the novel. Just as in *Romeo and Juliet*, William Shakespeare set the confrontation of Tybalt and Mercutio and its deadly consequences on the hottest summer day under a burning sun, in *The Great Gatsby*, Fitzgerald did the same with Tom Wilson's deadly confrontation with Gatsby. Both works are ostensible love stories carrying socially critical themes about the destructiveness of pointless and misguided behaviors—family feuds in the former, pursuit of money in the latter.

In Victor Hugo's novel *Les Misérables*, the overall metamorphosis of protagonist Jean Valjean from a cynical ex-convict into a noble benefactor demonstrates Hugo's theme of the importance of love and compassion for others. Hugo also reflects this in more specific plot events. For example, Valjean's love for Cosette sustains him through many difficult periods and trying events. Hugo illustrates how love and compassion for others beget the same in them: Bishop Myriel's kindness to Valjean eventually inspires him to become honest. Years later, Valjean, as M. Madeleine, has rescued Fauchelevent from under a fallen carriage, Fauchelevent returns the compassionate act by giving Valjean sanctuary in the convent. M. Myriel's kindness also ultimately enables Valjean to rescue Cosette from the Thénardiers. Receiving Valjean's father-like love enables Cosette to fall in love with and marry Marius. And the love between Cosette and Marius enables the couple to forgive Valjean for his past crimes when they are revealed.

In one of his shortest stories, Poe used economy of language to emphasize the murderer-narrator's obsessive focus on bare details like the victim's cataract-milky eye, the sound of a heartbeat, and insistence he is sane. The narrator begins by denying he is crazy, even citing his extreme agitation as proof of sanity. Contradiction is then extended: the narrator loves the old man, yet kills him. His motives are irrational—not greed or revenge, but to relieve the victim of his "evil eye." Because "eye" and "I" are homonyms, readers may infer that eye/I symbolizes the old man's identity, contradicting the killer's delusion that he can separate them. The narrator distances himself from the old man by perceiving his eye as separate, and dismembering his dead body. This backfires in another body part when he imagines the victim's heartbeat, which is really his own. Guilty and paranoid, he gives himself away. Poe predated Freud in exploring the paradox of killing those we love and the concept of projecting our own processes onto others.

William Faulkner contrasts the traditions of the antebellum South with the rapid changes of post-Civil War industrialization in his short story *A Rose for Emily*. The central character, Emily Grierson, denies the reality of modern progress, living inside the isolated world of her house. Contradictorily, she is both a testament to time-honored history and a mysterious, eccentric, unfathomable burden. Faulkner portrays her with deathlike imagery even in life, comparing her to a drowned woman and referring to her skeleton. Emily symbolizes the Old South; as her social status is degraded, so is the antebellum social order. Like Miss Havisham in Charles Dickens' *Great Expectations*, Emily preserves her bridal bedroom, denying change and time's passage. Emily tries to control death through denial, shown in her necrophilia with her father's corpse and her killing Homer Barron to stop him from leaving her, then also denying his death. Faulkner uses the motif of dust throughout to represent not only the decay of Emily, her house, and Old Southern traditions, but also how her secrets are obscured from others.

The great White Whale in *Moby-Dick* plays various roles to different characters. In Captain Ahab's obsessive, monomaniacal quest to kill it, the whale represents all evil, and Ahab believes it his duty and destiny to rid the world of it. Ishmael attempts through multiple scientific disciplines to understand the whale objectively, but fails—it is hidden underwater and mysterious to humans—reinforcing Melville's theme that humans can never know everything; here the whale represents the unknowable and may be interpreted as symbolizing God. Melville reverses white's usual connotation of purity in Ishmael's dread of white, associated with crashing waves, polar animals, albinos—all frightening and unnatural. White is often viewed as an absence of color, yet white light is the sum total of all colors in the spectrum. In the same way, white can signify both absence of meaning, and totality of meaning incomprehensible to humans. As a creature of nature, the whale also symbolizes how 19th-century white men's exploitative expansionistic actions were destroying the natural environment.

Because of the old fisherman Santiago's struggle to capture a giant marlin, some people characterize Ernest Hemingway's story as telling of man against nature. However, it can more properly be interpreted as telling of man's role as part of nature. Both man and fish are portrayed as brave, proud, and honorable. In Hemingway's world, all creatures, including humans, must either kill or be killed. Santiago reflects, "man can be destroyed but not defeated," following this principle in his life. As heroes are often created through their own deaths, Hemingway seems to believe that while being destroyed is inevitable, destruction enables living beings to transcend it by fighting bravely with honor and dignity. Hemingway echoes Romantic poet John Keats' contention that only immediately before death can we understand beauty as it is about to be destroyed. He also echoes ancient Greek and Roman myths and the Old Testament with the tragic flaw of overweening pride/overreaching. Like Icarus, Prometheus, and Adam and Eve, the old man "went out too far."

> **Review Video: Thematic Development**
> Visit mometrix.com/academy and enter code: 576507

UNIVERSAL THEME IN ANCIENT RELIGIOUS TEXTS

The Old Testament book Genesis, the Quran, and the Epic of Gilgamesh all contain flood stories. Versions differ somewhat: Genesis describes a worldwide flood, attributing it to God's decision that mankind, his creation, had become incontrovertibly wicked in spirit and must be destroyed for the world to start anew. The Quran describes the flood as regional, caused by Allah after sending Nuh (notice the similarity in name to Noah) as a messenger to his people to cease their evil. The Quran stipulates Allah only destroys those who deny or ignore messages from his messengers. Marked similarities also exist: in the Gilgamesh poems Utnapishtim, like Noah, is instructed to build a ship to survive the flood. Both men send out birds afterward as tests, and both include doves and a raven, though with different outcomes. Historians and archeologists believe a Middle Eastern tidal wave was a real basis for these stories. However, their universal themes remain the same: the flood was seen as God's way of wiping out humans whose behavior had become ungodly.

FIRST-PERSON NARRATION

First-person narratives let narrators express inner feelings and thoughts, especially when the narrator is the protagonist as Lemuel Gulliver is in Jonathan Swift's *Gulliver's Travels*. The narrator may be a close friend of the protagonist, like Dr. Watson in Arthur Conan Doyle's *Sherlock Holmes*. Or the narrator can be less involved with the main characters and plot, like Nick Carraway in F. Scott Fitzgerald's *The Great Gatsby*. When a narrator reports others' narratives secondhand or more, s/he is a "frame narrator," like the nameless narrator of Joseph Conrad's *Heart of Darkness* or Mr. Lockwood in Emily Brontë's *Wuthering Heights*. First-person plural is unusual but can be effective, as in Isaac Asimov's *I, Robot;* William Faulkner's *A Rose for Emily;* Maxim Gorky's *Twenty-Six Men and a Girl;* or Jeffrey Eugenides' *The Virgin Suicides*. Author Kurt Vonnegut is the first-person narrator in his semi-autobiographical novel *Timequake*. Also unusual but effective is a first-person omniscient (rather than the more common third-person omniscient) narrator, like Death in Markus Zusak's *The Book Thief* and the dead girl's ghost in Alice Sebold's *The Lovely Bones*.

SECOND-PERSON NARRATION

While second-person address is very commonplace in popular song lyrics, it is the least used form of narrative voice in literary works. Popular serial books of the 1980s like *Fighting Fantasy* or *Choose Your Own Adventure* employed second-person narratives. In some cases, a narrative combines both second-person and first-person voices, speaking of "you" and "I." This can draw readers into the story, and it can also enable the authors to compare directly "your" and "my" feelings, thoughts, and actions. When the narrator is also a character in the story, as in Edgar Allan Poe's short story "The Tell-Tale Heart" or Jay McInerney's novel *Bright Lights, Big City,* the narrative is better defined as first-person despite its also addressing "you."

THIRD-PERSON NARRATION

Narration in the third person is the most often-used type, as it allows authors the most flexibility. It is so common that readers simply assume without needing to be informed that the narrator is not a character in, or involved in the story. Third-person singular is used more frequently than third-person plural, though some authors have also effectively used plural. However, both singular and plural are most often included in stories according to which character(s) is/are being described. The third-person narrator may be either objective or subjective, and either omniscient or limited. Objective third-person narration does not include what the characters described are thinking or feeling, while subjective third-person narration does. The third-person omniscient narrator knows everything about all characters, including their thoughts and emotions, and all related places, times, and events, whereas the third-person limited narrator may know everything about a particular character of focus, but is limited to that character; in other words, the narrator cannot speak about anything that character does not know.

ALTERNATING-PERSON NARRATION

Although authors more commonly write stories from one point of view, there are also instances wherein they alternate the narrative voice within the same book. For example, they may sometimes use an omniscient third-person narrator and a more intimate first-person narrator at other times. In J. K. Rowling's series of *Harry Potter* novels, she often writes in a third-person limited narrative, but sometimes changes to narration by characters other than protagonist Harry Potter. George R. R. Martin's series *A Song of Ice and Fire* (the basis for the popular HBO TV series *Game of Thrones*) changes the point of view to coincide with divisions between chapters. The same technique is used by Erin Hunter (a pseudonym for several authors of the *Warriors, Seekers,* and *Survivors* book series). Authors using first-person narrative sometimes switch to third-person to describe significant action scenes, especially those where the narrator was absent or uninvolved, as Barbara Kingsolver does in her novel *The Poisonwood Bible.*

CLASSIC ANALYSIS OF PLOT STRUCTURE

In *Poetics,* Aristotle defined plot as "the arrangement of the incidents." He meant not the story, but how it is structured for presentation. In tragedies, Aristotle found results driven by chains of cause-and-effect preferable to those driven by the protagonist's personality/character. He identified "unity of action" as necessary for a plot's wholeness; its events must be internally connected, not episodic or relying on *deus ex machina* or other external intervention. A plot must have a beginning, middle, and end. Gustav Freytag adapted Aristotle's ideas into his Triangle/Pyramid (1863). The beginning, today called the exposition/incentive/inciting moment, emphasizes causes and de-emphasizes effects. Aristotle called the ensuing cause-and-effect *desis,* or tying up, today called complication(s) which occur during the rising action. These culminate in a crisis/climax/reversal/turning point, Aristotle's *peripateia.* This occurs at the plot's middle, where cause and effect are both emphasized. The falling action, which Aristotle called the *lusis* or unraveling, is today called the dénouement. The resolution comes at the catastrophe/outcome or end, when causes are emphasized and effects de-emphasized.

STORY VS. DISCOURSE

In terms of plot, "story" is the characters, places, and events originating in the author's mind, while "discourse" is how the author arranges and sequences events—which may be chronological or not. Story is imaginary; discourse is words on the page. Discourse allows story to be told in different ways. One element of plot structure is relating events differently from the order in which they occurred. This is easily done with cause-and-effect; for example, in the sentence, "He died following a long illness," we know the illness preceded the death, but the death precedes the illness in words. In Kate Chopin's short story "The Story of an Hour" (1894), she tells some of the events out of chronological order, which has the effect of amplifying the surprise of the ending for the reader. Another element of plot structure is selection. Chopin omits some details, such as Mr. Mallard's trip home; this allows readers to be as surprised at his arrival as Mrs. Mallard is.

ANALYSIS OF PLOT STRUCTURES THROUGH RECURRING PATTERNS IN ACTIONS OR EVENTS

Authors of fiction select characters, places, and events from their imaginations and arrange them in ways that will affect their readers. One way to analyze plot structure is to compare and contrast different events in a story. For example, in Kate Chopin's "The Story of an Hour," a very simple but key pattern of repetition is the husband's leaving and then returning. Such patterns fulfill the symmetrical aspect that Aristotle said was required of sound plot structure. In James Baldwin's short story, "Sonny's Blues," the narrator is Sonny's brother. In an encounter with one of Sonny's old friends early in the story, the brother initially disregards his communication. In a subsequent flashback, Baldwin informs us that this was the same way he had treated Sonny. In Nathaniel Hawthorne's "Young Goodman Brown," a pattern is created by the protagonist's recurrent efforts not to go farther into the wood; in Herman Melville's "Bartleby the Scrivener," by Bartleby's repeated refusals; and in William Faulkner's "Barn Burning," by the history of barn-burning episodes.

CONFLICT

A conflict is a problem to be solved. Literary plots typically include one conflict or more. Characters' attempts to resolve conflicts drive the narrative's forward movement. Conflict resolution is often the protagonist's primary occupation. Physical conflicts like exploring, wars, and/or escapes tend to make plots most suspenseful and exciting. Emotional, mental, and/or moral conflicts tend to make stories more personally gratifying or rewarding for many audiences. Conflicts can be external or internal. A major type of internal conflict is some inner personal battle, or "man against himself." Major types of external conflicts include "man against nature," "man against man," and "man against society." Readers can identify conflicts in literary plots by asking themselves who the protagonist is, who or what the antagonist is, why the antagonist is an antagonist, why the protagonist and antagonist conflict, what events develop the conflict, which event is the climax, what the outcome tells them about the protagonist, and whether they sympathized or identified with the protagonist or antagonist and why.

MOOD AND TONE

Mood is a story's atmosphere, or the feelings the reader gets from reading it. The way authors set the mood in writing is comparable to the way filmmakers use music to set the mood in movies. Instead of music, though, writers judiciously select evocative or descriptive words to evoke certain moods. The mood of a work may convey joy, anger, bitterness, hope, gloom, fear, an ominous feeling, or any other emotion the author wants the reader to feel. In addition to vocabulary choices, authors also use figurative expressions, particular sentence structures, and choices of diction that project and reinforce the moods they want to create. Whereas mood is the reader's emotions evoked by reading what is written, tone is the emotions and attitudes of the writer that s/he expresses in the writing. Authors use the same literary techniques to establish tone as they do to establish mood. An author may use a humorous tone, an angry or sad tone, a sentimental or unsentimental tone, or something else entirely.

PURPOSES OF GOOD DIALOGUE

In literary fiction, effectively written dialogue serves at least one but usually several purposes. It advances the story and moves the plot. It develops the characters. It sheds light on the work's theme(s) or meaning(s). It can, often subtly, account for the passage of time not otherwise indicated. It can alter the direction that the plot is taking, typically by introducing some new conflict(s) or changing (an) existing one(s). Dialogue can establish a work's narrative voice and/or the characters' voices and set the tone of the story or of particular characters. When fictional characters display enlightenment or realization, dialogue can give readers an understanding of

23

what those characters have discovered, and how. Dialogue can illuminate the motivations and wishes of the story's characters for its readers. By using consistent thoughts and syntax, dialogue can support character development. Skillfully created, it can also represent real-life speech rhythms in written form. Via conflicts and ensuing action, dialogue also provides drama.

In fictional literary works, effectively written dialogue should not have only the effect of breaking up or interrupting sections of narrative. Well-written dialogue does not reproduce verbatim things said in an author's real-life experiences. While dialogue may supply exposition for readers, it must nonetheless be believable. Dialogue should be dynamic, not static, and it should not resemble regular prose not representing conversation. Authors should not use dialogue as prose contexts for self-consciously "clever" similes or metaphors, which is unnatural and awkward. Dialogue should not slow down the movement of the plot or the story. When narrative would better establish a story's setting, authors should not substitute dialogue, which would be inappropriate. Authors should not express their own opinions in characters' dialogue. They should not try to imitate what real-life characters would say; dialogue must seem and sound natural, rather than actually duplicating natural speech. Dialogue should also not simply consist of conversations enclosed in quotation marks that do not serve the purpose of the story.

EFFECTS OF STORY EVENTS ON WORKS' MEANINGS

Novelist E. M. Forster has made the distinction between story as relating a series of events, such as a king dying and then his queen dying, versus plot as establishing motivations for actions and causes for events, such as a king dying and then his queen dying from grief over his death. Thus plot fulfills the function of helping readers understand cause-and-effect in events and underlying motivations in characters' actions, which in turn helps them understand life. This affects a work's meaning by supporting its ability to explain why things happen, why people do things, and ultimately explain some of the meaning in life. Some authors find that while story events convey meaning, they do not tell readers there is any one meaning in life or way of living, but rather are mental experiments with various meanings and ways of life enabling readers to explore. Hence stories may not necessarily be constructed to impose one definitive meaning, but rather to find some shape, direction, and meaning within otherwise random events.

ANALYSIS OF CHARACTER DEVELOPMENT

To understand the characters in a literary text, we can consider what kinds of observations the author makes about each character. We can look for contradictions in what a character thinks, says, and does. We can notice whether the author's observations about a character differ from what other characters in the story say about that character. We can note how the author describes each character. A character may be dynamic in that s/he changes in some significant way(s) during the story, or static in that s/he remains the same from the beginning of the story to the end. Characters may be perceived as "flat" or, in other words, not fully developed and/or without salient personality traits, or "round," as in more well developed, with characteristics that stand out vividly. Another thing to consider is whether characters in a story symbolize any universal properties. In addition, as readers we can think about whether we could compare and/or contrast the attributes of two characters in the same story to analyze how authors develop characters.

FIGURATIVE LANGUAGE

Figurative language is any language that extends past the literal meanings of the words. It serves the function of offering readers new insight into the people, things, events, and subjects covered in a work of literature. Figurative language also enables readers to feel they are sharing the authors' experiences. It can stimulate the reader's senses, make comparisons that readers find intriguing or even startling, and enable readers to view the world in different ways. Seven specific types of

24

figurative language include: imagery, similes, metaphors, alliteration, personification, onomatopoeia, and hyperbole. Imagery is descriptive language that accesses the senses. Imagery can describe people, animals, or things. For example, the images T. S. Eliot uses in his poem "The Waste Land" of towers crumbling, wells dried up, and tombstones toppled over create mental images for the reader of the decay of a civilization.

ALLITERATION, PERSONIFICATION, IMAGERY, AND SIMILE

Alliteration is using a series of words containing the same sounds—assonance with vowels, and consonance with consonants. Personification is describing a thing or animal as a person. Imagery is description using sensory terms that create mental images for the reader of how people, animals, or things look, sound, feel, taste, and/or smell. This verse from Alfred Tennyson's poem "The Eagle" uses all of these types of figurative language: "He clasps the crag with crooked hands." Tennyson used alliteration, repeating /k/ and /kr/ sounds. These hard-sounding consonants reinforce the imagery giving visual and tactile impressions of the eagle. Tennyson also used personification, describing a bird as "he" and calling its talons "hands." Similes are stated comparisons using "like" or "as." William Wordsworth's poem about "Daffodils" begins, "I wandered lonely as a cloud." This simile compares his loneliness to that of a cloud. It is also personification, giving a cloud the human quality loneliness.

METAPHOR AND ONOMATOPOEIA

Metaphor is an implied comparison that does not use "like" or "as" the way a simile does. Henry Wadsworth Longfellow echoes the ancient Greeks in "O Ship of State": the metaphor compares the state and its government to a nautical ship and its sailing. Onomatopoeia uses words imitating the sounds of things they name/describe. For example, in his poem "Come Down, O Maid," Alfred Tennyson writes of "The moan of doves in immemorial elms, / And murmuring of innumerable bees." The word "moan" sounds like some sounds doves make, "murmuring" represents the sounds of bees buzzing, and "buzzing" is also an onomatopoetic word. And in his play *The Tempest,* in scene 2 of Act One, William Shakespeare's character Ariel says, "Hark, hark! / Bow-wow. / The watch-dogs bark! / Bow-wow. / Hark, hark! I hear/ The strain of strutting chanticleer / Cry, 'cock-a-diddle-dow!'" Onomatopoetic words represent the sounds of a dog barking and a rooster crowing, respectively. ("Strain" is also imagery describing a rooster's crow as song; "strain" paired with "strutting" is alliteration.)

HYPERBOLE

Hyperbole is excessive exaggeration used for humor or emphasis rather than for literal meaning. For example, in *To Kill a Mockingbird*, Harper Lee narrated, "People moved slowly then. There was no hurry, for there was nowhere to go, nothing to buy and no money to buy it with, nothing to see outside the boundaries of Maycomb County." This was not literally true; Lee exaggerates the scarcity of these things for emphasis. In "Old Times on the Mississippi," Mark Twain wrote, "I... could have hung my hat on my eyes, they stuck out so far." This is not literal, but makes his description vivid and funny. In his poem "As I Walked Out One Evening", W. H. Auden wrote, "I'll love you, dear, I'll love you / Till China and Africa meet, / And the river jumps over the mountain / And the salmon sing in the street." He used things not literally possible to emphasize his meaning that he will love the person addressed forever.

COUPLETS AND METER TO ENHANCE MEANING IN POETRY

When a poet uses a couplet—a stanza of two lines, rhymed or unrhymed—it can function as the answer to a question asked earlier in the poem, or the solution to a problem or riddle. Couplets can also enhance the establishment of a poem's mood, or clarify the development of a poem's theme. Another device to enhance thematic development is irony, which also communicates the poet's tone and draws the reader's attention to a point the poet is making. The use of meter gives a poem a rhythmic context, contributes to the poem's flow, makes it more appealing to the reader, can represent natural speech rhythms, and produces specific effects. For example, in "The Song of Hiawatha," Henry Wadsworth Longfellow uses trochaic (/ ᴗ) tetrameter (four beats per line) to evoke for readers the rhythms of Native American chanting: "*By* the *shores* of *Gitche Gum*ee, / *By* the *shin*ing *Big*-Sea-*Wat*er / *Stood* the *wig*wam of No*ko*mis." (Italicized syllables are stressed; non-italicized syllables are unstressed.)

EFFECTS OF FIGURATIVE DEVICES ON MEANING IN POETRY

Through exaggeration, hyperbole communicates the strength of a poet's or persona's feelings and enhances the mood of the poem. Imagery appeals to the reader's senses, creating vivid mental pictures, evoking reader emotions and responses, and helping to develop themes. Irony also aids thematic development by drawing the reader's attention to the poet's point and communicating the poem's tone. Thematic development is additionally supported by the comparisons of metaphors and similes, which emphasize similarities among things compared, affect readers' perceptions of images and enhance the imagery, and are more creative than writing in only literal terms. The use of mood communicates the atmosphere of a poem, can build a sense of tension, and evokes the reader's emotions. Onomatopoeia appeals to the reader's auditory sense and enhances sound imagery even when the poem is visual (read silently) rather than auditory (read aloud). Rhyme connects and unites verses, gives the rhyming words emphasis, and makes poems more fluent. Symbolism communicates themes, develops imagery, and evokes readers' emotional and other responses.

POETIC STRUCTURE TO ENHANCE MEANING IN POETRY

The opening stanza of Romantic English poet, artist and printmaker William Blake's famous poem "The Tyger" demonstrates how a poet can enhance the meaning of the work through creating tension by using line length and punctuation independently of one another: "Tyger! Tyger! burning bright / In the forests of the night, / What immortal hand or eye / Could frame thy fearful symmetry?" The first three lines of this stanza are trochaic (/ ᴗ), with "masculine" endings—that is, strongly stressed syllables at the ends of each of the lines. But Blake's punctuation contradicts this rhythmic regularity by not providing any divisions between the words "bright" and "In" or between "eye" and "Could." This irregular punctuation foreshadows how Blake disrupts the meter at the end of this first stanza by using a contrasting dactyl (/ᴗᴗ), with a "feminine" (unstressed) ending syllable in the last word, "symmetry." Thus Blake uses structural contrasts to heighten the intrigue of his work.

In enjambment, one sentence or clause in a poem does not end at the end of its line or verse, but runs over into the next line or verse. Clause endings coinciding with line endings give readers a feeling of completion, but enjambment influences readers to hurry to the next line to finish and understand the sentence. In his blank-verse epic religious poem "Paradise Lost," John Milton wrote: "Anon out of the earth a fabric huge / Rose like an exhalation, with the sound / Of dulcet symphonies and voices sweet, / Built like a temple, where pilasters round / Were set, and Doric pillars overlaid / With golden architrave." Only the third line is end-stopped. Milton, describing the palace of Pandemonium bursting from Hell up through the ground, reinforced this idea through phrases and clauses bursting through the boundaries of the lines. A caesura is a pause in mid-verse. Milton's commas in the third and fourth lines signal caesuras. They interrupt flow, making the narration jerky to imply that Satan's glorious-seeming palace has a shaky and unsound foundation.

MAKING PREDICTIONS

When we read literature, making predictions about what will happen in the writing reinforces our purpose(s) for reading and prepares us mentally for beginning to read, and for continuing to read further. We can make predictions before we begin reading and during our reading. As we read on, we can test the accuracy of our predictions, revise them in light of additional reading, and confirm or refute our predictions. Some things that can help readers to make predictions about literary works include: thinking about the title of the book, poem, or play; looking at the illustrations when there are any; considering the structure of the text as we read; making use of our existing knowledge relative to the subject of the text; asking ourselves questions about the story, characters, and subject matter, particularly "why" and "who" questions; and then answering these questions for ourselves by referring to the text.

MAKING CONNECTIONS TO ENHANCE READING COMPREHENSION

Reading involves thinking. For good comprehension, readers make text-to-self, text-to-text, and text-to-world connections. Making connections helps readers understand text better and predict what might occur next based on what they already know, such as how characters in the story feel or what happened in another text. Text-to-self connections with the reader's life and experiences make literature more personally relevant and meaningful to readers. Readers can make connections before, during, and after reading—including whenever the text reminds them of something similar they have encountered in life or other texts. Knowing a work's genre (mystery, fantasy, or whatever it may be); common practices of a certain author; a story's geographical, historical, and social setting; characters that remind us of other people; familiar plot elements; literary structure and devices (such as flashbacks); themes encountered in other works; and similar use of language and tone to other works are all means for connections. Venn diagrams and other graphic organizers help visualize connections. Readers can also make double-entry notes: key content, ideas, events, words, and quotations on one side, and the connections with these on the other.

SUMMARIZING LITERATURE TO SUPPORT COMPREHENSION

When reading literature, especially demanding works, summarizing helps readers identify important information and organize it in their minds; briefly monitor understanding; identify the main theme(s), problems and solutions; and sequence the story. Readers can summarize before, during, and after they read. They can refer to examples of other occasions in life for summarizing: giving others directions, generally describing our weekends or summers in limited time, and explaining news items/articles we read, to name a few. To summarize literary content, readers should use their own words. Previewing a text's organization before reading by examining the book cover, table of contents, and illustrations also aids summarizing. So does making notes of key words and ideas in a graphic organizer while reading. Graphic organizers can also be used after reading: readers skim the text, pick out the most important parts of three to five sentences, and determine what can be omitted with the aid of the organizer. Unimportant details should be omitted in summaries. Summaries of nonfiction can include description, problem-solution, comparison-contrast, sequence, main ideas, and cause-and-effect.

EVALUATION OF SUMMARIES OF LITERARY PASSAGES

A summary of a literary passage is a condensation in the reader's own words of the passage's main points. Some guidelines for evaluating a summary of a literary passage include: The summary should be complete yet concise. It should be accurate, balanced, fair, neutral, and objective, excluding the reader's own opinions or reactions. It should reflect in similar proportion how much each point summarized was covered in the original passage. Summary writers should include tags of attribution, like "Macaulay argues that" to reference the original author whose ideas are represented in the summary. Summary writers should not overuse quotations: they should only quote central concepts or phrases they cannot precisely convey in words other than those of the original author. Another aspect in evaluating a summary is whether it can stand alone as a coherent, unified composition, albeit a brief one. In addition, evaluation of a summary should include whether its writer has cited the original source of the passage so that readers of the summary can find it.

TEXTUAL EVIDENCE TO EVALUATE PREDICTIONS

Textual evidence to evaluate reader predictions about literature includes specific synopses of the work, paraphrases of the work or parts of it, and direct quotations from it. The best literary analysis shows special insight into a theme, character trait, or change. The best textual evidence supporting analysis is strong, relevant, and accurate. Analysis that is not best, but enough, shows reasonable understanding of theme, character trait, or change; contains supporting textual evidence that is relevant and accurate, if not strong; and shows a specific and clear response. Analysis that partially meets criteria also shows reasonable understanding, but the textual evidence is generalized, incomplete, only partly relevant or accurate, or connected only weakly. Or there may be only relevant, accurate textual evidence, but no analysis and a vague or unclear response. Analysis that is vague, too general or incorrect, with an unclear response and irrelevant or incomplete textual evidence; that only summarizes the plot; and/or that answers the wrong question, or answers no question, is not enough to be adequate.

LITERARY THEORIES AND CRITICISM AND INTERPRETATION

Literary theory gives a rationale for the literary subject matter of criticism, and also for the process of interpreting literature. For example, Aristotle's *Poetics'* requirement of unity underlies any discussion of unity in Sophocles' *Oedipus Rex.* Postcolonial theory, assuming historical racism and exploitation, informs Nigerian novelist and critic Chinua Achebe's contention that in *Heart of Darkness,* Joseph Conrad does not portray Africans with complete humanity. Gender and feminist theories support critics' interpretation of Edna Pontellier's drowning at the climax of Kate Chopin's novel *The Awakening* (1899) as suicide. Until the 19th century, critics largely believed literature referenced objective reality, holding "a mirror up to nature" as William Shakespeare wrote. Twentieth-century Structuralism and New Historicism were predated and influenced by radical, non-traditional, historicized, cross-cultural comparative interpretations of biblical text in 19th-century German "higher criticism." Literary critic Charles Augustin Saint-Beuve maintained that biography could completely explain literature; contrarily, Marcel Proust demonstrated in narrative that art completely transformed biography. A profound 19th-century influence on literary theory was Friedrich Nietzsche's idea that facts must be interpreted to become facts.

GEOFFREY CHAUCER'S "THE PARLEMENT OF FOULES"

In his dream-vision, Cicero views the universe with his famous grandfather, learning philosophical principles of virtue during earthly, illusory, and deathlike life, toward Heaven's rewards in the afterlife's true life. Geoffrey Chaucer uses less grand designs in his dream-vision: Hoping to learn something from Cicero's work and influenced by it, he also dreams of Scipio Africanus. However, instead of touring the universe and Stoic philosophy, Africanus takes Chaucer to the temple of Venus—connecting with Chaucer's preface statement that he writes about love. This poem is noteworthy for the first known reference to St. Valentine's Day as being for lovers. Leaving Venus's temple, Chaucer witnesses Nature's comic "parliament" wherein birds, symbolizing human suitors, select mates. He alludes to sexual maturity at two years for male predator birds contrasting with one year for females: Nature grants the female eagle's request to defer choice for another year, but lets other birds form couples. Chaucer's awakening by morning birdsong celebrates summer, and illustrates the phenomenon that dreams often retroactively incorporate real sounds heard just before waking.

ARISTOTLE'S CRITERIA FOR TRAGEDY IN DRAMA

In his *Poetics,* Aristotle defined five critical terms relative to tragedy. (1) *Anagnorisis:* Meaning tragic insight or recognition, this is a moment of realization by a tragic hero(ine) when s/he suddenly understands how s/he has enmeshed himself/herself in a "web of fate." (2) *Hamartia:* This is often called a "tragic flaw," but is better described as a tragic error. *Hamartia* is an archery term meaning a shot missing the bull's eye, used here as a metaphor for a mistake—often a simple one—which results in catastrophe. (3) *Hubris:* While often called "pride," this is actually translated as "violent transgression," and signifies an arrogant overstepping of moral or cultural bounds—the sin of the tragic hero who over-presumes or over-aspires. (4) *Nemesis:* translated as "retribution," this represents the cosmic punishment or payback that the tragic hero ultimately receives for committing hubristic acts. (5) *Peripateia:* Literally "turning," this is a plot reversal consisting of a tragic hero's pivotal action, which changes his/her status from safe to endangered.

THEORY OF TRAGEDY PROPOSED BY HEGEL

Georg Wilhelm Friedrich Hegel (1770-1831) proposed a different theory of tragedy than Aristotle (384-322 BCE) which was also very influential. Whereas Aristotle's criteria involved character and plot, Hegel defined tragedy as a dynamic conflict of opposite forces or rights. For example, if an individual believes in the moral philosophy of the conscientious objector, i.e., that fighting in wars is morally wrong, but is confronted with being drafted into military service, this conflict would fit Hegel's definition of a tragic plot premise. Hegel theorized that a tragedy must involve some circumstance in which two values, or two rights, are fatally at odds with one another and conflict directly. Hegel did not view this as good triumphing over evil, or evil winning out over good, but rather as one good fighting against another good unto death. He saw this conflict of two goods as truly tragic. In ancient Greek author Sophocles' tragedy *Antigone,* the main character experiences this tragic conflict, between her public duties and her family and religious responsibilities.

REVENGE TRAGEDY

Along with Aristotelian definitions of comedy and tragedy, ancient Greece was the origin of the revenge tragedy. This genre became highly popular in Renaissance England, and is still popular today in contemporary movies. In a revenge tragedy, the protagonist has been done some serious wrong, such as the assault and murder of a family member. However, the wrongdoer has not been punished. In contemporary plots, this often occurs when some legal technicality has interfered with the miscreant's conviction and sentencing, or when authorities are unable to locate and apprehend the criminal. The protagonist then faces the conflict of suffering this injustice, or exacting his or her own justice by seeking revenge. Greek revenge tragedies include *Agamemnon* and *Medea.* Playwright Thomas Kyd's *The Spanish Tragedy* (1582-1592) is credited with beginning the Elizabethan genre of revenge tragedies. Shakespearean revenge tragedies include *Hamlet* (1599-1602) and *Titus Andronicus* (1588-1593). A Jacobean example is Thomas Middleton's *The Revenger's Tragedy* (1606, 1607). The 1974 movie *Death Wish* is a contemporary example.

HAMLET'S "TRAGIC FLAW"

Despite virtually limitless interpretations, one way to view Hamlet's tragic error generally is as indecision: He suffers the classic revenge tragedy's conflict of whether to suffer with his knowledge of his mother's and uncle's assassination of his father, or to exact his own revenge and justice against Claudius, who has assumed the throne after his crime went unknown and unpunished. Hamlet's famous soliloquy, "To be or not to be" reflects this dilemma. Hamlet muses "Whether 'tis nobler in the mind to suffer the slings and arrows of outrageous fortune, / Or to take arms against a sea of troubles, / And by opposing end them?" He sees the final sleep of death as "the rub; / For in that sleep of death what dreams may come... Must give us pause... that the dread of something after death... makes us rather bear those ills we have / Than fly to others that we know not of? / Thus conscience does make cowards of us all." Hamlet's excessive conscience leads to paralyzing indecision, at least temporarily.

For much of William Shakespeare's tragedy, Hamlet suffers anxiety over what to do about his uncle Claudius's murdering his (Hamlet's) father, Hamlet. During this time, Hamlet's tragic error might be considered a lack of action, as he seems paralyzed by his quandary. But making matters worse, Hamlet attempts to kill Claudius surreptitiously by stabbing him through a tapestry, accidentally killing Polonius instead. However, he eventually becomes inspired with a solution to avoid direct confrontation: "The play's the thing / Wherein I'll catch the conscience of the king." He presents a play depicting a similar murder. By observing his reaction, Hamlet can confirm or deny Claudius's guilt (reported by the late King Hamlet's ghost, which Hamlet was unsure was a true ghost or the devil) to inform his decision. During the presentation, Gertrude fatally drinks wine that Claudius poisoned and intended for Hamlet. Then Laertes kills Hamlet, to avenge Hamlet's accidental murder of Laertes' father Polonius, and his sister Ophelia's madness and eventual suicide in reaction to Hamlet's behavior. Hamlet's indecision delays action, but his actions have more tragic outcomes.

THEME OF OVERREACHING

A popular theme throughout literature is the human trait of reaching too far or presuming too much. In Greek mythology, Daedalus constructed wings of feathers and wax that men might fly like birds. He permitted his son Icarus to try them, but cautioned the boy not to fly too close to the sun. The impetuous youth (in what psychologist David Elkind later named adolescence's myth of invincibility) ignored this, flying too close to the sun: the wax melted, the wings disintegrated, and Icarus fell into the sea and perished. In the Old Testament, God warned Adam and Eve not to eat fruit from the tree of knowledge of good and evil, that they might remain pure and innocent. Ignoring this banished them from Eden's eternal perfection, condemning them to mortality and suffering. The Romans were themselves examples of over-reachers in their conquest and assimilation of most of the then-known world and ultimate demise. In Christopher Marlowe's *Dr. Faustus* and Johann Wolfgang von Goethe's *Faust,* the protagonist sells his soul to the Devil for unlimited knowledge and success.

CARPE DIEM TRADITION IN POETRY

Carpe diem is Latin for "seize the day." A long poetic tradition, it advocates making the most of time because it passes swiftly and life is short. It is found in multiple languages, including Latin, Torquato Tasso's Italian, Pierre de Ronsard's French, and Edmund Spenser's English, and is often used in seduction to argue for indulging in earthly pleasures. Roman poet Horace's Ode 1.11 tells younger woman Leuconoe to enjoy the present, not worrying about inevitable aging. Two Renaissance Metaphysical Poets, Andrew Marvell and Robert Herrick, treated *carpe diem* more as a call to action. In "To His Coy Mistress," Marvell points out that time is fleeting, arguing for love, and concluding that because they cannot stop time, they may as well defy it, getting the most out of the short time they have. In "To the Virgins, to Make Much of Time," Herrick advises young women to take advantage of their good fortune in being young by getting married before they become too old to attract men and have babies.

"To His Coy Mistress" begins, "Had we but world enough, and time, / This coyness, lady, were no crime." Using imagery, Andrew Marvell describes leisure they could enjoy if time were unlimited. Arguing for seduction, he continues famously, "But at my back I always hear/Time's winged chariot hurrying near; / And yonder all before us lie / Deserts of vast eternity." He depicts time as turning beauty to death and decay. Contradictory images in "amorous birds of prey" and "tear our pleasures with rough strife / Thorough the iron gates of life" overshadow romance with impending death, linking present pleasure with mortality and spiritual values with moral considerations. Marvell's concluding couplet summarizes *carpe diem*: "Thus, though we cannot make our sun / Stand still, yet we will make him run." "To the Virgins, to Make Much of Time" begins with the famous "Gather ye rosebuds while ye may." Rather than seduction to live for the present, Robert Herrick's experienced persona advises young women's future planning: "Old time is still a-flying / And this same flower that smiles today, / Tomorrow will be dying."

REFLECTION OF CONTENT THROUGH STRUCTURE

Wallace Stevens' short yet profound poem "The Snow Man" is reductionist: the snow man is a figure without human biases or emotions. Stevens begins, "One must have a mind of winter," the criterion for realizing nature and life does not inherently possess subjective qualities; we only invest it with these. Things are not as we see them; they simply are. The entire poem is one long sentence of clauses connected by conjunctions and commas, and modified by relative clauses and phrases. The successive clauses and phrases lead readers continually to reconsider as they read. Stevens' construction of the poem mirrors the meaning he conveys. With a mind of winter, the snow man, Stevens concludes, "nothing himself, beholds nothing that is not there, and the nothing that is" (ultimate reductionism). Linguist and poetics expert Jay Keyser once remarked (NPR, 2005) that he wrote all the words of "The Snow Man" on white cards and made them into a mobile; it was "perfectly balanced, like an Alexander Calder creation." He said the mobile visually represented the poem's content.

CONTRAST OF CONTENT AND STRUCTURE

Robert Frost's poem "Stopping by Woods on a Snowy Evening" (1923) is deceptively short and simple, with only four stanzas, each of only four lines, and short and simple words. Reinforcing this is Frost's use of regular rhyme and meter. The rhythm is iambic tetrameter throughout; the rhyme scheme is AABA in the first three stanzas and AAAA in the fourth. In an additional internal subtlety, B ending "here" in the first stanza is rhymed with A endings "queer," "near," and "year" of the second; B ending "lake" in the second is rhymed in A endings "shake", "mistake," and "flake" of the third. The final stanza's AAAA endings reinforce the ultimate darker theme. Though the first three stanzas seem to describe quietly watching snow fill the woods, the last stanza evokes the seductive pull of mysterious death: "The woods are lovely, dark and deep," countered by the obligations of living life: "But I have promises to keep, / And miles to go before I sleep, / And miles to go before I sleep." The last line's repetition strengthens Frost's message that despite death's temptation, life's course must precede it.

ASPECTS THAT COMBINE TO TOTAL EFFECT IN THEODORE ROETHKE'S "THE WAKING"

"The Waking" is a villanelle, with five tercets, one quatrain, and only two rhymes. Roethke alternately repeats two main lines: "I wake to sleep, and take my waking slow," and "I learn by going where I have to go" throughout, gradually revealing meaning. Continuous overall rhythm and revolving sound patterns of interconnected rhyming and assonance create perpetual motion, reflecting the life cycle. Roethke's use of villanelle form perfectly suits this cyclical effect: repetition, becoming hypnotically chant-like, reinforces the poem's mystical quality. Waking to sleep, learning by going, and "think[ing] by feeling" represent paradoxes: meaning, like form, becomes circular. These symbolize abandoning conscious rationalism to embrace spiritual vision. We wake from the vision to "Great Nature," and "take the lively air" in life's dance. "This shaking keeps me steady"—another paradox—juxtaposes and balances fear of mortality with ecstasy in embracing experience. The transcendent vision of all life's interrelationship demonstrates, "What falls away is always. And is near." Readers experience the poem holistically, like music, through Roethke's integration of theme, motion, and sound.

SYLVIA PLATH'S USE OF VILLANELLE FORM TO CONVEY MEANING IN "MAD GIRL'S LOVE SONG"

Sylvia Plath wrote the poem "Mad Girl's Love Song" in college to exemplify young love. The two repeated lines, "I shut my eyes and all the world drops dead" and "(I think I made you up inside my head.)" reflect the existential viewpoint that nothing exists in any absolute reality outside of our own perceptions. In the first stanza, the middle line, "I lift my lids and all is born again," in its recreating the world, bridges between the repeated refrain statements—one of obliterating reality, the other of having constructed her lover's existence. Unlike other villanelles wherein key lines are subtly altered in their repetitions, Plath repeats these exactly each time. This reflects the young woman's love, also not changing throughout the poem. The final quatrain expresses some regret: "I should have loved a thunderbird instead; / At least when spring comes they roar back again." Plath contrasts the thunderbirds' rebirth with the unchanging love she depicts, and reinforces it. The unchanging repeated lines mirror the lack of progress in her love.

TED HUGHES' ANIMAL METAPHORS

Hughes frequently used animal metaphors, as in "Crow" and collected poems about the mythic creature-character Crow. In "The Thought Fox," a model of concise, structured beauty, Hughes characterizes the poet's creative process with succinct, striking imagery of an idea as a fox entering his head. Repeating "loneliness" in the first two stanzas emphasizes the poet's lonely work: "Something else is alive / Beside the clock's loneliness." He treats an idea's arrival as separate from himself. Three stanzas detail in vivid images a fox's approach from the outside winter forest at starless midnight —its nose, "Cold, delicately" touching twigs and leaves; "neat" paw prints in snow; "bold" body; wide, deep, brilliant green eyes; and self-contained, focused progress—"Till, with a sudden sharp hot stink of fox," he metaphorically depicts poetic inspiration as the fox's physical entry into "the dark hole of the head." Hughes ends by summarizing his vision of poet as an interior, passive idea recipient, with the outside world unchanged: "The window is starless still; the clock ticks, / The page is printed."

LITERARY EXAMPLES OF METAPHOR

A metaphor is an implied comparison, i.e. it compares something to something else without using "like", "as", or other comparative words. For example, in "The Tyger" (1794), William Blake writes, "Tyger Tyger, burning bright, / In the forests of the night;" this is a metaphor as Blake compares the tiger to a flame not by saying it is like a fire, but by simply describing it as "burning." Henry Wadsworth Longfellow's poem "O Ship of State" (1850) uses an extended metaphor by referring consistently throughout the entire poem to the state, union, or republic as a seagoing vessel, referring to its keel, mast, sail, rope, anchors, and to its braving waves, rocks, gale, tempest, and "false lights on the shore". Within the extended metaphor, Wordsworth uses a specific metaphor: "...the anchors of thy hope!" This is a metaphor because, like Blake (above), Wordsworth does not say the state's hope is like a ship's anchors; he equates them without using comparative words.

LITERARY EXAMPLES OF SIMILES

A simile is a directly stated comparison of one thing to another thing, often using "like" or "as". In his novel *Lord Jim* (1900), Joseph Conrad writes in Chapter 33, "I would have given anything for the power to soothe her frail soul, tormenting itself in its invincible ignorance like a small bird beating about the cruel wires of a cage." Conrad uses the word "like" to compare the girl's soul to a small bird. His description of the bird beating at the cage shows the similar helplessness of the girl's soul to gain freedom. In his poetic Scots song "A Red, Red Rose" (1794), Robert Burns writes, "O my

32

Luve's like a red, red rose, / That's newly sprung in June: / O my Luve's like the melodie, / That's sweetly play'd in tune." Burns uses "like" to compare his beloved to a beautiful, freshly blooming flower. In a second simile, he compares her to a beautiful musical melody. In the poem *The Daffodils* (1888), Wordsworth writes, "I wandered lonely as a cloud / that floats on high o'er vales and hills," comparing his persona's loneliness to that of a single cloud in the sky.

When an author uses similes to compare one thing to another, this gets readers' attention; stimulates readers' imaginations; and appeals to readers' senses by describing sensations of sight, sound, touch, smell, and/or taste. Similes lend more lifelike characteristics to fictional and poetic characters. Readers can more easily relate emotions expressed by authors to their own personal experiences when they read similes authors use. Consequently, readers can better understand literary subject matter when authors compare things to other things using similes. Additionally, similes offer readers ways to introduce more variety into the way they think, and show them different/new perspectives for perceiving reality. In his "Sonnet 18" (1609), Shakespeare writes, "Shall I compare thee to a summer's day? / Thou art more lovely and more temperate". This simile does not use "like" or "as" the way many similes do, yet it does directly state a comparison by using the verb "compare".

LITERARY EXAMPLES OF PERSONIFICATION

Personification is the device of attributing human qualities and/or behaviors/actions to something that is not human. While personification is the literary term for this, a synonym used in the social sciences is anthropomorphism. In his romantic tragedy *Romeo and Juliet* (1597), Shakespeare writes dialogue spoken by Capulet (Act 1, Scene 2): "When well-appareled April on the heel / Of limping winter treads..." This contains three instances of personification: (1) April is a month, not a lady, yet he describes April as being well-dressed and as (2) treading (walking); (3) winter is a season, does not have a physical heel, and cannot limp. In his poem "Loveliest of Trees" (1896), A. E. Housman describes the cherry tree as "Wearing white for Eastertide." He personifies the tree's white flowers as white clothing, as a human would wear for Easter. In her short story, "How Pearl Button Was Kidnapped" (1912), Katherine Mansfield describes "...little winds playing hide-and-seek..." She personifies breezes as playing children.

Personification, i.e. attributing human qualities and actions to inanimate objects, non-human living things, or abstract concepts, imbues text with more profound meanings. We humans tend to be anthrocentric; i.e., we view the world from our human perspective, seeing non-human entities in a human light as well. When authors and poets use personification, they bring inanimate objects to life and characterize plants, animals, and ideas with human traits. Readers can better understand the nature and behaviors of non-human things/creatures by reading about them through the lens of personification. We can more easily relate to human beings, qualities, traits, and behaviors than non-human ones. Moreover, author use of personification opens up new, divergent, varied, and creative perspectives for readers. As an example, in his poem "Ode: Intimations of Immortality from Recollections of Early Childhood" (1807), William Wordsworth writes, "The Moon doth with delight / Look round her when the heavens are bare". He personifies the inanimate object of the moon as a human female looking around "her", creating a vivid visual image and investing the scene with emotional mood and tone.

Analyzing and Interpreting Literature Knowledge

WILLIAM SHAKESPEARE

William Shakespeare lived in England from 1564-1616. He was a poet and playwright of the Renaissance period in Western culture. He is generally considered the foremost dramatist in world literature, and the greatest author to write in the English language. He wrote many poems, particularly sonnets, of which 154 survive today, and approximately 38 plays. Though his sonnets were larger in number and are very famous, he is best known for his plays, including comedies, tragedies, tragicomedies and historical plays. His play titles include: *All's Well That Ends Well, As You Like It, The Comedy of Errors, Love's Labour's Lost, Measure for Measure, The Merchant of Venice, The Merry Wives of Windsor, A Midsummer Night's Dream, Much Ado About Nothing, The Taming of the Shrew, The Tempest, Twelfth Night, The Two Gentlemen of Verona, The Winter's Tale, King John, Richard II, Henry IV, Henry V, Richard III, Romeo and Juliet, Coriolanus, Titus Andronicus, Julius Caesar, Macbeth, Hamlet, Troilus and Cressida, King Lear, Othello, Antony and Cleopatra,* and *Cymbeline.*

WILLIAM FAULKNER

William Faulkner lived in the state of Mississippi in the United States of America from 1897-1962. He is known as one of the greatest authors of Southern literature in America, and of American literature in general. Faulkner wrote one play, poems, essays, screenplays, and especially novels and short stories. He based his writing on his experience living in Mississippi during the early 20th century. Many of his short stories and novels are set in a fictional Southern county modeled on the two counties where he lived. Faulkner was awarded the 1949 Nobel Prize for Literature and two Pulitzer Prizes for Fiction, both for novels: one for *A Fable* in 1954, and another for *The Reivers*, his final novel, in 1962. Titles of some of his best-known works include the novels *The Sound and the Fury; As I Lay Dying; Light in August; Absalom, Absalom!;* and the short story *A Rose for Emily.*

GEOFFREY CHAUCER

THE CANTERBURY TALES

Medieval poet Geoffrey Chaucer (c. 1343-1400), called the "Father of English Literature," chiefly wrote long narrative poems, including *The Book of the Duchess, Anelida and Arcite, The House of Fame, The Parlement of Foules, The Legend of Good Women,* and *Troilus and Criseyde.* His most famous work is *The Canterbury Tales.* Its historical and cultural context is life during the Middle Ages, representing a cross-section of society—tradespeople, professionals, nobility, clergy, and housewives, among others, and religious pilgrimages, a common practice of the time. Its literary context is a frame-tale, that is, a story within a story. Chaucer described a varied group of pilgrims all on their way to Canterbury, taking turns telling stories to amuse the others. Tales encompass a broad range of subjects: bawdy comedy, chivalry, romance, and religion. These include *The Knight's Tale, The Miller's Tale, The Reeve's Tale, The Cook's Tale, The Man of Law's Tale, The Wife of Bath's Tale, The Friar's Tale, The Summoner's Tale, The Clerk's Tale, The Merchant's Tale, The Squire's Tale, The Franklin's Tale, The Physician's Tale, The Pardoner's Tale, The Nun's Priest's Tale,* and others.

THE PARLEMENT OF FOULES

In the brief preface to his poem "The Parlement of Foules," Geoffrey Chaucer refers to ancient Classical Roman author Cicero's "The Dream of Scipio." This was a philosophical dialogue Cicero wrote as a kind of epilogue to his famous longer book, *De re publica* ("*The Republic*"). It narrates that Roman senator and general Scipio the Younger dreams that his grandfather, the renowned general Scipio Africanus, visits him and escorts him to heaven. While viewing the spheres, he tells his grandson how the afterlife is the true life, earthly virtue earns the reward of Heaven, and earthly delights are less important. This reflects Stoic philosophy: Romans adapted Platonic ideals from the Greeks. Whereas "The Dream of Scipio" is a dream-vision on the nature of the universe as macrocosm, Chaucer's poem is a dream-vision on a smaller part of the universe as microcosm. He describes reading "The Dream of Scipio," then also dreaming of a visit from Scipio Africanus, who praises him and promises to reward him for reading Cicero's work.

INFLUENCE OF CICERO'S "DREAM OF SCIPIO": During Geoffrey Chaucer's lifetime (1300s), Cicero's philosophical dialogue "The Dream of Scipio," found at the end of his major work *De re publica* (*The Republic*) was a very popular, admired, and influential work. Medieval Christians appreciated Greek and Latin Stoic philosophies for their assigning more importance to spiritual virtues than materialism. They adapted these easily to Christianity for their similarity to Christian values, as they did with many other pagan traditions. Chaucer wrote several dream-vision poems influenced by the Classics, including "The House of Fame," influenced by Virgil's *Aeneid,* and "The Book of the Duchess," influenced by Ovid's *Metamorphoses.* He introduces *The Parlement of Foules* by recounting "The Dream of Scipio," and his own similar dream from the influence of reading this work, as homage to Cicero. He then segues to writing that though personally unsuccessful in love, he writes about love. He contrasts the brevity of life with the lengthiness of learning the poetic art. He concludes his preface asking help from Venus, Roman Goddess of Love.

> **Review Video: <u>Historical Authors (Chaucer, Thomas Browne, William Blake, William Wordsworth, Samuel Coleridge, Lord Byron, Percy Shelley, John Keats)</u>**
> Visit mometrix.com/academy and enter code: 752719

DRAMA
EARLY DEVELOPMENT

Interestingly, early English drama originally developed from religious ritual. Early Christians established traditions of presenting pageants or mystery plays, each traveling on wagons and carts through the streets of its city, depicting events of the Judeo-Christian Old and New Testaments. Medieval tradition assigned responsibility for performing specific plays to the different guilds. In Middle English, "mystery" meant both religious ritual/truth, and craft/trade. Historically, mystery plays were to be reproduced exactly the same every time as religious rituals. However, by human nature, some performers introduced individual interpretations of roles and/or even improvised. Thus drama was born. Narrative detail and nuanced acting were evident in mystery cycles by the Middle Ages. As individualized performance evolved, plays on other subjects also developed. Middle English mystery plays extant include the York Cycle, Coventry Cycle, Chester Mystery Plays, N-Town Plays, and Towneley/Wakefield Plays. Mystery plays have been revived in the 20th and 21st centuries. Dame Judi Dench (born in York) and other actors began their careers in mystery play revivals.

DEFINING CHARACTERISTICS

In the Middle Ages, it was common to compose plays in verse. Early Christian mystery plays were always written in verse. By the time of the Renaissance, Shakespeare and other dramatists wrote plays that mixed prose, rhymed verse, and blank verse. Shakespeare also often used rhyming couplets in his plays. The traditions of costumes and masks were seen in ancient Greek drama, medieval mystery plays, and Renaissance drama. Conventions like asides, wherein actors make comments directly to the audience unheard by other characters, and soliloquies, i.e., dramatic monologues, were also common during Shakespeare's Elizabethan dramatic period. Monologues dated back to ancient Greek drama. Elizabethan dialogue tended to use colloquial prose for lower-class characters' speech and stylized verse for upper-class characters. Another Elizabethan convention was the play-within-a-play, like in *Hamlet*. As drama moved toward realism, dialogue became less poetic and more conversational, as in most modern English-language plays. Contemporary drama, both onstage and onscreen, includes a convention of breaking the fourth wall, wherein actors directly face and address audiences.

POETRY

Unlike prose, which traditionally (except in forms like stream of consciousness) consists of complete sentences connected into paragraphs, poetry is written in verses. These may form complete sentences, clauses, or phrases. Poetry may be written in rhyming verses or unrhymed verse. It can be metered, i.e., following a particular rhythmic pattern, such as iambic, dactylic, spondaic, trochaic, or anapestic, or without regular meter. The terms iamb and trochee, among others, identify stressed and unstressed syllables in each verse. Meter is also described by the number of beats or stressed syllables per verse: dimeter (2), trimeter (3), tetrameter (4), pentameter (5), and so forth. With ᴗ = unstressed, /= stressed, iambic = ᴗ/; trochaic = /ᴗ; spondaic =//; dactylic =/ᴗᴗ; anapestic =ᴗᴗ/. Poetry with neither rhyme nor meter is called free verse. Poems may be in free verse, metered but unrhymed, rhymed but without meter, or using both rhyme and meter. In English, the most common meter is iambic pentameter. Unrhymed iambic pentameter is called blank verse. Rhyme schemes identify which lines rhyme, such as ABAB, ABCA, AABA, and so on.

MAJOR FORMS

The ballad is a form historically and currently used in both musical songs and poems. The *ballade* was very popular in 14th- and 15th-century France; ballads were also common in traditional English and American folk songs and poems. Poetry ballads often are rhymed and metered and cover subjects like love, death, murder, or religious topics. In dramatic monologue poems, the poet speaks in the voice of a character/persona. Elegies are mourning poems, traditionally with three parts: a lament, praise of the deceased, and solace for loss. Epic poems are long, recount heroic deeds and adventures, use very stylized language, and combine dramatic and lyrical conventions. Epigrams are memorable, one- or two-line rhymes. Epistolary poems are written and read as letters. Odes evolved from early poems with music and dance to Romantic poems expressing strong feelings and contemplative thoughts. Pastoral poems (and novels) idealize nature and country living. Limericks typically are two lines of iambic trimeter, two lines of iambic dimeter, and one line of iambic trimeter, usually humorous and/or bawdy.

HAIKU

Haiku was originally a Japanese poetry form. In the 13th century, haiku was the opening phrase of renga, a 100-stanza oral poem. By the 16th century, haiku diverged into a separate short poem. When Western writers discovered haiku, the form became popular in English and other languages. A haiku has 17 syllables, traditionally distributed across three verses as 5/7/5, with a pause after the first or second line. Haiku are syllabic and unrhymed. Haiku philosophy and technique are that brevity's compression forces writers to express images concisely, depict a moment in time, and evoke illumination and enlightenment. An example is 17th-century haiku master Matsuo Basho's classic: "Oh, old pond! / A frog jumps in— / the sound of water." Modern American poet Ezra Pound revealed the influence of haiku in his two-line poem "In a Station of the Metro"—line 1 has 5+7 syllables, line 2 has 7, but it still preserves haiku's philosophy and imagistic technique: "The apparition of these faces in the crowd; / Petals on a wet, black bough."

SONNETS

The sonnet traditionally has 14 lines of iambic pentameter, tightly organized around a theme. The Petrarchan sonnet, named for 14th-century Italian poet Petrarch, has an eight-line stanza, the octave, and a six-line stanza, the sestet. There is a change or turn, known as the volta, between the eighth and ninth verses setting up the sestet's answer or summary. The rhyme scheme is ABBA/ABBA/CDECDE or CDCDCD. The Petrarchan sonnet was introduced to 16th-century England by Sir Thomas Wyatt. The English or Shakespearean sonnet has three quatrains and one couplet, with the rhyme scheme ABAB/CDCD/EFEF/GG. This format better suits English, which has fewer rhymes than Italian. The final couplet often contrasts sharply with the preceding quatrains, as in Shakespeare's sonnets—for example, Sonnet 130, "My mistress' eyes are nothing like the sun." Variations on these two forms include 16th-century Edmund Spenser's Spenserian sonnet; 17th-century John Milton's Miltonic sonnet; and sonnet sequences, as used by 17th-century poet John Donne in *La Corona*, 19th-century poet Elizabeth Barrett Browning in *Sonnets from the Portuguese*, 19th-20th-century poet Rainer Maria Rilke, and 20th-century poets Robert Lowell and John Berryman.

LITERARY TERMINOLOGY

In works of prose such as novels, a group of connected sentences covering one main topic is termed a paragraph. In works of poetry, a group of verses similarly connected is called a stanza. In drama, when early works used verse, these were also divided into stanzas or couplets. Drama evolved to use predominantly prose. Overall, whether prose or verse, the conversation in a play is called dialogue. Large sections of dialogue spoken by one actor are called soliloquies or monologues. Dialogue that informs audiences but is unheard by other characters is called an aside. Novels and plays share certain common elements, such as characters—the people in the story; plot—the action of the story; a climax—when action and/or dramatic tension reaches its highest point; and denouement—the resolution following the climax. Sections dividing novels are called chapters, while sections of plays are called acts. Subsections of plays' acts are called scenes. Novels' chapters are usually not subdivided, although some novels have larger sections divided into groups of chapters.

NOVELS

MAJOR FORMS

Historical novels set fiction in particular historical periods—including prehistoric and mythological—and contain historical, prehistoric, or mythological themes. Examples include Walter Scott's *Rob Roy* and *Ivanhoe*; Leo Tolstoy's *War and Peace*; Robert Graves' *I, Claudius*; Mary Renault's *The King Must Die* and *The Bull from the Sea* (an historical novel using Greek mythology); Virginia Woolf's *Orlando* and *Between the Acts*; and John Dos Passos's *U.S.A* trilogy. Picaresque novels recount episodic adventures of a rogue protagonist or *pícaro,* like Miguel de Cervantes' *Don Quixote* or Henry Fielding's *Tom Jones.* Gothic novels originated as a reaction against 18th-century Enlightenment rationalism, featuring horror, mystery, superstition, madness, supernatural elements, and revenge. Early examples include Horace Walpole's *Castle of Otranto,* Matthew Gregory Lewis' *Monk*, Mary Shelley's *Frankenstein*, and Bram Stoker's *Dracula.* In America, Edgar Allan Poe wrote many Gothic works. Contemporary novelist Anne Rice has penned many Gothic novels under the pseudonym A. N. Roquelaure. Psychological novels, originating in 17th-century France, explore characters' motivations. Examples include Abbé Prévost's *Manon Lescaut;* George Eliot's novels; Fyodor Dostoyevsky's *Crime and Punishment;* Tolstoy's *Anna Karenina;* Gustave Flaubert's *Madame Bovary;* and the novels of Henry James, James Joyce, and Vladimir Nabokov.

NOVEL OF MANNERS

Novels of manners are fictional stories that observe, explore, and analyze the social behaviors of a specific time and place. While deep psychological themes are more universal across different historical periods and countries, the manners of a particular society are shorter-lived and more varied; the novel of manners captures these societal details. Novels of manners can also be regarded as symbolically representing, in artistic form, certain established and secure social orders. Characteristics of novels of manners include descriptions of a society with defined behavioral codes; the use of standardized, impersonal formulas in their language; and inhibition of emotional expression, as contrasted with the strong emotions expressed in romantic or sentimental novels. The novels of Jane Austen are examples of some of the finest novels of manners ever produced. In the 20th century, Evelyn Waugh's *Handful of Dust* is a novel of social manners, and his *Sword of Honour* trilogy is a novel of military manners. Another 20th-century example is *The Unbearable Bassington* by Saki (the pen name of writer H. H. Munro), focusing on Edwardian society.

WESTERN-WORLD SENTIMENTAL NOVELS

Sentimental love novels originated in the movement of Romanticism. Eighteenth-century examples of novels that depict emotional rather than only physical love include Samuel Richardson's *Pamela* (1740) in English, and Jean-Jacques Rousseau's *Nouvelle Héloïse* (1761) in French. Also in the 18th century, Laurence Sterne's novel *Tristram Shandy* (1760-1767) is an example of a novel with elements of sentimentality. The Victorian era's rejection of emotionalism caused the term "sentimental" to have undesirable connotations. In the 19th century, William Makepeace Thackeray and Charles Dickens, while not considered sentimental novelists by any means, both included sentimental elements in some of their novels: for example, in Dickens' *A Christmas Carol*. A 19th-century author of genuinely sentimental novels was Mrs. Henry Wood (e.g., *East Lynne*, 1861). In the 20th century, Erich Segal's sentimental novel *Love Story* (1970) was a popular bestseller, staying on the New York Times Best Seller List for 41 weeks, and was adapted into a movie (also released in 1970) which was also well received by both movie audiences and film critics, receiving numerous award nominations.

EPISTOLARY NOVEL

Epistolary novels are told in the form of letters written by their characters rather than in narrative form. Samuel Richardson, the best-known author of epistolary novels like *Pamela* (1740) and *Clarissa* (1748), widely influenced early Romantic epistolary novels throughout Europe that freely expressed emotions. Richardson, a printer, published technical manuals on letter-writing for young gentlewomen; his epistolary novels were natural fictional extensions of those nonfictional instructional books. Nineteenth-century English author Wilkie Collins' *The Moonstone* (1868) was a mystery written in epistolary form. By the 20th century, the format of well-composed written letters came to be regarded as artificial and outmoded. English novelist Christopher Isherwood tried to revive the form in *Meeting by the River* (1967), but this was criticized for using chatty and informal letters to tell a story with a serious religious theme. A 20th-century evolution of letters was tape-recording transcripts in French playwright Samuel Beckett's drama *Krapp's Last Tape*. Though evoking modern alienation, Beckett still created a sense of fictional characters' direct communication without author intervention as Richardson had.

PASTORAL NOVELS

Pastoral novels and fiction (as well as poetry) lyrically idealize country life as idyllic and utopian, akin to the Garden of Eden. *Daphnis and Chloe*, written by Greek novelist Longus around the second or third century, was pastoral and influenced Elizabethan pastoral romances like Philip Sidney's *Arcadia* and Thomas Lodge's *Rosalynde* (both 1590). William Shakespeare based his play *As You Like It* on *Rosalynde*. Jacques-Henri Bernardin de St. Pierre's French work *Paul et Virginie* (1787) demonstrated the early Romantic view of the innocence and goodness of nature. Later non-pastoral novels like *The Rainbow* (1915) and *Lady Chatterley's Lover* (1928), both by D. H. Lawrence, contain pastoral elements. Growing realism transformed pastoral writing into less ideal and more dystopian, distasteful and ironic depictions of country life in George Eliot's and Thomas Hardy's novels. Saul Bellow's novel *Herzog* (1964) may demonstrate how urban ills highlight an alternative pastoral ideal. Some scholars feel the pastoral satire *Cold Comfort Farm* (1932) by Stella Gibbons (also adapted into a movie) has made British novelists less able to take the pastoral tradition's lyricism seriously.

BILDUNGSROMAN

Bildungsroman is German, literally meaning "education novel." This term is also used in English to describe "apprenticeship" novels focusing on coming-of-age stories, including youth's struggles and searches for things such as identity, spiritual understanding, or the meaning in life. Johann Wolfgang von Goethe's *Wilhelm Meisters Lehrjahre* (1796) is credited as the origin. Charles Dickens' two novels *David Copperfield* (1850) and *Great Expectations* (1861) also fit this form. H. G. Wells wrote *bildungsromans* about questing for apprenticeships to address modern life's complications in *Joan and Peter* (1918), and from a Utopian perspective in *The Dream* (1924). School *bildungsromans* include Thomas Hughes' *Tom Brown's School Days* (1857) and Alain-Fournier's *Le Grand Meaulnes* (1913). Many Hermann Hesse novels, including *Demian, Steppenwolf, Siddhartha, Magister Ludi,* and *Under the Wheel* are *bildungsromans* about struggling/searching youth. Samuel Butler's *The Way of All Flesh* (written in 1885 and published in 1903) and James Joyce's *A Portrait of the Artist as a Young Man* (1916) are two outstanding modern examples. Variations include J. D. Salinger's *The Catcher in the Rye* (1951), set both within and beyond school, and William Golding's *Lord of the Flies* (1955), a novel not set in a school but one that is a coming-of-age story nonetheless.

ROMAN À CLEF

Roman à clef, French for "novel with a key," means the story needs a real-life frame of reference, or key, for full comprehension. In Geoffrey Chaucer's *Canterbury Tales,* the Nun's Priest's Tale contains details that confuse readers unaware of history about the Earl of Bolingbroke's involvement in an assassination plot. Other literary works fitting this form include John Dryden's political satirical poem *Absalom and Achitophel* (1681), Jonathan Swift's satire *A Tale of a Tub* (1704), and George Orwell's political allegory *Animal Farm* (1945), all of which cannot be understood completely without knowing their camouflaged historical contents. *Roman à clefs* disguise truths too dangerous for authors to state directly. Readers must know about D. H. Lawrence's enemies to comprehend *Aaron's Rod* (1922). To appreciate Aldous Huxley's *Point Counter Point* (1928), readers must realize that the characters Mark Rampion and Denis Burlap respectively represent author Huxley and real-life critic John Middleton Murry. Marcel Proust's *Remembrance of Things Past (À la recherché du temps perdu,* 1871-1922) is informed by his social context. James Joyce's *Finnegans Wake* is an enormous *roman à clef* via multitudinous personal references.

REALISM

Realism is a literary form whose goal is to represent reality as faithfully as possible. Its genesis in Western literature was a reaction against the sentimentality and extreme emotionalism of the works written in the literary movement of Romanticism, which championed feelings and their expression. Realists focused in great detail on immediacy of time and place, on specific actions of their characters, and the justifiable consequences of those actions. Some techniques of realism include writing in the vernacular, i.e., the characters' ordinary conversational language; writing in specific dialects used by some characters; and emphasizing the analysis and development of characters more than the analysis and development of plots. Realistic literature often addresses various ethical issues. Historically, realistic works have often concentrated on the middle classes of the authors' societies. Realists eschew treatments that are too dramatic or sensationalistic as exaggerations of the reality that they strive to portray as closely as they are able.

SATIRE

Satire uses sarcasm, irony, and/or humor as social criticism to lampoon human folly. Unlike realism, which intends to depict reality as it exists without exaggeration, satire often involves creating situations or ideas deliberately exaggerating reality to be ridiculous to illuminate flawed behaviors. Ancient Roman satirists included Horace and Juvenal. Alexander Pope's poem "The Rape of the Lock" satirized the values of fashionable members of the 18th-century upper-middle class, which Pope found shallow and trivial. The theft of a lock of hair from a young woman is blown out of proportion: the poem's characters regard it as seriously as they would a rape. Irishman Jonathan Swift satirized British society, politics, and religion in works like *A Tale of a Tub.* In *A Modest Proposal,* Swift used essay form and mock-serious tone, satirically "proposing" cannibalism of babies and children as a solution to poverty and overpopulation. He satirized petty political disputes in *Gulliver's Travels.* Swift was known as a master of the ancient Roman Horatian and Juvenalian satirical styles.

HISTORICAL CONTEXT OF CHANGE BETWEEN MIDDLE AGES AND RENAISSANCE

The ancient Greek Athenian elite were a highly educated society, developing philosophies and writing about principles for creating poetry and drama. During the Roman Empire, the Romans assimilated and adapted the culture of the Greeks they conquered into their own society. For example, the gods of Roman mythology were essentially the same as in Greek myth, only renamed in Latin. However, after the fall of the Roman Empire, the many European countries formerly united under Roman rule became fragmented. There followed a 1,000-year period of general public ignorance and illiteracy—called the Dark Ages as well as the Middle Ages. Only the Church remained a bastion of literacy: monks and priests laboriously copied manuscripts one at a time by hand. Johannes Gutenberg's 1450 invention of the movable-type printing press changed everything: multiple copies of books could be printed much faster. This enabled a public return to literacy, leading to the Renaissance, or "rebirth"—reviving access and interest for Greek and Roman Classics, and generating a creative explosion in all arts.

CHRISTOPHER MARLOWE

Christopher Marlowe was born the same year as William Shakespeare (1564), but died at the age of 29. Some people have proposed Marlowe could have falsified his death and continued writing under Shakespeare's name. Most scholars reject this theory. In the 19th century, an anonymous author also suggested Shakespeare temporarily wrote under the name Christopher Marlowe. In *As You Like It,* Shakespeare pays homage to Marlowe, quoting "Hero and Leander"; in Touchstone's dialogue, mentioning death over a "reckoning," thought to allude to Marlowe's presumed murder over money he owed; and including "in a little room," words from Marlowe's *Jew of Malta.* Shakespeare recycled Marlowe's themes from *Dido* in *Antony and Cleopatra,* from *Jew of Malta* in *The Merchant of Venice,* from *Edward II* in *Richard II,* and from *Dr. Faustus* in *Macbeth.* A speech in *Hamlet* echoes *Dido.* Shakespeare's character Marcadé in *Love's Labour's Lost* acknowledges the god Mercury in Marlowe's play *The Massacre at Paris,* with whom Marlowe identified himself in his poem "Hero and Leander."

COMEDY

Today, most people equate the idea of comedy with something funny, and of tragedy with something sad. However, the ancient Greeks defined these differently. Comedy needed not be humorous or amusing: it needed only a happy ending. The Classical definition of comedy, as included in Aristotle's works, is any work that tells the story of a sympathetic main character's rise

40

in fortune. According to Aristotle, protagonists needed not be heroic or exemplary: he described them as not evil or worthless, but as ordinary people—"average to below average" morally. Comic figures who were sympathetic were usually of humble origins, proving their "natural nobility" through their actions as their characters were tested, rather than characters born into nobility—who were often satirized as self-important or pompous. Comedy's mirror-image was tragedy, portraying a hero's fall in fortune. While by Classical definitions, tragedies could be sad, Aristotle went further, requiring their depicting suffering and pain to cause "terror and pity" in audiences; that tragic heroes be basically good, admirable, and/or noble; and that their downfalls be through personal action, choice, or error, not by bad luck or accident.

SHAKESPEAREAN COMEDY

Aristotle defined comedy not as a humorous drama, but as one in which the protagonist experiences a rise in fortune, and which has a happy ending. Such Classical definitions of drama were very popular during the Renaissance and the Elizabethan period within it, when William Shakespeare was writing. All of Shakespeare's comedies, as opposed to his tragedies, had happy endings. Not all of them are equally funny, although many are. His play *A Comedy of Errors* fits the comedic genre of the farce. Based and expanding on a Classical Roman comedy, it includes slapstick humor and mistaken identity—not deliberate, but accidental, and is generally light and "fluffy," with disturbing topics only hinted at but soon dissolved in laughter and love. Shakespeare's *Much Ado About Nothing* is a romantic comedy. It incorporates some more serious themes, including social mores; perceived infidelity; marriage's duality as both trap and ideal; and honor and its loss, public shame, and deception, but also much witty dialogue and a happy ending.

DRAMATIC COMEDIES

Three types of dramas classified as comedy include the farce, the romantic comedy, and the satirical comedy. The farce is a zany, goofy type of comedy that includes pratfalls and other forms of slapstick humor. The characters appearing in a farce tend to be ridiculous or fantastical in nature, markedly more so than characters in other types of comedies. Another aspect of farce is inclusion in the plot of situations so improbable as to be unbelievable—albeit still highly entertaining. Farcical plots frequently feature complications and twists that can go on almost indefinitely. They also often include wildly incredible coincidences that rarely if ever would occur in real life. Mistaken identity, deceptions, and disguises are common devices used in farcical comedies. Shakespeare's play *The Comedy of Errors,* with its cases of accidental mistaken identity and slapstick, is an example of farce. Contemporary examples of farce include the Marx Brothers' movies, the Three Stooges movies and TV episodes, and the *Pink Panther* movie series.

ROMANTIC COMEDY

Romantic comedies are probably the most popular of the types of comedy, in both live theater performances and movies. They include not only humor and a happy ending, but also love. In the typical plot of a romantic comedy, two people well suited to one another are either brought together for the first time, or reconciled after being separated. They are usually both sympathetic characters, and seem destined to be together yet separated by some intervening complication—such as an ex-lover(s), interfering parents or friends, or differences in social class. The happy ending is achieved through the lovers' overcoming all these obstacles. William Shakespeare's *Much Ado About Nothing;* Walt Disney's version of *Cinderella* (1950); Broadway musical *Guys and Dolls* (1955); and movies *When Harry Met Sally* (1989), starring Billy Crystal and Meg Ryan, written by Nora Ephron; *Sleepless in Seattle* (1993) and *You've Got Mail* (1998), both directed by Nora Ephron and starring Tom Hanks and Meg Ryan; and *Forget Paris* (1995), co-written, produced, directed by and starring Billy Crystal, are examples of romantic comedies.

SATIRICAL COMEDY AND BLACK COMEDY

Satires generally mock and lampoon human foolishness and vices. Satirical comedies fit the classical definition of comedy by depicting a main character's rise in fortune, but they also fit the definition of satire by making that main character either a fool, morally corrupt, or cynical in attitude. All or most of the other characters in the satirical comedy display similar foibles. These include cuckolded spouses, dupes, and other gullible types; tricksters, con artists, and criminals; hypocrites; fortune seekers; and other deceptive types who prey on the latter, who are their willing and unwitting victims. Some classical examples of satirical comedies include *The Birds* by ancient Greek comedic playwright Aristophanes, and *Volpone* by 17th-century poet and playwright Ben Jonson, who made the comedy of humors popular. When satirical comedy is extended to extremes, it becomes black comedy, wherein the comedic occurrences are grotesque or terrible. Contemporary movie examples include Quentin Tarantino's *Pulp Fiction* (1994) and the Coen brothers' *Fargo* (1996).

METAPHYSICAL POETS

Dr. Samuel Johnson, a famous 18th-century figure, who wrote philosophy, poetry, and authoritative essays on literature, coined the term "Metaphysical Poets" to describe a number of mainly 17th-century lyric poets who shared certain elements of content and style in common. The poets included John Donne (considered the founder of the Metaphysical Poets), George Herbert, Andrew Marvell, Abraham Cowley, John Cleveland, Richard Crashaw, Thomas Traherne, and Henry Vaughan. These poets encouraged readers to see the world from new and unaccustomed perspectives by shocking and surprising them through their use of paradoxes; contradictory imagery; original syntax; combinations of religious, philosophical, and artistic images; subtle argumentation; and extended metaphors called conceits. Unlike their contemporaries, they did not allude to classical mythology or nature imagery in their poetry, but to current geographical and scientific discoveries. Some, like Donne, showed Neo-Platonist influences—like the idea that a lover's beauty reflected Eternity's perfect beauty. They were called metaphysical for their transcendence—Donne in particular—of typical 17th-century rationalism's hierarchical organization through their adventurous exploration of religion, ideas, emotions, and language.

SIR THOMAS BROWNE

Sir Thomas Browne (1605-1682) was a British polymath, a practicing medical physician, scientist, religious philosopher, and author. His writing style was extraordinary and varied widely across his works. Browne was knighted in 1671 by King Charles II in recognition of his accomplishments. Among English-language writers, he has received widespread regard for his high originality. His thinking was paradoxical in that his interests embraced mysticism and other ancient esoteric disciplines, yet also a strong Christian religiosity and the nascent field of inductive scientific reasoning. His original mind produced many fresh ideas and perspectives, expressed with great complexity of both thought and language. Today he is less known and understood than many great authors, due not only to his advanced ideas and wording, but also to his many references to Biblical, Classical, and esoteric sources. The Oxford English Dictionary credits him with coining over 100 new English vocabulary words, most of which are commonly recognized today. Famous authors have consistently admired and cited him across all four centuries since his death.

Sir Thomas Browne's writing style influenced the literary world from his lifetime in the 17th century through the 21st century today. Eighteenth-century literary authority Dr. Samuel Johnson noted Browne's diverse linguistic sources, as well as his transfer of terminology among different artistic disciplines. He credited Browne with having "augmented our philosophical diction"; defended Browne's "uncommon words and expressions," observing that "he had uncommon sentiments"; and explained that Browne coined new vocabulary because he "was not content to express, in many

42

words, that idea for which any language could supply a single term." The Oxford English Dictionary lists Browne as number 70 of top-cited sources; contains 803 Browne entries; quotes him in 3,636 entries; and credits him with originating over 100 English words, including the following 38: ambidextrous, analogous, approximate, ascetic, anomalous, carnivorous, coexistence, coma, compensate, computer, cryptography, cylindrical, disruption, electricity, exhaustion, ferocious, follicle, generator, gymnastic, herbaceous, insecurity, indigenous, jocularity, literary, locomotion, medical, migrant, mucous, prairie, prostate, polarity, precocious, pubescent, therapeutic, suicide, ulterior, ultimate, and veterinarian. (Hilton, OED, 8/12)

ROMANTICISM

The height of the Romantic movement occurred in the first half of the 19th century. It identified with and gained momentum from the French Revolution (1789) against the political and social standards of the aristocracy and its overthrowing of them. Romanticism was also part of the Counter-Enlightenment, a reaction of backlash against the Enlightenment's insistence on rationalism, scientific treatment of nature, and denial of emotionalism. Though expressed most overtly in the creative arts, Romanticism also affected politics, historiography, natural sciences, and education. Though often associated with radical, progressive, and liberal politics, it also included conservatism, especially in its influences on increased nationalism in many countries. The Romantics championed individual heroes, artists, and pioneers; freedom of expression; the exotic; and the power of the individual imagination. American authors Edgar Allan Poe and Nathaniel Hawthorne, Laurence Sterne in England, and Johann Wolfgang von Goethe in Germany were included among well-known Romantic authors. The six major English Romantic poets were William Blake, William Wordsworth, Samuel Taylor Coleridge, Lord Byron, Percy Bysshe Shelley, and John Keats.

WILLIAM BLAKE

William Blake (1757-1827) is considered one of the major English Romantic poets. He was also an artist and printmaker. In addition to his brilliant poetry, he produced paintings, drawings, and notably, engravings and etchings, impressive for their technical expertise, artistic beauty, and spiritual subject matter. Because he held many idiosyncratic opinions, and moreover because he was subject to visions, reporting that he saw angels in the trees and other unusual claims, Blake was often thought crazy by others during his life, though others believed him angelic and/or blessed. His work's creative, expressive character, and its mystical and philosophical elements, led people to consider him both precursor to and member of Romanticism, and a singular, original, unclassifiable artist at the same time. Blake illustrated most of his poetry with his own hand-colored, illuminated printing. He also partially illustrated Dante's *Divine Comedy* a year before dying; the small portion he completed was highly praised. His best-known poetry includes *Songs of Innocence and of Experience*, *The Book of Thel*, *The Marriage of Heaven and Hell*, and *Jerusalem*.

WILLIAM WORDSWORTH

William Wordsworth (1770-1850) was instrumental in establishing Romanticism when he and Samuel Taylor Coleridge, another major English Romantic poet, collaboratively published *Lyrical Ballads* (1798). Wordsworth's "Preface to Lyrical Ballads" is considered a manifesto of English Romantic literary theory and criticism. In it, Wordsworth described the elements of a new kind of poetry, which he characterized as using "real language of men" rather than traditional 18th-century poetic style. In this Preface he also defined poetry as "the spontaneous overflow of powerful feelings [which] takes its origin from emotion recollected in tranquility." *Lyrical Ballads* included the famous works "The Rime of the Ancient Mariner" by Coleridge, and "Tintern Abbey" by Wordsworth. His semi-autobiographical poem, known during his life as "the poem to Coleridge," was published posthumously, entitled *The Prelude* and regarded as his major work. Wordsworth was England's Poet Laureate from 1843-1850. Among many others, his poems included "Tintern Abbey," "I Wandered Lonely as a Cloud" (often called "Daffodils"), "Ode: Intimations of Immortality," "Westminster Bridge," and "The World Is Too Much with Us."

SAMUEL TAYLOR COLERIDGE

One of the six major Romantic English Poets, Samuel Taylor Coleridge (1772-1834) was also a philosopher and literary critic, and close friends fellow Romantic poet William Wordsworth, with whom he collaborated in publishing *Lyrical Ballads,* launching the Romantic movement. He wrote very influential literary criticism, including the major two-volume autobiographical, meditative discourse *Biographia Literaria* (1817). Coleridge acquainted English-language intellectuals with the German idealist philosophy. He also coined many now familiar philosophical and literary terms, like "the willing suspension of disbelief," meaning that readers would voluntarily withhold judgment of implausible stories if their authors could impart "human interest and a semblance of truth" to them. He strongly influenced the American Transcendentalists, including Ralph Waldo Emerson. Coleridge's poem *Love,* a ballad (written to Sara Hutchinson), inspired John Keats' poem "La Belle Dame Sans Merci." He is credited with the origin of "Conversational Poetry" and Wordsworth's adoption of it. Some of his best-known works include "The Rime of the Ancient Mariner," "Christabel," "Kubla Khan," "The Nightingale," "Dejection: An Ode," and "To William Wordsworth."

JOHN KEATS

John Keats (1795-1821), despite his short life, was a major English Romantic poet. He is known for his six Odes: "Ode on a Grecian Urn," "Ode on Indolence," "Ode on Melancholy," "Ode to a Nightingale," "Ode to Psyche," and "To Autumn." Other notable works include the sonnet "O Solitude," "Endymion," "La Belle Dame Sans Merci," "Hyperion," and the collection *Lamia, Isabella, The Eve of St. Agnes and Other Poems*. The intensity and maturity he achieved in his poetry within a period of only around six years are often remarked since his death, though during life he felt he accomplished nothing lasting. He wrote a year before dying, "I have left no immortal work behind me—nothing to make my friends proud of my memory—but I have lov'd the principle of beauty in all things, and if I had had time I would have made myself remember'd." He was proven wrong. His verse from "Ode on a Grecian Urn" is renowned: "'Beauty is truth, truth beauty'—that is all / Ye know on earth, and all ye need to know."

GEORGE GORDON, LORD BYRON

George Gordon Byron, commonly known as Lord Byron (1788-1824) was a major English Romantic poet. He is known for long narrative poems "Don Juan," "Childe Harold's Pilgrimage," and the shorter lyric poem "She Walks in Beauty." The aristocratic Byron travelled throughout Europe, living in Italy for seven years. He fought in the Greek War of Independence against the Ottoman Empire, making him a national hero in Greece, before dying a year later from a fever contracted there. He was the most notoriously profligate and flamboyant Romantic poet, with reckless behaviors including multiple bisexual love affairs, adultery, rumored incest, self-exile, and incurring enormous debts. He became friends with fellow Romantic writers Percy Bysshe Shelley, the future Mary Shelley, and John Polidori. Their shared fantasy writing at a Swiss villa the summer of 1816 resulted in Mary Shelley's *Frankenstein*, Byron's *Fragment of a Novel*, and was the inspiration for Polidori's *The Vampyre* establishing the romantic vampire genre. Byron also wrote linguistic volumes on American and Armenian grammars. He loved and kept many animals. His name is synonymous today with the mercurial Romantic.

PERCY BYSSHE SHELLEY

Percy Bysshe Shelley (1792-1822), a major English Romantic poet, was not famous during life but became so after death, particularly for his lyric poetry. His best-known works include

44

"Ozymandias," "Ode to the West Wind," "To a Skylark," "Music," "When Soft Voices Die," "The Cloud," "The Masque of Anarchy"; longer poems "Queen Mab"/"The Daemon of the World" and "Adonaïs"; and the verse drama *Prometheus Unbound.* Shelley's second wife, Mary Shelley, was the daughter of his mentor William Godwin and the famous feminist Mary Wollstonecraft (*A Vindication of the Rights of Woman*), and became famous for her Gothic novel *Frankenstein.* Early in his career Shelley was influenced by William Wordsworth's Romantic poetry, and wrote the long poem *Alastor, or the Spirit of Solitude.* Soon thereafter he met Lord Byron, and was inspired to write "Hymn to Intellectual Beauty". He composed "Mont Blanc," inspired by touring the French Alpine commune Chamonix-Mont-Blanc. Shelley also encouraged Byron to compose his epic poem *Don Juan.* Shelley inspired Henry David Thoreau, Mahatma Gandhi, and others to civil disobedience, nonviolent resistance, vegetarianism, and animal rights.

WILLIAM BUTLER YEATS

William Butler Yeats (1865-1939) was among the greatest influences in 20th-century English literature. He was instrumental in the Celtic Revival/Irish Literary Revival, founding and initially running the Abbey Theatre, and was the first Irishman awarded the Nobel Prize for Literature (1923). An Irish Nationalist, he was passionately involved in politics. Yeats was believed transitional from Romanticism to Modernism. His earlier verses were lyrical, but later became realistic, symbolic, and apocalyptic. He was fascinated with Irish legend, occult subjects, and historical cycles—"gyres." He incorporated Irish folklore, mythology, and legends in "The Stolen Child," "The Wanderings of Oisin," "The Death of Cuchulain," "Who Goes with Fergus?" and "The Song of Wandering Aengus." Early collections included *The Secret Rose* and *The Wind Among the Reeds.* His later, most significant poetry collections include *The Green Helmet, Responsibilities, The Tower,* and *The Winding Stair.* Yeats's visionary, apocalyptic (1920) poem "The Second Coming" reflects his belief that his times were the anarchic end of the Christian cycle/gyre: "what rough beast, its hour come round at last, / Slouches toward Bethlehem to be born?"

ELIZABETHAN LITERATURE

Elizabethan literature is English literature written during the reign of Elizabeth I. This includes the Early Tudor period and ends with the death of Shakespeare. Elizabethan literature reflects the national pride felt during the reign of the Virgin Queen. The language of the period is highly colored, rich, and ornamented. Elizabethan poetry saw the birth of the sonnet and the epic poem "The Faerie Queen," written by Edmund Spenser. The crowning achievement of the period was Elizabethan drama, which became hugely popular with the people. Authors such as Thomas Kyd and Christopher Marlowe ushered in this golden age of drama, followed by Thomas Dekker, George Chapman, and Thomas Heywood. William Shakespeare's elegant histories, comedies, and tragedies displayed the genius of this dramatic period. The death of the queen, followed closely by Shakespeare's passing, brought a close to this golden period of drama.

GEOFFREY CHAUCER

Geoffrey Chaucer is regarded as the greatest of the Middle English authors. Chaucer wrote works of narrative poetry, and his greatest achievement is "The Canterbury Tales." "The Canterbury Tales" presents 24 stories told by a group of pilgrims traveling to Canterbury. The tales range over many subjects, including romances, religious themes, and bawdy verses. The genius of the work is the rich characterization of the pilgrims, done with consummate skill, insight, and humor. Chaucer was influenced by Dante and Boccacio, whom he read on visits to Italy. Chaucer's writing expanded the scope of Middle English writing beyond provincial life and moral ideals to a more inclusive view of the world. Chaucer was born in England in 1343 and entered royal service in his teens. He held numerous political and diplomatic posts over the years, traveling and serving across Europe.

Chaucer was widely read, and he incorporated much that he learned in his travels in his writing. Chaucer died in England in 1400.

SIR THOMAS MALORY

Sir Thomas Malory is thought to be Sir Thomas Malory of Warwickshire, although this is still the subject of academic debate. His major work, *Le Morte D'Arthur*, is a collection of prose stories based on Arthurian legend and oral traditions. These tales were the first collection of works on the legends of King Arthur and the Knights of the Round Table. They tell the stories of the kingdom of Camelot and the epic adventures of its characters. Famous characters—such as King Arthur, Sir Lancelot, Sir Gawain, and Queen Guinevere—have served as models for countless adaptations and are familiar figures in folk literature. The details of Thomas Malory's life are a mystery, but certain facts are known, chiefly from his works. Born in 1408 in England, Malory completed his literary masterpiece while imprisoned for criminal activity. Malory petitioned for release upon completion of his manuscript, but this was denied, and he died in jail in 1471. His great work was published posthumously in 1485.

CHRISTOPHER MARLOWE

Christopher Marlowe was an English author and playwright who produced a remarkable body of work in his short life. He gained acclaim as the most important Elizabethan dramatist before Shakespeare. His most successful plays include *Edward II, Tamburlaine the Great, Dr. Faustus*, and *The Jew of Malta*. Marlowe's writing is characterized by passionate protagonists, the strength of his verse, and his brilliant plotting. Scholars believe that some works attributed to Shakespeare may have been written in whole or part by Marlowe. Marlowe's poetry is accomplished, the best known being the verse that begins, "Come live with me and be my love." Marlowe, the son of a cobbler, was born in Canterbury in 1564 and educated at Cambridge. He lived a turbulent and sometimes violent life, engaging in criminal activity ranging from forgery to espionage. He was killed in 1593 at age 29 in a brawl over a tavern bill, cutting short a brilliant talent.

WILLIAM SHAKESPEARE

William Shakespeare, arguably the greatest playwright ever, has influenced world literature for the last 400 years. Shakespeare's genius was the ability to create works that capture the drama of human conflict and weakness while developing characters that suffer man's deepest existential anxieties. Master of drama and poetry alike, his writing is without peer in literary history. He wrote tragedies, histories, comedies, sonnets, and narrative poems. His works have been translated into scores of languages and adapted for film, opera, and ballet. Some of his best-known works include *Hamlet, Henry V, Romeo and Juliet*, and *Macbeth*. Shakespeare was born in Stratford-upon-Avon in 1564 and received a classical education. He married Anne Hathaway and spent most of his professional life in London, where he used the Globe Theatre as his base from 1599 on. He was well established as an actor and playwright as early as 1592 and wrote a series of brilliant sonnets in 1609. Shakespeare died in England in 1616 and is buried in Stratford.

EDMUND SPENSER

Edmund Spenser was one of the greatest Elizabethan poets, famed for his evocative sonnets and rich epic poetry. His most famous work is "The Faerie Queen," a heroic romance narrating the exploits of 12 knights. Published in 1596, it introduced a new poetic form, the Spenserian stanza based on an Italian poetic scheme. "The Faerie Queen" includes a moral allegory in an epic narrative. Spenser was a prolific author, penning sonnet sequences and notable short verse.

Born in London in 1552, Spenser was educated at Cambridge and joined the household of the Earl of Leicester, where he wrote his first work, *The Shepherdess Calendar,* comprised of 12 pastoral poems, in 1579. Spenser moved to Ireland in 1590, where he ran an estate in Cork. There he wrote an elegy for his friend Sir Philip Sidney called "Astrophel." Spenser returned to London, where he died in 1599, his place in literary history assured.

SAMUEL PEPYS

Samuel Pepys's fame rests on his *Diary*, published in full in 1828. This work provides an insightful and unusually candid view of 17th-century court life. Pepys chronicled events in his own life as well as important historical occasions, such as the coronation of Charles II. Pepys left us the most dramatic account of the great fire in London and the Black Plague. His legacy is to provide a window into the history of his time through his *Diary*. Pepys was born in London in 1633, the son of a tailor. Educated at Cambridge, he served as a naval officer, member of Parliament, and president of The Royal Society. These positions gave him an entree into the high society of London, where he was feted and honored over the years. His personal life was marred by tragedy with the death of a beloved young wife. Pepys's *Diary* went undiscovered for over 100 years until it was found in Cambridge in 1825. Pepys died in London at age 70 in 1703, at the height of his fame.

JOHN DRYDEN

John Dryden was a man for all seasons, a poet, playwright, and literary critic. He wrote a number of popular plays, the most important being *The Wild Gallant, All for Love, The Maiden Queen*, and *The Indian Queen*. Equally adept as a poet, Dryden won royal favor with his poem "To His Sacred Majesty," written for Charles II's restoration to the throne. His verse satires were considered masterpieces. He served as Poet Laureate of England from 1668 to 1688 and was revered in English society. Born in rural England in 1631, Dryden moved to London in 1655, where he remained for the rest of his life. He was appointed the royal historiographer in 1670. When James II was crowned, Dryden converted to Catholicism in the 1680s. His last years were spent translating several of the ancient classics. He died in London in 1700. His career was illustrious, and he became one of the most honored men in England.

JOHN BUNYAN

John Bunyan's literary reputation rests on his masterpiece, *The Pilgrim's Progress*, written in 1684. This work is a religious allegory that became the best seller of its day. Read by both Catholics and Protestants, it recounts the spiritual journey of humankind. Bunyan was born in 1628 in Bedford, in the English countryside, and served in Cromwell's army during the English Civil War. A spiritual maverick, he joined a nonconformist church in 1653 and became a popular preacher. In 1660, Bunyan was arrested for preaching without a permit and spent 12 years in prison. This was a time of productive writing for Bunyan, who penned *Grace Abounding to the Chief of Sinners, The Holy War*, and other spiritual tracts. Bunyan also began work on his magnum opus, *The Pilgrim's Progress*, while in prison. He was a vocal opponent of Quakerism, which he denounced in *A Vindication* in 1657. Bunyan was an active writer and preacher until his death in 1688.

ALEXANDER POPE

Alexander Pope, the great English poet and satirist, was born in London in 1688. Pope's style features biting wit, excellent command of formal poetry, and a particular kind of verse that is both insightful and dramatic. Among his numerous works is his great satire, "The Rape of the Lock," narrating a feud started over a lock of hair. "An Essay on Criticism," Pope's poem about writing, launched his career in 1711. He was to produce a body of work noted chiefly for satire and brilliant essays, including translations of Homer's "Iliad" and "Odyssey." Pope also edited a controversial edition of Shakespeare, which won him notoriety. Pope had little formal education and was raised a Catholic at a time that anti-Catholic feeling ran high in England. He contracted an unknown illness

when he was a child, leaving him a semi-invalid and stunting his growth. Despite these handicaps, Pope became one of the giants of English literature until his death in London in 1744.

DANIEL DEFOE

Daniel Defoe, born in London, had a varied and prolific literary career. He produced more than 500 books, the most important being *Robinson Crusoe* and *Moll Flanders*. Generally considered England's first novelist, Defoe was a keen observer of life and was able to translate this into riveting characters in his novels. Defoe was an eclectic author, writing essays and nonfiction, and working as a journalist during his productive years. His editorship of the *Review* from 1704 to 1713 made him the finest journalist of his day. Defoe was successful in both business and politics, becoming a strong supporter of William of Orange. His political pamphlets earned him a short term in prison. Rescued by a Tory politician, Defoe became a well-known political pamphleteer, writing arguments for the Tory party. Defoe died in London in 1731, at the apex of his journalistic career.

JONATHAN SWIFT

Jonathan Swift, Irish satirist, wrote on a wide variety of subjects, including economics, politics, society, and manners. His legacy was established by *Gulliver's Travels*, his blistering satire on the human condition published in 1726. Other well-known works include *Tale of a Tub*, a satire on the church; *Drapier's Letters*, an influential tract on Irish politics; and *A Modest Proposal*, a suggestion that Irish children be fattened and used as food for the rich. Born in Dublin in 1667, Swift received an excellent education at Trinity College and Oxford. Ordained a priest in the Church of Ireland in 1694, Swift served for ten years before becoming secretary to a prominent diplomat. Swift lived for years in both London and Dublin, where his reputation as a satirist grew. His health began to decline in the 1730s, and he was declared incompetent and assigned a guardian. Upon his death in 1745, his estate granted a large sum to found a hospital for the mentally ill.

HENRY FIELDING

Henry Fielding, English novelist and playwright, is considered a pioneer in novel writing. Fielding wrote more than 25 plays before turning his talent to novels. His best-known work is *Tom Jones*, and other notable works include *Joseph Andrews, Amelia, Shamela*, and *The Life of Mr. Jonathan Wild the Great*. He also published a newspaper, *The Champion*, which was highly successful. He was adept in social satire and comedy, which are best exemplified by *Tom Jones*. Born in Somerset in 1707, Fielding became active in politics in his late twenties. His strong anti-Jacobite essays gained Fielding political favor, and he served for many years as a judge in London. When political favor turned against him, Fielding concentrated on his writing, producing several late novels of note. Fielding died in 1754.

SAMUEL JOHNSON

Samuel Johnson—the English poet, essayist, biographer, and lexicographer—dominated the literary period of mid-18th-century England. In 1746, he began to organize the first dictionary of the English language. He completed the task in 1755, and it was hailed as a major literary accomplishment and made Johnson's reputation. A prolific essayist and journalist, his prose was celebrated for its keen observation of human folly and frailty. Johnson's other major works include *Lives of the Poets*, *Rasselas*, and "The Vanity of Human Wishes," considered his greatest poem. "Irene," a verse tragedy, was produced for the stage in 1746. Johnson was born in Lichfield in 1709 and worked as a schoolmaster there for many years. He moved to London to become a writer and succeeded beyond his dreams. Johnson was immortalized by James Boswell, his friend and confidant, in *The Life of Samuel Johnson*. Johnson was such a giant literary figure that, upon his death in 1784, his era became known as the Age of Johnson.

ROBERT BURNS

Robert Burns, the famed Scottish poet, became the most well-known literary figure in Scotland. Burns's work includes some of the best-known poetry in the English language, including "Auld Lang Syne," "A Red, Red, Rose," and the long narrative poem "Tam o' Shanter." His first anthology of poetry was *Poems, Chiefly in the Scottish Dialect*, which became an instant success and led to his long and distinguished career. Burns spent much of his life collecting and editing traditional Scottish airs. Born to a poor family in 1759, Burns spent much of his life working the land on the family farm. He was a rebel by nature and supported the French Revolution openly. Burns died in 1796, having lived only 37 years but enshrining his poetry in the hearts of all Scots. His reputation has grown over the generations, and Burns is recognized as a major poet who transcended his nationalistic feelings.

JAMES BOSWELL

James Boswell was a Scottish biographer and essayist. His most important work is *The Life of Samuel Johnson*, still regarded as one of the finest biographies in the English language. He also wrote a political history, *An Account of Corsica*, which narrates that island's movement for independence. Boswell's diaries, which include astute observations on society and manners of his day, were published after his death. Born in Edinburgh in 1740, Boswell immigrated to England, where he met Samuel Johnson in 1763. Boswell neglected his own law practice to devote his life to Johnson and his biography. He spent much of the next 25 years traveling and living with Johnson. This was a unique friendship of two notable literary figures that resulted in a biography of great power and feeling. Boswell died at age 54, leaving a legacy for all future biographers.

WILLIAM BLAKE

William Blake, poet and artist, launched his career in 1789 with the publication of *Songs of Innocence*. His most important prose work, *The Marriage of Heaven and Hell*, rejects rationalism in favor of mystical faith. His masterpiece, *Songs of Innocence and Experience*, was written in 1794. Blake pioneered what he termed prophetic books, which purport to predict the futures of America and Europe. His epic poem "Jerusalem" sought to imagine the existence of spirit after death.

Blake was a master illustrator and true mystic. Born in 1757, he had visions of angels, devils, and poets as a young child. His illustrations were extraordinary, and he worked on Dante's "Divine Comedy" and other major works. Blake's art and poetry are a heady mix of symbolism, mystic vision, and powerful emotion. Thought by many to be mad, Blake remained true to his vision and died in England in 1827 at the age of 69. Few men or women equaled Blake's extravagant perceptions and his ability to put them into words and art.

WILLIAM WORDSWORTH

William Wordsworth was a catalyst for the Romantic movement in English literature. A close friendship with Samuel Taylor Coleridge resulted in the publication of a joint venture, *Lyrical Ballads*, which sounded a new voice in poetry. The neoclassical model then in vogue was renounced for poetry written in the manner in which people actually spoke. Wordsworth's best-known volumes include *Poems: in Two Volumes* and his greatest work, *The Prelude*, an epic based on the author's life. Wordsworth was born in the Lake District of England in 1770. Educated at Cambridge, he traveled extensively in Europe and became fired up with the spirit of the French Revolution. In his early thirties, Wordsworth married and retired to his home in Grasmere, where he lived the remainder of his life. He held the position of Poet Laureate of England from 1843 until his death in 1850. One of the most loved poems in the English language is "Tintern Abbey," published in his first slender volume of poems in 1798.

SAMUEL TAYLOR COLERIDGE

Samuel Taylor Coleridge was a leading figure in English Romanticism. His partnership with the young William Wordsworth blossomed with the publication of *Lyrical Ballads* in 1798. The first poem in this book is Coleridge's "The Rime of the Ancient Mariner," a spectacular start to a most successful career. Coleridge's creative ideas on poetic form and his original and striking use of language are his contributions to English literature. Other poems of this period include "Christobel" and "Kubla Kahn." Coleridge was a tragic figure in English literature. Born in the West Country in 1772, and educated at Cambridge, he married hastily and unhappily. In later life, he moved to the Lake District to be close to William Wordsworth, his lifetime friend. Coleridge became an opium addict and his marriage failed during this time. He had an unrequited love affair with Sara Hutchinson, the sister of Wordsworth's fiancée. These travails prevented Coleridge from creative work for many years, and his body of poetry is small. This unhappy but brilliant figure died in 1834.

JANE AUSTEN

Jane Austen was an English novelist of enduring popularity. Considered by some to be a founder of the modern novel, Austen narrated the everyday life of country gentry in the latter part of the 18th century. She combined keen observation, sharp wit, and memorable characters to create a much-loved body of work. *Northanger Abbey, Sense and Sensibility*, and *Pride and Prejudice* were written in the 1790s but not published until 10 years later. *Emma, Mansfield Park*, and *Persuasion* were the fruits of her later work. Her parodies of Gothic romances and novels of courtship are unequaled in English literature. A brilliant plotter, her view of character relationships against the complex web of social manners and mores of the day is unequaled. Austen was born in 1775. She was educated at home in the Bath area, where she lived her entire life. All of her novels were published anonymously, and she wrote productively until her death in 1817. Austen's works were a critical success as well as being loved by the public. They have been adapted for the theatre, television, and the cinema.

LORD BYRON

George Gordon Byron was an English poet who captured the imagination of the literary world. His most famous work is *Childe Harold's Pilgrimage*, a work of fiction set as a travelogue. Perhaps his masterpiece is the epic satire "Don Juan," a lengthy poem largely autobiographical. Later works of note include *The Prisoner of Chillon and other Poems*, "Manfred," and the satirical poem "Beppo." Byron was born in 1788 in London and reared in Scotland. He was educated at Cambridge. He was unusually handsome but suffered from a clubfoot. Byron took his seat in the House of Lords briefly before setting out on travels in Europe. He left England for good in 1816, traveling widely in Switzerland, Italy, and Greece. Byron engaged in passionate love affairs, became a revolutionary, and generally captured the imagination of the literary world. He died of a fever in Greece in 1824, and his body was sent back to England for burial.

SIR WALTER SCOTT

Sir Walter Scott was a Scottish poet and novelist. He began his literary career by collecting traditional ballads of Scotland and publishing them in an anthology. He specialized in narrative poetry with a romantic theme, usually set in medieval times. His breakthrough poems include "The Lady of the Lake" and "The Lay of the Last Minstrel." Scott is best known for his historical novels published as the *Waverley Novels*. Included in this group are *Rob Roy, Ivanhoe, Kenilworth*, and *The Bride of Lammermoor*. Scott was born in 1771 in Edinburgh and spent his early life there. His formal training was as a barrister, but he did not practice law for a living. He relied on his popular fiction for his income and was most successful at first. A publishing partnership failed, and Scott was burdened with large debts he spent most of his life repaying. He eventually became financially stable through his popular fiction and works of literary criticism. He died in Scotland in 1832.

PERCY SHELLEY

Shelley was a renowned English poet who used the themes of love, romance, and imagination as his topics. Shelley had a powerful lyrical voice, and his best-known poems—"To a Skylark," "Prometheus Unbound," "Ode to the West Wind," and "Adonais"—exhibit this narrative power. He has remained an inspiration to Romantic poets for centuries. Born in England in 1792, Shelley attended Eton and Oxford before being expelled for publishing a tract on atheism. He traveled widely in Europe, sometimes in the company of Lord Byron. He had a passionate relationship with Mary Shelley, whom he would marry after the death of his first wife. Tragedy stalked Shelley, with the loss of two children and his wife's subsequent breakdown. Besieged by creditors, and in failing health, he continued to write productively until his death by drowning in Italy in 1822. His 29 years were filled with literary accomplishment and personal sorrow.

MARY SHELLEY

Mary Wollstonecraft Godwin (later Shelley) was an English novelist who won lasting fame with her Gothic horror story *Frankenstein*, published in 1818. This classic narrates the creation of a monster from human body parts. This work has been adapted countless times in many ways, always retaining the flavor of horror and responsibility. Shelley's later works include *Valperga, The Last Man*, and *Lodore*. She also edited numerous editions of Percy Shelley's prose and poetry.

Shelley was born in England in 1797, the only child of radical reformer William Godwin and feminist pioneer Mary Wollstonecraft. She eloped to Europe with Percy Shelley, whom she married in 1813. Mary Shelley suffered greatly from several miscarriages, the death of two children, and ultimately her husband's drowning. She continued to write effectively through these travails, but never again equaled the success of *Frankenstein*. She died in 1851.

JOHN KEATS

John Keats was an English poet of great imagination and a romantic nature. His work is best known for six odes written in 1819: "Ode to a Grecian Urn," "Ode to a Nightingale," "Ode to Psyche," "Ode on Melancholy," "Ode on Indolence," and "To Autumn." This poetry abounds in symbolism exploring the frailty of life and the power of creative art. They are felt to be some of the best English poetry extant. Keats's other notable works include "Lamia," "The Eve of St. Agnes," and "Hyperion."

Keats was born in London in 1795 and studied medicine for a time. He soon turned to poetry, mentored by the political radical and writer Leigh Hunt. In 1818, he published his first poetry, "Endymion," an epic based on Greek mythology. Keats contracted tuberculosis, and fell upon hard times. His engagement to Fanny Brawne would end as his health failed. As his disease advanced, Keats moved to Rome hoping the change would help heal him. He died there in 1821 at the tender age of 25.

CHARLES DICKENS

Charles Dickens is thought by some to be England's greatest novelist. In 1837, *The Pickwick Papers*, a comic novel, launched his career. This was followed quickly by *Oliver Twist* (1838), *Nicholas Nickelby* (1839), and *A Christmas Carol* (1843). Dickens had a genius for creating memorable characters, and his ability to evoke a sense of 19th-century England is unmatched. His later works include *David Copperfield* (1850), *Great Expectations* (1861), and *A Tale of Two Cities* (1859). Charles Dickens was born in Portsmouth in 1812. He worked as a journalist until the success of his novels. Dickens founded and edited several literary magazines, including *Household Words* and *All the Year Round*. Dickens gave reading tours in Europe and the United States that were very popular and drew large crowds. Dickens died in Gad's Hill Place in 1870 and is buried in Westminster Abbey.

LORD ALFRED TENNYSON

Tennyson was an important English poet of his day, publishing his first work, *Poems, Chiefly Lyrical* in 1830. His subsequent volumes of poetry include *Maud, and Other Poems* (1855), and *Idylls of the King* (1885), an epic poem based on the legend of King Arthur. Later works of note are *Enoch Arden* (1864) and *Demeter and Other Poems* (1889). His best-loved individual poems are "The Charge of the Light Brigade," "Crossing the Bar," and "Mariana." Tennyson wrote of history, honor, and faith, championing Victorian values and mastering the technical elements of poetry. Born in a small village in the north of England in 1809, he was educated at Cambridge and published his first book of verse there. Tennyson was named Poet Laureate of England by Queen Victoria in 1850, succeeding William Wordsworth. He died in England in 1892, his place in history secure.

CHARLOTTE BRONTË

Charlotte Brontë, beloved English novelist, wrote stories of independent women in a very personal voice. Her characters were enmeshed in romance and love affairs, even as they lived lives of creativity unusual for the period. Her first novel, *The Professor*, was not published until after her death. Her most powerful work is *Jane Eyre* (1847), a narrative of a young woman and her travails in love and society. Other works include *Shirley* (1849) and *Villete* (1853), based on her sister Emily's experiences living in Europe. Brontë was born in 1816, the daughter of a Yorkshire clergyman. She was sent to a boarding school with harsh living conditions and strict rules of behavior. She would later use the school as a model in *Jane Eyre*. The death of her three siblings in quick succession clouded her life with sadness. She died in England in 1855 at the tender age of 38.

EMILY BRONTË

Emily Brontë, sister of Charlotte Brontë, and English novelist and poet, produced only one novel in her lifetime. However, her novel *Wuthering Heights* (1847) stands as a testament to her literary talent. A harsh tale, it is the story of the passionate bond between Catherine and Heathcliff, in which two families are jealously destroyed. It is a signature novel of English Romanticism. Emily Brontë was a poet of some skill, her works appearing jointly with her sister's in *Poems by Currer, Ellis, and Acton Bell* (1846). Emily Brontë was born in 1818 in Yorkshire. A unique and mysterious personality, she had few friends except her sister Anne, with whom she maintained a strong bond. Together they created the world of Gondal, an imaginary society that she used extensively in her poetry. In Charlotte's words, "Emily was stronger than a man, simpler than a child." Emily contracted tuberculosis and died at age 30 in 1848.

WILLIAM MAKEPEACE THACKERAY

William Thackeray was a gifted Victorian English novelist and satirist. He started his writing career doing satirical pieces for magazines and weeklies. *The Book of Snobs* (1848) and his masterwork, *Vanity Fair* (1849), both appeared first as serials in periodicals. *Vanity Fair* follows Becky Sharp as she attempts to climb the social ladder of English society. Thackeray's later work includes *Barry Lyndon* (1852), *The Virginians* (1859), and the fictional autobiography *Pendennis* (1850).

Thackeray was born in India, but returned to England for his education at Cambridge. Thackeray was a popular lecturer, and he toured England and America giving talks. His strength as a writer was his ability to describe the moralistic hypocrisy of British society. *Vanity Fair* is his lasting legacy and remains a popular vehicle for adaptations today. Thackeray died in London in 1863.

ANTHONY TROLLOPE

Trollope was an English novelist of great dexterity. Famed for his evocation of Victorian life and his vivid characters, Trollope was one of the most popular writers of his day. His finest works were two novel sequences, *The Barsetshire Novels*, consisting of four volumes, and the politically themed *Palliser Novels*. His fiction created characters that have stood the test of time and remain fresh today. Trollope's stories have been adapted many times for film, television, and the stage.

Trollope was born in rural London in 1815 and reared there in modest circumstances. He became a civil servant, working for the Royal Mail for many years. He wrote with great energy during his life, producing prose collections, travel books, biographies, and 47 novels. His two-volume *Autobiography* appeared posthumously in 1883. Anthony Trollope died in 1882 at the age of 67.

ELIZABETH BARRETT BROWNING

Browning, the well-known poet of Victorian England, is best remembered for her lyrics of love in her *Sonnets from the Portuguese* published in 1850. Her verse "How do I love thee? Let me count the ways" has inspired lovers for over 150 years. Her other major works include "Aurora Leigh" (1857), a verse novel, clearly autobiographical, and *Last Poems* (1852). Browning's poetry evokes England and Italy, where she also lived, and has themes of social justice throughout. Browning was born in Hertfordshire in 1806 and reared on the family farm. Smothered by an overly protective father, the poet suffered poor health and was a semi-recluse. She met Robert Browning in 1845, and they wed the next year. The couple moved to Italy, where Browning improved both her health and disposition. She spent the next 16 years with Browning in a devoted and tender marriage. Elizabeth died in 1861 at age 55.

ROBERT BROWNING

Robert Browning was a major Victorian poet known for his skill in characterization, psychological nuances, and colorful and dramatic dialogue. His early work was not well received, but Browning persisted, publishing the successful *Dramatic Lyrics* in 1842. His next collection, *Dramatis Personae* (1864), was his most popular. His technical skill as a poet remains his greatest legacy. Browning was born in London in 1812 and was largely self-educated. He did not achieve public acclaim until later in life. In 1845, Browning began a correspondence with the reclusive Elizabeth Barrett. Against all odds, the couple married in 1846 and created one of the great literary romances. The pair lived a full and devoted life together until Elizabeth's death in 1861. Robert Browning survived and enjoyed his greatest success until his passing in 1889, 28 years after Elizabeth died.

WILKIE COLLINS

Willkie Collins, English novelist, is considered the pioneer of the mystery story and novel. His first novels were *Antonia, or The Fall of Rome* (1850) and *Basil* (1852), his first novel of suspense. Collins's reputation was made with the publication of *The Woman in White* in 1860. He followed this success with the hugely popular *The Moonstone* in 1868. His later works include *Armadale* (1866), *The New Magdalen* (1873), *The Haunted Hotel* (1879), and *Heart and Science* (1883).

Collins was born in London in 1824 and studied law in college. Although admitted to the bar, he never practiced and soon turned his energies to writing. Befriended by Charles Dickens, who published much of his early work serially in his literary magazines, Collins soon became popular, and the demand for mystery and suspense fiction has never waned. He died in London in 1889.

CHRISTINA ROSSETTI

Christina Rossetti was an accomplished English Victorian poet. Her best-known poetry is contained in *Goblin Market and other Poems* (1862) and *The Prince's Progress and other Poems* (1862).

Rossetti published a successful book of children's poetry, *Sing-Song*, in 1872. Her later work is highlighted by *Time Flies*, published in 1885. In 1904, William Rossetti compiled his sister's *Poetical Works* followed by a collection of her letters. A devout high Anglican, her work often reflects her piety. Rossetti was born England in 1830 into a cultured and well-to-do family. After her initial successes, Rossetti was afflicted with Graves' disease and never really recovered her health. Increasingly reclusive, she devoted herself to melancholy religious prose. Rossetti never married, spurning several Catholic suitors, and died at her family home in 1894. She was 64 years old.

LEWIS CARROLL

Lewis Carroll is the pen name of Charles Lutwidge Dodgson, author of *Alice's Adventures in Wonderland* (1865) and its sequel *Through The Looking Glass* (1871). His literary reputation rests on these two children's books although he wrote several other works, including "The Hunting of the Snark" (1876), *A Tangled Tale* (1885), and *Sylvie and Bruno* (1889). Carroll also wrote several significant works on logic and mathematics. The character of Alice was inspired by his favorite child-friend, Alice Liddell, and her two sisters, to whom he related the story. Carroll was born in England in 1832 and became a mathematics teacher and resident scholar of Christ Church College, Oxford. He assumed his pen name to protect his academic reputation, which might have been affected by authoring children's books. *Alice* brought him instant celebrity and served as an entrée to Victorian society. Carroll remained at Guildford until his death in 1898.

MATTHEW ARNOLD

Matthew Arnold, English poet and critic, published six volumes of collected verse in his life, covering a wide range of subjects and moods. Much of his poetry evokes sadness and despair. Best remembered for "Dover Beach" (1867), a poem concerning the loss of faith in the modern age, Arnold was a critic of great importance. Arnold believed that literature and culture should be inculcated into society for moral and spiritual reasons. He was a prolific essayist, writing on religion, social issues, literature, and economics. His literary criticism was influential throughout the world. Arnold was born in Middlesex and educated at Rugby School and Oxford University. He worked for many years as an inspector of schools, a position he valued highly. In 1857, he became professor of poetry at Oxford, where he taught for ten years. His lectures at Oxford became the basis for many of his influential essays over the years. Arnold died in 1888.

W. S. GILBERT

Gilbert was an English playwright and humorist who teamed with Arthur Sullivan to produce the most popular light verse and comic opera in the English language. The partnership was formed in 1870, and they produced 17 operettas together. The most popular include *The Pirates of Penzance* (1879), *The Mikado* (1884), *H.M.S. Pinafore* (1878), and *The Yeoman of the Guard* (1888). Gilbert and Sullivan became the most successful writers of light opera ever. Gilbert was born in London in 1836 and educated at King's College. He began his writing career as a journalist, creating humorous pieces for magazines and weeklies. In 1866, he wrote his first play, *Dulcamara*, for a Christmas presentation. His partnership with Sullivan lasted 20 years and proved to be one of the most successful in music history. Gilbert died in London in 1911.

GEORGE ELIOT

George Eliot, the pen name of Mary Ann Evans, English novelist and essayist, started her literary career with the publication of *Scenes of a Clerical Life* in 1858. Her most beloved novel is *Middlemarch* (1872), a richly evocative narration of life in an English country town. Her characters are vivid and memorable, particularly her protagonist Dorothea Brooke. Eliot went on to publish a number of fine novels, including *Silas Marner* (1861), *Daniel Deronda* (1876), and *The Mill on the Floss* (1860), thought to be largely autobiographical. Her writing was bold and powerful, and

brought new prestige to the 19th-century English novel. Eliot was born in the English countryside in 1819. After her father's death, she served as an editor of *The Westminster Review*, a leading literary journal. Eliot was a free thinker who had a long relationship with a married man, causing a scandal in English society. She died in London in 1880.

ROBERT LOUIS STEVENSON

Robert Louis Stevenson was a Scottish essayist, novelist, poet, and short-story writer. After writing for weeklies for a few years, his *Treasure Island* (1883) brought him acclaim and wealth. Stevenson followed this success with *Kidnapped* (1886), *The Strange Case of Dr. Jekyll and Mr. Hyde* (1886), and *The Master of Ballantrae* (1889), all critical and financial successes. Stevenson also wrote a book of verse for children, *A Child's Garden of Verses* (1885). His swashbuckling tales and colorful language engaged the fancy of the public, and he retired a wealthy man. Stevenson was born in Edinburgh in 1850 and educated in law. His life was tainted by chronic tuberculosis, and he sought cures and more healthy climates all over the world. Stevenson finally found the relief he sought in Samoa, where he settled and lived the last years of his life. He died there in 1894, at the young age of 44.

SIR ARTHUR CONAN DOYLE

Conan Doyle's contribution to literature was the enigmatic detective, Sherlock Holmes. Conan Doyle based his character on a former professor at the University of Edinburgh. Holmes first appeared in 1887 in "A Study in Scarlet," and more stories of the master of deductive reasoning appeared in magazines of the day. These stories were collected and published as *The Adventures of Sherlock Holmes* in 1892. Most memorable among the Holmes novels include *The Hound of the Baskervilles* (1902), *The Valley of Fear* (1915), and *The Sign of Four* (1890). Conan Doyle also wrote a number of popular historical romances. Conan Doyle was born in Edinburgh in 1859 and educated at Edinburgh. He trained as a physician and practiced medicine in Southsea from 1882 to 1890. The success of his writing allowed him to largely retire from medicine.

THOMAS HARDY

Hardy was an English novelist, playwright, and short-story writer. His dark works, often drawn from his own experience, include his first novel *Far from the Madding Crowd* (1874), a tale of a strong woman and her three lovers. Hardy followed this modest success with four powerful novels, *Jude the Obscure* (1895), *The Return of the Native* (1878), *Tess of the D'Urbervilles* (1891), and *The Mayor of Casterbridge* (1896). All these volumes showcase Hardy's skills as storyteller and creator of strong characters. Hardy's poetry is also considered some of the best of his time. Hardy was born in Dorchester in southwest England in 1840. He was trained as an architect, which he gave up for writing when he achieved success. Following the death of his wife, Hardy was guilt-ridden, and his grief fueled the writing of his greatest poetry, *Poems of 1912–13*. Hardy married again and lived until 1928.

OSCAR WILDE

Oscar Wilde (originally named Fingal O'Flahertie Wills Wilde) was an Irish writer, poet, critic, and, playwright. Famed for his wit, repartee, and flamboyant lifestyle, Wilde's first success was *The Importance of Being Earnest*, produced in 1895. Some of Wilde's most famous works include *The Picture of Dorian Gray* (1891), a moral allegory, *An Ideal Husband* (1895), *The Happy Price* (1888), and a French drama *Salome* (1896). "De Profundis" (1905) was taken from a letter written in prison. His final work, "The Ballad of Reading Gaol" (1897), is his most famous poem. Wilde was born in Dublin in 1854 and had a classical education. He moved to London, becoming a leader in the Aesthetic movement. Wilde was imprisoned for his homosexual activity, after losing a libel suit against the father of his lover, and spent two years at hard labor. On his release from prison, he moved to France, where he resided until his death in 1900 at the age of 46.

H. G. WELLS

H. G. Wells was an English journalist and novelist. Known as a founding father of science fiction, he is now best known for *The Time Machine* (1895), *The Island of Dr. Moreau* (1886), and *The War of the Worlds* (1898), futuristic novels that captured the fancy of the public. He was also admired in his day for his traditional novels, chief of which is *Tono-Bungay* (1909). Wells wrote the respected *The Outline of History* (1920), which is a warning to society to recognize and remedy its problems.

Wells was born in London in 1866 and attended the Normal School of Science. He incorporated his scientific knowledge in his work, which gave it a ring of truth. Wells was a socialist who believed the salvation of society would be its technology. He was active politically his entire life and became an influential advocate of socialism. Wells died in London in 1946, having witnessed the birth of the atomic age.

BRAM STOKER

Bram Stoker, born Abraham Stoker, was an Irish novelist. His reputation is based on the creation of one of the most feared and imitated characters in literature, Count Dracula of Transylvania. Count Dracula was a polished and urbane aristocrat and a supernatural creature who feasted on human blood to transform his victims into monsters. The Gothic novel *Dracula*, published in 1897, is based on folklore and the historical figure Vlad the Impaler. Born in Dublin in 1847, Stoker received a classical education at Trinity College, Dublin. He worked in local government for a short time and then became secretary and manager of Sir Henry Irving, a prominent actor in London. Their association would last 27 years before Stoker retired to concentrate on his writing. Bram Stoker died in 1912, his legacy assured in the ever-popular figure of Dracula.

RUDYARD KIPLING

Kipling, the favorite writer of the British Empire, was a novelist, poet, and short-fiction writer of great skill. His novels of British imperialism, such as *Kim* (1901), carved a unique literary niche for Kipling. His poetry was much beloved; outstanding examples are "Gunga Din," "Mandalay," and "Danny Deever." Kipling's story collections for children include *The Jungle Book* (1894) and *Just So Stories* (1902). Kipling's descriptions of British colonial life became a window for the world to understand the glory and excesses of the empire. Kipling was born in Bombay in 1865 and educated in England. He returned to India for several years, working as a journalist and fledgling poet. Returning to England, his prose collection captured the fancy of the nation. Kipling lived for four productive years in Vermont and then went home for good. The first English writer to win a Nobel Prize for Literature, he died in England in 1936.

JOSEPH CONRAD

Joseph Conrad, born Josef Teodor Konrad Korziniowski, was a Polish-born English novelist who found success with his early adventure novels of the sea, such as *Almayer's Folly* (1895), *Lord Jim* (1900), and *Typhoon* (1903). He is perhaps best known for his adventure and psychological thrillers, such as *Heart of Darkness* (1902) and *The Secret Agent* (1907). Conrad was noted for his treatment of moral questions and the adroit use of language in his work. Born in Poland in 1857, Conrad moved with his exiled family to Russia. Conrad went to sea with both the French Merchant Marine and the British Merchant Navy, eventually commanding a ship. His travels provided the raw material for his fiction, which is now highly regarded by critics. Conrad became a British subject and lived in Bishopsbourne until his death in 1924.

SAMUEL BUTLER

Samuel Butler, English essayist, critic, and novelist, is best known for his biting satire and savage wit. His first major work, *Erewhon*, published in 1872, was a satire on the public's belief in universal progress. He wrote two additional novels, *The Fair Haven* (1873), an attack on the Resurrection, and *Erewhon Revisited* (1901), before the publication of his best-known work, *The Way of All Flesh*, published posthumously in 1903. *The Way of All Flesh* is a largely autobiographical work describing Victorian middle-class life. Samuel Butler was born in Nottinghamshire in 1835 and educated at Cambridge. He emigrated to New Zealand and became a sheep farmer and occasional writer on scientific theory. Returning to England in 1864, he turned to writing full time, and produced most of his major work. Butler died in England in 1902.

FORD MADOX FORD

Ford Madox Ford, born Ford Hermann Hueffer, was an English novelist and critic. His most honored work is *The Good Soldier*, published in 1915. *The Good Soldier* narrates an unhappy marriage in the English upper class. Ford collaborated on two novels with Joseph Conrad, *The Inheritors* (1901) and *Romance* (1903). His other major works include *Parade's End*, a trilogy of novels set in America and Europe. Editor and founder of the *Transatlantic Review*, a literary journal of excellent reputation, Ford spent his later productive years writing a general survey of world literature for lay readers.

Ford was born in England in 1873 and fought in France in World War I. He returned and settled in Paris after the war, where he was active in literary society. He lived for a time in America before returning to Europe. He died in 1939.

D. H. LAWRENCE

D. H. Lawrence, English novelist, poet, essayist, and short-fiction writer, brought an intensity to his work and life that sometimes scandalized his peers. His autobiographical novel, *Sons and Lovers*, was published in 1913. His greatest works, *The Rainbow* (1915), *Women in Love* (1921), and *Lady Chatterley's Lover* (1928) (banned in England and America for 30 years), focus on love, class, social standing, and sexuality. *The Complete Poems of D. H. Lawrence* (1964) is the best anthology of his verse. Lawrence was born in industrial England in 1885. His childhood was marred by an unhappy home. In 1915, Lawrence and his wife left England for good and traveled extensively. Suffering from tuberculosis, Lawrence sought a climate that would benefit his health. He died of the disease in 1930.

GEORGE BERNARD SHAW

George Bernard Shaw was an Irish playwright and critic. Shaw published his collections of drama in *Plays Pleasant and Unpleasant* (1898), which included some of his best work, including his critical prefaces. Shaw's plays also include *Caesar and Cleopatra* (1901), *Major Barbara* (1907), *Pygmalion* (1913), and *St. Joan* (1924). He was awarded the Nobel Prize in literature in 1925. Shaw chose controversial topics for his dramas, stressing realistic social problems. He satirized social class and gender discrimination, but with a light touch that made its points without anger. Shaw was born in Dublin in 1856 and soon moved to London. An ardent progressive, he spoke and wrote passionately on the social issues of the day. He was renowned for his literary criticism, and was a major contributor to literary digests of his day. A leading figure in world literature, Shaw died in Hertfordshire in 1950.

JAMES JOYCE

James Joyce, Irish novelist and short-story writer, developed a style rich in innovative literary technique and creative language. His first major work was a collection of short stories, *The Dubliners* (1914), followed by an autobiographical novel, *A Portrait of the Artist as a Young Man*

(1916), and a drama, *Exiles* (1918). Joyce published *Ulysses* in 1922 to critical acclaim. Joyce spent many years on his next novel, finally publishing *Finnegans Wake* in 1939. James Joyce was born in Dublin in 1882, and most of his fiction is set in that city. Rebelling against the constraints of Catholic society, Joyce left Ireland and lived in Europe most of his life. He lived in a number of European cities with his wife Nora Barnacle, often in poor circumstances and plagued by an eye disorder that caused near blindness. Joyce died in 1941.

Virginia Woolf

Virginia Woolf, born Adele Virginia Stephen—English novelist, short-fiction writer, essayist, and critic—was one of the most creative and influential writers of the 20th century. After publishing two traditional novels, Woolf wrote *Jacob's Room* (1922), using her stream of consciousness method of interior monologues to develop an absent character. She continued her experimentation in *Mrs. Dalloway* (1925), *To the Lighthouse* (1927), and *The Waves* (1931). Woolf was born in England in 1882 and educated by her father, a distinguished literary figure in his own right. After her father's death, she and her family moved to the Bloomsbury section of London, where their home became the center of the group of authors, artists, and thinkers known as the Bloomsbury Group. She married Leonard Woolf, with whom she would found the Hogarth Press, a publisher of many important Modernist writers. Woolf committed suicide in 1941 by drowning.

Gerald Manley Hopkins

Gerald Manley Hopkins, English poet, published his first successful poem, "The Wreck of the Deutschland," in 1875. He followed this with a series of sonnets, including "The Windhover," "Pied Beauty," "God's Grandeur," and "Carrion Comfort." His later poems were written in a period of personal depression and religious doubt. He developed a style called sprung rhythm, which attempts to duplicate human speech. The first collection of his work, *Poems*, was published 30 years after his death. His reputation has grown over the decades, and he is now seen as a major influence on modern poetry. Hopkins was born in Stratford, Essex, in 1844. He attended Oxford where he received a classical education. Following his decision to convert to Catholicism and study for the priesthood, Hopkins abandoned poetry for seven years. Poverty and spiritual doubt haunted him the rest of his life. He died in England in 1889.

Wilfred Owen

Wilfred Owen is regarded as the greatest English poet of World War I. Owen's work is best known as a scathing indictment against war based on his experiences in France during 1917–18. Stylistically innovative, his language is starkly realistic in depicting the horrors of war. Most of Owen's work was published after his death, with the collected *Poems* introduced by Siegfried Sassoon, which include "Strange Meeting" and "Anthem for Doomed Youth." Owen's verse was used in Benjamin Britten's *War Requiem*, a powerful choral piece that became an instant classic.

Wilfred Owen was born in Shropshire and had a mundane education at Shrewsbury Technical College. He taught until 1915, when he enlisted in the army. Wounded in 1917, he was recovering in Scotland, where he met Sassoon, who encouraged his poetry. Returning to the front in 1918, he was killed only a week before the war ended.

Katherine Mansfield

Born Kathleen Mansfield Beauchamp, Mansfield was a New Zealand short story writer. Her first collection of short fiction, *In a German Pension* (1911), was well received. She was to publish a number of anthologies of her work, including *Bliss* (1920), *The Garden Party and Other Stories* (1922), and *Prelude* (1918). Her style and strength was the complex and subtle development of her characters, probing their psychological depths. She was a prolific contributor to magazines, working with her editor-husband, John Middleton Murry. He collected all of her letters and journals and published them after her death. Mansfield was born in New Zealand in 1888. She emigrated to England in 1907, where she would spend the rest of her life. Mansfield died in Fontainebleau in 1923.

AGATHA CHRISTIE

Dame Agatha Christie, English novelist and playwright, is one of the most successful writers of all time. The author of more than 80 detective novels, her work has been translated into more than 100 languages. She created two memorable characters, the eccentric Hercule Poirot and the elderly spinster Miss Jane Marple, who are the protagonists of most of her books. Christie wrote and adapted many works for the stage, including her famous *The Mousetrap*, which is the longest running play in the history of drama. The play is still running in London, where it opened in 1952. Many of her works have been adapted for television and film. Born and raised in the West Country in 1890, she worked as a nurse and chemist in World War I, during which time she gained a working knowledge of poisons, which she utilized in her fiction. Christie died in Wallingford in 1976.

E. M. FORSTER

Edward Morgan Forster—English novelist, essayist, and critic—a major figure in modern literature, published his first four novels between 1905 and 1910: *Where Angels Fear To Tread* (1905), *The Longest Journey* (1907), *A Room With A View* (1908), and *Howard's End* (1910). Forster addressed subjects such as social justice, materialism and spirituality, and the dissolution of the English upper classes. His masterpiece, *A Passage to India* (1924), was inspired by several visits to India and Forster's service in Egypt in World War I. Forster also published volumes of literary criticism and essays. Forster was born in 1879 in London into an upper-middle-class household. He was educated at King's College, Cambridge, and became a contributor to a number of literary journals. His eclectic and prolific work made him a major figure in world literature. Forster died in England in 1970, at age 91.

WILLIAM BUTLER YEATS

William Butler Yeats, Irish poet and playwright, originally made his name as a dramatist with such plays as *The Countess Cathleen* (1892), *The Land of Heart's Desire* (1894), and *Cathleen in Houlihan* (1902). The poetry of Yeats's later years shows a spare, realistic style, with much symbolism. Examples of this are "Easter 1916" (1916), celebrating the Easter rising in Dublin, and "The Second Coming" (1921). Yeats was awarded the Nobel Prize for Literature in 1923. Yeats was born in Dublin in 1865 and raised in London. He maintained a strong interest in Irish nationalism, folklore, mysticism, and painting his entire life. In love with the political activist Maud Gonne, he suffered when his love was not returned. Yeats was a founder of what became the Abbey Theatre in Dublin, a center of Irish literary life. Yeats died in France in 1939.

ALDOUS HUXLEY

Aldous Huxley, English novelist and social critic, created a hellish vision of the future in *Brave New World*, published in 1932. Describing a society based on technology and social control, *Brave New World* was the summation of a generation's fears about the future. Huxley's early novels are full of biting satire and criticism of society. His later works include *Island* (1962), reflecting his interest in Eastern spirituality and metaphysics. *After Many A Summer Dies The Swan* (1939) indicates Huxley's growing distrust of politics and social trends. Two later works discuss his experiments with hallucinogenic drugs. Huxley was born in Surrey, England, in 1894 and educated at Eton and Oxford. He emigrated to America in 1937, where he lived for the rest of his life. Huxley remained active as a teacher, writer, and social critic until his death in 1963.

W. H. Auden

Wystan Hugh Auden was an English-born man of letters, an accomplished poet, playwright, critic, editor, and translator. Perhaps best known for his verse, which was witty, musical, and innovative in the use of rhythms, Auden published a number of collections. *The Age of Anxiety* (1947) won him a Pulitzer Prize for Poetry. Other important works include *Another Time* (1940), *The Double Man* (1941), *Nuns* (1951), and the National Book Award winner *The Shield Of Achilles* (1955). An opera librettist of great skill, he worked with such luminaries as Britten and Stravinsky. Born in England in 1907, Auden was educated at Oxford, where he became a political activist for leftist movements. He moved to the United States, becoming a popular teacher and lecturer while producing work of the first order. Auden died in 1973 at the age of 65.

George Orwell

George Orwell, the pen name of Eric Arthur Blair—English novelist, critic, and playwright—is best known for his novels damning totalitarian regimes, and doing so with crushing satire. His two major works are *Animal Farm* (1945) and *1984* (1949), which established him as a leading satirist and novelist. His writing was fueled by his passionate economic and political views, and they are the keystones of his work. Aside from his two successful novels, he wrote several lesser ones, a collection of essays, and his four-volume *Collected Essays, Journalism, and Letters of George Orwell* (1968). Orwell was born Bengal, India in 1903 and educated at Eton. He then joined the Indian Imperial police in Burma but became disillusioned by imperialism and returned to Europe to live. Orwell fought for the Republicans in the Spanish Civil War and wrote of his experiences. After his success in the 1940s, he enjoyed an all too brief period of fame until his death in 1950.

Anthony Powell

Anthony Powell, English novelist, contributed to the staggering achievements of 20th-century fiction with his writing of the 12-volume opus *A Dance to the Music of Time,* published between 1951 and 1975. Grouped in three series of four novels each, it is the story of a man's life over 50 years, from public school through adulthood. His narration is sometimes humorous, often melodramatic, and it has been consistently overlooked by critics. His earlier works focus on satirizing the British upper class. After completing his master work, Powell remained productive, producing a four-volume memoir. Anthony Powell was born in London in 1905 and educated at Eton and Oxford. He worked for many years in journalism and publishing until his success allowed him to concentrate on his novels. He had a long and active career that ended with his death in 2000.

Samuel Beckett

Samuel Beckett was an Irish-French novelist, playwright, short-story writer, and poet. His work explores the degradation of modern man, with a focus on the essential meaninglessness and absurdity of life. Beckett's work contains little action, with meaning coming from dialogue and silences. His best-known work, the play *Waiting for Godot* (1953), is an allegory of life waiting only on death. Beckett was a prolific author, writing short fiction, drama, and prose for almost 50 years. He left a huge body of work behind that attests to his technical skills as a writer. He was awarded the Nobel Prize for Literature in 1969 for his contributions. Born in Ireland in 1906, Beckett was educated at Trinity College, Dublin. He moved to Paris, where he befriended James Joyce, who had an important influence on his work. He fought in the French Resistance during the war and was forced to flee Paris, to which he returned in 1945. He died in France in 1989.

Dylan Thomas

Dylan Thomas, Welsh poet and prose writer, was a figure bigger than life. Thomas produced his first volume of poetry in his twenties and won a reputation as a fresh voice in modern poetry. Later

60

volumes include *Death And Embraces* (1946) and *In Country Sleep* (1952), which included his best-known verse, "Do Not Go Gentle Into That Good Night." Thomas was an eclectic writer, developing stories and radio scripts that were very successful. His short-story volumes include *Under Milk Wood* (1954) and *A Child's Christmas in Wales* (1955). Thomas was born in Swansea, Wales, in 1914, the son of a teacher. Perhaps best known by the public for his bouts of drinking, strife-ridden relationships, and flamboyant personality, his work is sometimes overshadowed by his personality. Thomas died of alcoholism on a poetry-reading tour in New York City in 1953 at the age of 39.

J. R. R. TOLKIEN

John Ronald Reuel Tolkien, English novelist, became famous for his mythological fantasies *The Hobbit* (1937), and *The Lord of the Rings* trilogy (1954–55). His fantasies were based on bedtime stories he told his children. At the urging of his friend and colleague C. S. Lewis, Tolkien wrote *The Hobbit* and spent the next 12 years writing the sequels, *The Lord of the Rings*. His own favorite among his novels was the Middle Earth romance *The Silmarillion*, published by his son after Tolkien's death. Tolkien was an academic, an Oxford professor of Anglo-Saxon and English language and literature. Born in South Africa in 1892, he attended Oxford on a scholarship and fought in World War I. His fantasies changed his life, but he continued his interest in medieval literature. Tolkien died in 1973 at age 81.

WORLD LITERATURE FROM 1200 A.D. THROUGH MILTON'S PARADISE LOST

1200 A.D. - European mystery plays combine biblical themes with social satire.

1297 A.D. - Marco Polo's "Travels" introduces Europeans to Asian culture.

1400 A.D. - Chaucer's "The Canterbury Tales" collects stories of pilgrims in a rich evocation of medieval life.

1450 A.D. - Gutenberg invents movable metal type and the printing press.

1516 A.D. - Martin Luther launches the Protestant Reformation in Wittenberg, Germany.

1558 A.D. - The reign of Elizabeth I begins the golden age of English literature.

1589 A.D. - William Shakespeare's first plays are produced in London.

1611 A.D. - The King James Bible is published and will have a lasting impact on English literature.

1660 A.D. - The Restoration Period of English literature begins.

1667 A.D. - Milton's "Paradise Lost" is published in blank verse in England.

BEN JONSON

Ben Jonson was a commanding figure in English letters. Playwright, poet, and critic, Jonson was famed for his elegant writing and brilliant intelligence. Jonson was the master of satires with his savage portrayals of human follies and corruption. The best known of these are <u>Valpone</u>, <u>Epicine</u>, and <u>The Alchemist</u>. Jonson also wrote epic poetry including the well known "Song to Celia" that was widely influential in the Restoration period. Jonson published his collected works in 1616 and was named Poet Laureate the same year. Born in London in 1572, Jonson had no formal education and went to war as a youth against the Spanish in Flanders. He became a popular writer of masques, a form of court entertainment that featured great spectacle, music, and poetry. Jonson was second only to Shakespeare in reputation among his peers. His followers, whom he served as a mentor, became known as "Sons of Ben."

FRANCIS BACON

Francis Bacon, Viscount St. Albans, Baron Verulam, was one of the greatest English essayists and philosophers. Bacon wrote primarily on science and scientific inquiry, championing the method of scientific investigation and empirical observation contrary to the scholastic philosophy favored by the Church. His greatest work was "Instaruratio Magna", a sweeping argument against the Renaissance and Scholastic philosophy. Bacon's "Essays," published in 1612, covered a wide range of subjects including English history, law, and society, and employed an aphoristic style. His vision of utopia was described in "New Atlantis" published in 1627. Bacon was born in London in 1561 and was active in politics, serving in Parliament several times. He served as Solicitor General under James I, but was charged with bribery in 1621 and barred from parliament. He remained an active writer until his death in London in 1626.

JOHN DONNE

John Donne, the greatest of the Metaphysical poets, wrote highly original verses on both religious and secular poetry. His love verses were written prior to his secret marriage to 17-year-old Ann More, of which the best known are "The Sunne Rising," "The Bait," and "To Catch a Falling Star." His reputation as a religious poet rests on "The Holy Sonnets" written in a period of spiritual search.

Donne was born into a Catholic family with strong ties to the Church. He converted to Anglicanism in 1614 after suffering a crisis of faith. Donne's marriage to Ann More without her father's consent caused a scandal for which he served a short prison sentence. His ambitions for a government career were dashed by this incident, and he turned to a career as an Anglican priest and dean of London's St. Paul's Cathedral. His reputation as a passionate preacher grew, but his poetry was not published until two years after his death. Donne wrote his own funeral sermon that was delivered in 1631.

JOHN MILTON

John Milton, the great English poet, wrote one of the great masterpieces of English literature in "Paradise Lost." This great Christian epic poem describing "mans first disobedience" was published in 1667. Milton followed this with the more severe "Paradise Regained", and his final work, the verse drama Samson Agonistes both published in 1671. Milton was born into a wealthy family and attended St. Paul's school and Cambridge before undertaking seven years of independent study. Several of his best known works including "L'Allegro" and "Il Penseroso" emerged from this period. Milton was a strong supporter of the Puritan and Commonwealth cause and wrote extensively defending civil freedom. He served as secretary in the Cromwell government but became severely disillusioned by the Restoration in 1660. Blind since 1652, he turned his power to the writing of his majestic work for which he is best remembered. Byron called him "the prince of poets" – a well deserved sobriquet.

WORLD LITERATURE FROM 500 BC THROUGH SAPPHO'S POEMS FROM THE ISLAND OF LESBOS

3500 B.C. - The first written language is developed by Sumerians in Mesopotamia.

3000 B.C. - The Egyptians begin using hieroglyphics on papyrus.

2000 B.C. - "Gilgamesh," an epic poem of Mesopotamia, is written.

1500 B.C. - The first alphabet is developed by the Phoenicians.

1200 B.C. - The Old Testament is written.

800 B.C. - Homer writes the epic poems the "Iliad" and the "Odyssey" on Greek heroism in the Trojan Wars.

800 B.C. - The Chinese spiritual text *The Way of Power* presents Taoist philosophy of harmonious living.

700 B.C. - Hesiod's "Theogony" presents the mythology of Greek gods.

610 B.C. - The earliest known record of Latin appears in Rome.

610 B.C. - Sappho's poems from the island of Lesbos are written.

WORLD LITERATURE FROM HERODOTUS THROUGH 1100 AD

450 B.C. - Herodotus's history is the first historical work written.

430 B.C. - Sophocles, Euripides, and Aristophanes write Greek drama.

400 B.C. - The Indian epic the *Bhagavad Gita* is composed.

380 B.C. - Plato's *Republic* elaborates the teaching of Socrates and lays the foundation for Western philosophy.

100 A.D. - Papermaking is invented in China.

100 A.D. - The New Testament is written in Greek.

633 A.D. - The Koran is recorded in Arabic.

750 A.D. - The epic poem "Beowulf," the oldest extant work in English, is composed orally.

1045 A.D. - Movable type is invented in China.

1100 A.D. - Old English evolves into Middle English.

HOMER

Homer is regarded as the greatest and earliest of the Greek epic poets and a literary giant whose innovations had lasting impact on Western culture. Very little is known of his life although it is generally agreed he was blind. He lived in the latter part of the eighth century B.C., and his greatest works are the "Iliad" and the "Odyssey." The authorship and means of composition of both epics are a source of academic debate, and few facts can be verified. Both of these epic poems relate the events of the Trojan War and are clearly derived from oral traditions. Some scholars believe they were not written down until long after the death of Homer. Others feel that Homer may have been a bardic singer, and the poems were derived from his recitals. These epics were so influential that they were the foundation of education in classical Greece and Rome, and they remain a core of liberal arts today.

SAPPHO

Sappho was one of the earliest and most influential of the Greek poets. She lived on the island of Lesbos, from which the word *lesbian* is derived. On Lesbos, she is thought to have led a community of young women whom she tutored in music and poetry. Sappho's poetry is usually dedicated to these young women for whom she served as a mentor. Sappho's poetry is intimate in tone and often treats themes of love and friendship. Very little is known of her life, and her poetry survives only in fragments. Some scholars think she was exiled to Sicily by a repressive government on Lesbos.

There is an apocryphal story about Sappho committing suicide by throwing herself off a cliff after a tragic love affair. All such stories must be classed as speculation, but what is certain is her poetic skill and dedication to her students with whom she lived on Lesbos.

SOPHOCLES

One of the greatest Greek playwrights, Sophocles wrote powerful tragedies that were considered the highest form of the art. He lived and wrote in the fourth century B.C. and was considered one of the leading citizens of Athens. His major works include *Oedipus the King, Antigone*, and *Electra*.

Although Sophocles wrote more than 100 plays, only seven complete dramas have survived. His tragic heroes value truth above all, even if it brings destruction and death. Sophocles was the master of writing tightly constructed plays and was an innovator in Greek drama. He added a third lead actor to the original two and produced self-contained plays rather than trilogies. Sophocles lived in Athens and was famous as a writer, musician, statesman, and priest. Aristotle considered Sophocles the greatest of the classical Greek dramatists, and his plays have been studied for centuries for their plotting and composition.

EURIPIDES

Euripides is the author of 92 plays, of which only 19 survive. His greatest works are *Medea, Electra*, and *Hippolytus*. Euripides lived in Athens from 484 B.C. until the last two years of his life, which he spent at the court of King Archelaus of Macedonia. Little is known of his early life, and he built his reputation as a playwright by competing in the dramatic contests in Athens, which he won 22 times. Euripides was a master at creating complex characters with rich emotional lives. His characterization of women was particularly artful. In Euripides's dramas, the gods are indifferent to earthly problems, and he portrays human weakness as the cause of suffering. Many of his plays are about the foolishness of war, and he championed unpopular social causes, such as the equality of women in society. His personal reputation as a pundit inspired two dramatic parodies of him by his rival Aristophanes. Embittered by these attacks, Euripides left Athens for Macedonia, where he died in 406 B.C.

ARISTOPHANES

Aristophanes was a Greek playwright who was the greatest comedic writer of his time. His plays were noted for their brilliant dialogue, poetic choral lyrics, sharp parodies, and topical allusions. Eleven of his plays survive, the best known being *The Clouds, The Wasps*, and *The Birds*. Others include *Lysistrata* and *The Frogs*. He wrote in the style of old comedy, combining mime, fantasy, chorus, and bawdy humor, which delighted his audiences. He loved to satirize social institutions, public figures, and the gods. The details of his life are largely unknown, and most of the information comes from his work. A citizen of Athens all his life, Aristophanes launched his dramatic career in 427 B.C. He wrote two parodies of Euripides's plays, which so incensed his rival that he left Athens. Aristophanes was a popular figure in Greece and his works are still occasionally staged today.

VIRGIL

Virgil was one of the greatest of Roman poets. He wrote the inscription for his own tomb, "One who sang of flocks and farms and heroes." Virgil's magnum opus is the epic poem the "Aeneid," which ranks as one of the most influential works in early classical literature. The "Aeneid" tells the tale of the adventures and triumphs of the Trojan hero Aeneas. Virgil's influence extends to the work of Dante, Spenser, Milton, and Shakespeare. His goal was to create works comparable to those of the Greek poets, and in this he succeeded. His work is uniquely his own and reflects his Roman culture.

Virgil was born in northern Italy and was well educated for a farmer's son. During the civil war of 41 B.C., his farm was confiscated, and he moved to Rome to become part of the Emperor Augustus's circle of artists. His first published work was the "Eclogues," followed by "Georgics," and finally the "Aeneid." Much of his early work was about farm life and the joys of a bucolic existence. He became ill on a trip to Greece and died upon his return in 19 B.C.

OVID

Publius Ovidius Naso, known as Ovid, was a great Roman poet applauded for his passionate, technically skilled, and witty poetry. His influence is seen in the works of Chaucer, Milton, Dryden, and Shakespeare. His masterpiece, "Metamorphoses," is written on the theme of transformation in Greek and Roman myth and is widely respected as a seminal work in Roman literature. His love narratives, "Amores," were kept alive during the Middle Ages despite the opposition of the Church. Ovid also wrote an instruction manual on the art of love, which established him as a major writer.

Born in Sulmo in eastern Italy, Ovid moved to Rome to join the court of Emperor Augustus. He was exiled to the Black Sea for unknown reasons in 8 ad. Ovid's pleas for forgiveness were published as his *Sorrows and Letters from Pontus*, but he was not pardoned and remained in exile until his death in 17 ad. His legacy is one of the most influential in all of classical poetry.

DANTE ALIGHIERI

Dante Alighieri, the greatest of the Italian poets, was a major figure in the Renaissance revolution of arts and letters. His epic masterpiece, the "Divine Comedy," ranks as one of the truly great literary works in history. The "Divine Comedy" presents a panoramic view of man and his place in the cosmos, describing a man's journey through the divine realms of Hell, Purgatory, and Paradise. The traveler is helped first by Virgil then by Beatrice, who was based on Beatrice Portinari, a figure Dante idealized as a figure of divine love. Combining deeply religious themes with sharp commentaries on social and political institutions, the "Divine Comedy" uses Tuscan dialect, which had a great influence on the development of the modern Italian language. Dante was an aristocrat born in Florence in 1265, and his political activism led to his exile in 1302. Thereafter, he lived in different Italian cities, finally settling in Ravenna, on the Adriatic. He was a prolific writer, treating subjects as varied as uses of the Italian language and Christian political philosophy. Dante died in Ravenna in 1321.

FRANCOIS RABELAIS

Francois Rabelais's major work was a five-volume masterpiece, *Gargantuan and Pantagreul*, published in Paris in 1564. This work is a unique combination of social satire, licentious comedy, and humanist philosophy. Shocked by this material, the Church placed the work on *Catholic Librium Prohibitorum*, and it was banned in France during his lifetime. His literature inspired the word *Rabelaisian*, which has come to mean a character with qualities of coarse humor, ribaldry, and boisterousness. His literary influence is seen in the works of Voltaire, Hugo, and Swift.

Rabelais was truly a Renaissance man, being a Benedictine monk, physician, teacher, and translator, and renowned for his knowledge in many fields. His role as a monk, no doubt, was part of the reason his work was seen as controversial by the church and banned. He died in France in 1553.

MICHEL DE MONTAIGNE

Michel de Montaigne's great contribution is the introduction of the essay to Western literature. His seminal work, *Essays*, introduced the genre, and the French term *essay*, meaning to try, was the name given the new form. *Essays* was published in three volumes from 1580 to 1588 and drew heavily from established literary forms, such as the treatise and religious confessions. Montaigne commented on social issues, as well as the human condition, in a brief, personal voice. His insights into major historical issues, such as religious conflict and exploration of the New World, were admired throughout Europe. The son of a wealthy landowner in southern France, Montaigne received a classical education and studied law. He counseled Parliament until 1571, when he retired to his family estate for study and writing. During the turbulent periods of civil war in France, he was drawn back to politics as a mediator and eventually became mayor of Bordeaux. He died on his family estate in 1592.

JEAN-JACQUES ROUSSEAU

Jean-Jacques Rousseau was a Swiss-born novelist, essayist, philosopher, and intellect who was very influential in the affairs of nations. Written in French, Rousseau's most important work is *The Social Contract*, his polemic for changing society. The ideas expressed in this work helped ignite the French and American revolutions. He wrote two hugely successful novels, *Julie* and *Emile*, and numerous essays on a wide variety of topics. His autobiography *Confessions* is a candid self-examination and self-criticism. Born in Geneva in 1712, Rousseau moved to Paris and established his reputation as a writer with his essay "Discourse on the Science and Arts," which argued that science and art degraded the natural man. Rousseau's works became increasingly controversial, and he was derided and exiled from several countries. Finally, he found refuge in England, but his last years were marked by paranoia and mental illness. He died in Ermenonville in 1778, a largely broken man.

JOHANN WOLFGANG VON GOETHE

Johann Wolfgang von Goethe was a German poet, novelist, and playwright. He was an initiator of the Sturm und Drang movement, which preceded German Romanticism. Goethe's best work includes the lyric poem "Hermann and Dorothea" and his drama *Faust*, which narrates the tale of the scholar who trades his soul for knowledge and pleasure. Goethe also wrote scientific essays and an autobiography, *Poetry and Truth*. One of his most popular works is the novel *The Sorrows of Young Werther*, which narrates the emotional pain of the protagonist/author. Goethe was born in Frankfurt in 1749 and served as a public official in Weimar for ten years. A long sojourn in Italy influenced his writing style and cultural outlook. Goethe developed a close friendship with the writer Friedrich von Schiller, and they remained confidants for many years. Goethe and Schiller shared many literary interests, and their relationship enriched both authors' work. Goethe remained active into old age and died in Weimar in 1832.

WILLIAM CULLEN BRYANT

William Cullen Bryant was an American poet, critic, and prose writer. His most famous work is "Thanatopsis," a reverie on death, published in 1817. He enjoyed nature, and much of his work touches on natural beauty. "To a Waterfowl" (1821) is an example of his affection for the natural world. This poem became a milestone in American poetry, viewing nature as the guiding principle of life. Bryant was also a critic, and his volume *Early American Verse* was instrumental in building the foundation for the American literary tradition. Bryant was born in Massachusetts in 1794. He began a career as a lawyer but soon realized his interests were in writing. He moved to New York in 1825, where he served as editor of the *New York Evening Post*, a liberal newspaper dedicated to the abolition of slavery and workers' rights. Bryant became a champion of these causes, and much of his energy was used to advocate for them. He became the dean of American journalism and was active until his death in New York in 1878.

WASHINGTON IRVING

Washington Irving was an American novelist, essayist, and short-story writer. Some of his best works are the now-familiar stories "Rip Van Winkle" and "The Legend of Sleepy Hollow," immortalized as children's fiction. Irving was an astute critic, essayist, and folklore expert. Irving's later works include *Tales of the Alhambra*, *Life and Voyages of Christopher Columbus*, and his impressions of the American west, *A Tour of the Prairies*. A well-known biographer, he wrote volumes about George Washington and Mohammed. Irving was born in 1783 and grew up in New York. Irving lived abroad for many years, serving as a diplomat in Spain for two separate periods of his life. He was a founder and co-publisher of a literary journal, *Salamagundi,* which was popular with American literary figures. He toured the American west several times and was an accurate observer of pioneer America. Upon his death in 1859, he was called "the first American man of letters."

JAMES FENIMORE COOPER

James Fenimore Cooper has a legitimate claim to being the first American novelist. Cooper was a prolific writer, and his best-known novels are *The Leatherstocking Tales*, which include *The Pioneers, The Last of the Mohicans, The Pathfinder*, and *The Deerslayer*. Cooper wrote a series of adventure novels in nautical settings, the most important being *The Pilot*. The three novels of *The Littlepage Manuscripts* address American social issues. His later work includes *The Sea Lions* and *Red Rover*, which enjoyed popular success. Cooper was born in New Jersey in 1789. Expelled from Yale University for unknown reasons, he spent eight years in the Navy, mustering out in 1809. Enriched by an inheritance from his father, Cooper devoted himself to politics and writing. Cooper's political writing embroiled him in many lawsuits, which he often won. He began a period of writing social criticism, including *The American Democrat* and *A Letter to His Countrymen* attacking American democracy. Cooper was active until the end of his life in 1851.

VICTOR HUGO

Victor Hugo—French playwright, novelist, and poet—was a giant figure in the Romantic revolution in the French arts. Best known for his great historical novels *Les Miserables* and *The Hunchback of Notre Dame*, Hugo also wrote drama, verse plays, and poetry. Important later works include *The Punishments* and an elegy for his drowned daughter, "Les Contemplations." Hugo was the most popular author in France for three decades. Born in Besancon, France, in 1802, Hugo began his literary career by founding *Conservateur Litteraire*, a literary journal, in 1819. Hugo was a giant figure in French letters and politics, becoming a vocal advocate of the republican cause. Hugo left France for 19 years after Napoleon III came to power. The creation of the Third French Republic in 1870 led to Hugo's triumphant return to Paris among adoring throngs. Hugo's revolutionary spirit can be seen in many of his works, particularly *Les Miserables* with its vivid depiction of the revolution. Hugo died in his beloved Paris in 1885.

HEINRICH HEINE

Heinrich Heine was perhaps the greatest poet of the German post-Romantic period. His first collection of poetry was published as *The Book of Songs* in 1827. His most controversial work was "Germany, A Winter's Tale," an epic satire on German politics. Heine wrote scores of impressive poems, and his works have been translated into most of the world's major languages. Heine's poetry was set to music by both Schubert and Schumann. Born in Dusseldorf, Germany, in 1797, Heine studied law in order to enter government service. He moved to Paris in 1831 and wrote articles on political, social, and economic issues of the day. Heine's works were banned in Germany in 1835, and he was forbidden to return to his homeland. His political views were considered radical for the time, and he was discriminated against for his Jewish heritage. Heine fell victim to a chronic illness that confined him to bed for the last years of his life. Despite this, he transcended his suffering in his last volume *Romanzero*. Heine died in Paris in 1856.

HONORÉ DE BALZAC

Balzac was a writer of prodigious output. He named his body of literature *The Human Comedy*. This French novelist wrote almost 100 works of fiction in his 51 years. His realistic description of 19th-century French society and manners provides a window to history. His first major success was *The Physiology of Marriage* in 1830. He followed this with *Lost Illusions*, an autobiographical novel of the corruption of a young poet in Paris, which is considered his greatest work. Later works include *The Black Sheep* and *Cousin Bette,* which were both successful. Balzac wrote in great detail and was an excellent plotter. His works were influential in the development of the novel. Balzac was born in Tours in 1799 and educated in Paris. He tried business and failed; he then gave his full attention to writing. Balzac was an obsessive worker, sometimes writing for days without rest. His tales could be melodramatic, but readers loved them, and his reputation soared. Balzac died in Paris in 1850 at age 51. His productivity in writing novels is unmatched.

STENDHAL

Stendhal was the pen name of Marie Henri Beyle, a French novelist of great technical skill. His novels reflect deep and subtle psychological themes, using irony, cool, detached prose, and great realism. His greatest works include *The Red and the Black* (1830) and *The Charterhouse of Parma* (1839). Both books narrate the adventures of young men and their rise and fall. Later important novels include *The Life of Henry Brulard*, an autobiographical novel, and *Memoirs of an Egotist*. Stendhal also wrote several excellent biographies, including one on Rossini. Born in Grenoble, Stendhal joined the Ministry of War and later fought with Napoleon in his European and Russian campaigns. After the fall of Napoleon, he worked as a minor diplomat in Italy from 1831 until his death in 1842. Unappreciated in his own time, Stendhal's reputation has grown with the years. Modern novelists feel he is a major figure in the development of the genre.

ALLEN GINSBERG

Allen Ginsberg, American poet, was a major figure in the Beat Generation. He, Jack Kerouac, and William S. Burroughs led a group of artists in opposing the conformist society of America in the 1950s. Ginsberg's epic poem "Howl" (1956) became a rallying cry for the counterculture revolution. Ginsberg's poetry draws from traditions of free verse and symbolism in a probing voice demanding to be heard. Always socially and politically engaged, Ginsberg's later works include "Kaddish" (1961), *The Fall Of America: Poems of These States* (1973), and *Reality Sandwiches* (1966).

Born in New Jersey in 1926 to a working class family, Ginsberg was educated at Columbia University. He moved to San Francisco in the 1950s, where he found a flourishing counterculture of rebellion. Ginsberg and his friends lived bohemian lives and challenged all the accepted mores of society. Ginsberg died in 1997.

EUGENE O'NEILL

Eugene O'Neill, American playwright, was a pioneer in American drama. O'Neill was an innovator and experimented with aspects of realism and naturalism in his work. He was one of the most critically honored dramatists of his time, winning four Pulitzer prizes and the Nobel Prize for Literature in 1936. Financial success did not come with his critical acclaim, and O'Neill struggled for a long time. His most outstanding play, *Long Day's Journey Into Night*, was written in 1941 but not produced until after his death. O'Neill was born in New York to a show business family in 1888 and attended Princeton University. Suffering from tuberculosis, O'Neill turned his attention to drama and by 1920 had a play in production in New York. His later success was highlighted by *The Iceman Cometh* (1946) and *Strange Interlude* (1928), for which he would win a Pulitzer Prize. O'Neill remained an active writer until his death in 1953.

VOLTAIRE

Voltaire was the pen name of Francois-Marie Arouet, French novelist, poet, playwright, and philosopher. Voltaire was a vocal and literate advocate for freedom of thought, political justice, and humanism in 18th-century France. Voltaire's fame is for his essays and letters defending human rights and arguing for reason and tolerance. Best known of his literary works are *Candide* and *Zadig*, fiction that blends philosophy and humanism. Nonfiction works include *Essays on the Manner* and *Spirit of Nations*, a seven-volume history, and a dictionary of philosophy. Voltaire was born in Paris in 1694 and educated by the Church. He soon abandoned the study of law for writing, philosophy, and advocating human rights. His sharp tongue and pen found ready targets in the Church, nobility, and government. A short stay in England exposed him to the ideas of John Locke and other liberal minds of the times. Many of his works were banned during his lifetime, which ended in Paris in 1778.

ALEXANDER PUSHKIN

Pushkin was an immensely talented poet, playwright, and short-story writer. Possibly the most revered Russian writer, Pushkin began his literary career with narrative poetry, including "The Prisoner of Caucasus" and "The Gypsies." In 1831, he wrote his famous verse-tragedy "Boris Godunov." His verse novel "Eugene Onegin" (1833) became his most important work. Master of the short story, Pushkin produced many great ones, including "The Queen of Spades" (1834). Pushkin's later work is innovative and experiments with language, form, and characterization.

Born in Moscow in 1799, he was educated at the Imperial Lyceum and served in the Russian government until his exile for writing poetry critical of the Tsar. Allowed to return to Moscow by the new Tsar in 1826, Pushkin married and continued his literary career. Pushkin was killed in a duel with his wife's lover in 1837, only 37 years old. His impact on Russian literature is immeasurable.

GEORGE SAND

George Sand, the pen name of Amandine Aurore Lucile Dupin, was a French woman of letters who was an accomplished essayist, novelist, and playwright. Her novels often touch on themes of love, romance, and early feminist philosophy. Best known are *She and He* (1859), *Little Fadette* (1849), and *The Country Waif* (1850). Her four-volume autobiography *Story of My Life* chronicles her exciting life in detail. Sand's novels mix socialist and feminist ideas with erotic language and criticisms of society. Sand was born in Paris in 1804 and received a Catholic education. She married at 18 but began a series of love affairs that ended in her divorce. She was a striking figure, wearing men's clothes and having open affairs with Musset, Chopin, and others. She fascinated the public with her personal escapades and was an extremely popular writer in her day. Sand died in Nohant in 1876.

RALPH WALDO EMERSON

Emerson was American essayist, poet, and transcendentalist philosopher. His first major work, *Nature*, was published in 1836. It proclaims the unity of nature and the universe and his belief that each man finds his way to the divine through individual apprehension. His two-volume *Essays* (1841–44) include his most famous essays, including "Love," "Friendship," and "The Oversoul." *Poems* (1847) and *May-Day* (1867) contain his best poetry. Emerson founded *The Dial*, a journal for transcendentalist writers, in 1840. Emerson was born in New England in 1803 and educated at Harvard University. Ordained as a Unitarian minister, he left the Church after being disillusioned with orthodox Christianity. Returning to America, he became a leading figure in the transcendentalist movement, joining such notables as Margaret Fuller, Henry David Thoreau, and Louisa May Alcott.

HENRY DAVID THOREAU

Thoreau was an American essayist and naturalist who published only two books in his life. His first book, *A Week on the Concord and Merrimac*, was a failure, and his prospects seemed dim. Then came *Walden* (1854), his masterpiece, which narrates Thoreau's experiment in simple living in a cabin on Walden Pond for two years. Initially unsuccessful, *Walden* became a classic and guide to a simpler, more natural life. Thoreau's *Journals* appeared in 1906. Thoreau was born in Concord, Massachusetts, in 1817 and graduated from Harvard in 1837. He was a teacher and major figure in the transcendentalist movement in New England. He wrote extensively on nature, society, and the spirit of individualism for many years. Often at odds with authorities, Thoreau spent a night in jail and defended his actions in a famous essay, "Civil Disobedience" (1849). He died in 1862 in his beloved Concord.

NATHANIEL HAWTHORNE

Nathaniel Hawthorne was an American fiction writer. Hawthorne had a tragic vision of life, believing man is imperfect and a mixture of good and evil. His work reflects this view, starting with the publication of *Twice Told Tales* in 1837. Hawthorne gained public fame with *The Scarlet Letter* (1850), a novel of adultery in puritan New England. He followed this with the successful *House of the Seven Gables*, a novel tracing the history of a family hiding a dark secret. Hawthorne was born in Salem, Massachusetts, in 1804 to a prosperous family. He graduated from Bowdoin College in 1825 and vowed to devote his life to literature. Living in semi-seclusion in Salem for 12 years, Hawthorne produced his first stories. After briefly working in government, he joined a utopian community at Brook Farm, later satirized in his novel *The Blithedale Romance* (1852). Appointed American counsel in Liverpool, he lived in Europe for many years.

HENRY WADSWORTH LONGFELLOW

Longfellow was one of the most popular American poets of his day. He gained lasting fame with his long narrative poems "Hiawatha" (1855) and "Evangeline" (1847). His *Tales of the Wayside Inn* (1863) contains "Paul Revere's Ride," a poem known and beloved by American schoolchildren. Among the best known of his shorter poems are "The Arsenal at Springfield," "The Wreck of the Hesperus," "A Psalm of Life," and "The Village Blacksmith." He also wrote essays and translated Dante's "Divine Comedy." Longfellow was born in Maine in 1807 to a wealthy family. He was educated at Bowdoin College and studied in Europe for several years before returning to Bowdoin to teach languages. He later became a faculty member at Harvard and was a well-respected professor. He died in New England in 1882.

EDGAR ALLEN POE

Poe was an American poet, novelist, and short-story writer of particular talent. His tales of terror and arresting poems have gained him lasting fame in American literature. Poe published a great anthology of short stories with *Tales of the Grotesque and Arabesque* in 1840. He cemented his fame with *The Raven and Other Poems* in 1845. Some of his greatest poems include "The Bells" (1849), "Annabel Lee" (1849), and "Ulaume" (1847). His best-known short stories include "The Pit and the Pendulum" (1843), "The Tell-Tale Heart" (1843), and "The Gold Bug" (1843). Poe was born in Boston and was orphaned at an early age. Raised by a wealthy Virginia businessman, he attended the University of Virginia and West Point. Poe's marriage to a young cousin would end with her early death. Poe would never recover from this loss and sank into a morass of drug addiction and alcohol abuse. He died in Baltimore in 1849.

NIKOLAI GOGOL

Gogol was a Russian playwright, novelist, and short-story author who wrote sharp satirical prose in an innovative style. Two collections of his short stories, *Mirgorod* and *Arabesques*, were published in 1835. His best-known work, the novel *Dead Souls*, a biting satire on feudal Russia, appeared in 1842. The sequel to *Dead Souls* was to have been Gogol's crowning work, but he burned the manuscript in 1852, shortly before his death. Only fragments of the manuscript remain.

Gogol was born in 1809 in Ukraine. Moving to St. Petersburg, he worked in civil service and teaching as he began to write. Gogol began displaying symptoms of mental illness in the 1840s. He became obsessed with religion and fell under the influence of a fanatical priest who urged him to destroy the manuscript of the second part of *Dead Souls* to atone for the original book. Increasingly, Gogol became delusional. He destroyed the manuscript and then starved himself to death in 1852.

ALEXANDRE DUMAS

Known as Alexandre Dumas père (father), this great French novelist and playwright was the most popular literary figure in France in his time. Best remembered for his exciting historical novels *The Three Musketeers* (1844), and *The Count of Monte Cristo* (1845), Dumas published many other popular novels, including *The Man in the Iron Mask* (1850), as well as many dramas based on his stories. His forte was the historical novel, usually with heroic figures and imaginative plots that captured the fancy of the public. Dumas was born in Paris in 1802, the son of one of Napoleon's great generals. Dumas led a life worthy of his novels, having many mistresses and winning and losing fortunes regularly. He was a flamboyant character in the café society of Paris, living with the joy that seemed to permeate his fiction. Dumas left several volumes of his memoirs documenting his exciting adventures. He died in Dieppe in 1870.

FYODOR DOSTOYEVSKY

Fyodor Dostoyevsky, Russian novelist, journalist, and short-story writer, was the master of the psychological character. He also had unusual skill as a prose writer and ranks as the greatest of Russian writers. His first major work was *Crime and Punishment* (1867), narrating a murder and its aftermath. This was followed quickly by a series of important works, including *The Idiot* (1874), *The Possessed* (1872), and *The Brothers Karamazov* (1880). All these works deal with the criminal mind and the struggles within the human psyche. Dostoyevsky was born in Moscow in 1821, the son of a physician who was murdered by serfs when Dostoyevsky was in his late teens. He suffered from epilepsy and was a chronic gambler, which left him in constant debt. Arrested for subversion, he spent eight years in Siberia before his release. With Tolstoy, he is considered the greatest Russian writer. He died in St. Petersburg in 1881.

HERMAN MELVILLE

Melville was one of America's rare talents, excelling in short stories, poetry, and, above all, the novel. Melville wrote adventure stories, *Typee* (1846) and *Omoo* (1847), before writing his master novel, *Moby Dick* (1851). This novel was an allegory about men, life, and obsession. It is usually considered one of the greatest American novels. Unpopular at first, it was rediscovered in the 1920s and given the accolades it so richly deserved. Melville's later work includes *The Piazza Tales*, a collection of short stories, and the novels *The Confidence Man* (1857) and *Billy Budd* (1888).

Melville was born in New York in 1819 and went to sea as a teenager. In 1866, Melville became a customs inspector in New York. Stalked by tragedy with the death of two sons and his financial reverses, Melville persisted with his writing. He is now considered one of literature's finest novelists. Melville died in New York in 1891.

Mometrix

HARRIET BEECHER STOWE

Harriet Beecher Stowe, American novelist, rests her reputation on *Uncle Tom's Cabin* (1852), a polemic that brought the horrors of slavery to the world. The book became a bible for the abolitionist cause, and some credit it as a catalyst for the American Civil War. Three million copies were sold in the decade after it was published, and it was translated into more than 25 languages. Stowe's later works include *Oldtown Folks* (1869) and *The Minister's Wooing* (1859).

Stowe was born in Litchfield, Connecticut, in 1811. In her late teens, she moved to Cincinnati and married a clergyman. She became heavily involved in the abolitionist movement, which led her to write *Uncle Tom's Cabin*. Enriched and honored by her book, Stowe continued to campaign for social justice until her death in 1896.

WALT WHITMAN

Whitman, the American poet and journalist, sought to develop an American voice for poetry. His style mirrored the American ideal: democratic, idealistic, free-flowing, and panoramic in perspective. His life's work, *Leaves of Grass* (1855), embodied what Whitman conceived as the American spirit. Using free verse, Whitman produced an American original. Whitman was born on Long Island, in New York state, and was reared in nearby Brooklyn. He worked as a teacher, typesetter, and journalist, becoming editor of the *Brooklyn Eagle* in 1846. He lived most of his life in Brooklyn, until the publication of *Leaves of Grass*. During the Civil War, he traveled to Virginia to nurse his wounded brother. He stayed on as a hospital volunteer until the end of the war. Crippled by a stroke in 1873, he retired to New Jersey, where he died in 1892.

CHARLES BAUDELAIRE

Baudelaire was a French essayist, poet, and critic. His reputation as one of the great French poets of his time was based on his seminal work, *The Flowers of Evil* (1857). *The Flowers of Evil* combines macabre imagery and a profane, cynical tone to produce a book of much power. Baudelaire was prosecuted and fined for obscenity following its publication, and a few of the poems were banned from future editions. Baudelaire was born in Paris in 1821 to a wealthy family. He turned to writing almost immediately and began friendships with Courbet, Delacroix, and Manet. After squandering a large inheritance, Baudelaire became addicted to opium and alcohol, and began to deteriorate. His later years were poverty stricken, and he was heavily in debt. The publication of *The Flowers of Evil* further alienated the public. His writing career was essentially over, and he died of syphilis in 1867 at the age of 46.

GUSTAVE FLAUBERT

Flaubert was a French author of fiction, a master of the novel and adept at short stories. After an unsuccessful first manuscript, Flaubert spent five years writing his best-known work, *Madame Bovary*, published in 1857. This narrative of the adulterous affairs of a middle-class French woman shocked much of France, and Flaubert was prosecuted for the book's "immorality." His other novels include *Salaambo* (1862) and *A Sentimental Education* (1869). Flaubert is recognized as a pioneer in modern fiction writing. Flaubert was born in Rouen, France, in 1821 and began writing fiction as a child. He enrolled in law school but soon suffered a breakdown and abandoned his education. He committed himself to writing with great energy and gave up many of the distractions of Paris life to concentrate on his craft. Flaubert died suddenly of a cerebral hemorrhage at his home in Croisset, France, in 1880. He was 58 years old.

EMILY DICKINSON

Emily Dickinson is ranked as one of America's greatest poets. Dickinson's poetry is highly formal, her language both subtle and creative, and it reflects the quiet life she led. Dickinson's topics

72

include death, art, love, pain, and betrayal, all couched in her wonderful poetic language. She wrote more than 1,800 poems, yet only ten are known to have been published in her lifetime. Her fame has grown through the generations, and she is at last recognized as a poetic genius. Born in Amherst, Massachusetts, in 1830, she was educated at Mt. Holyoke seminary. She returned to Amherst and went into virtual seclusion in her parents' home. She saw very few people socially and rarely left the house. Despite this isolation, Dickinson's work is vibrant and alive, reflecting her keen observation of the world. Dickinson is a true American literary voice, rivaling Walt Whitman. She died in Amherst in 1886.

IVAN TURGENEV

Ivan Turgenev—Russian novelist, playwright, and short-story writer—wrote politically inflammatory stories criticizing Russian serfdom and government. His work managed to inflame both the tsarist generation and the young radicals of his time. Best known for his *Fathers and Sons*, published in 1862, he continued writing fiction for over 30 years. Some of his more successful novels include *On the Eve* (1860), *Smoke* (1867), and *The Virgin Soil* (1877), a controversial novel about Russia. His best-known play is *A Month in the Country,* first produced in 1855. Turgenev was born in Oryol in 1818 and educated in universities in Moscow and St. Petersburg before moving to Berlin. Here he became a Westerner for life. This was reflected in his work, which became increasingly critical of Russian society and economics. He left Russia in 1863 and lived in France and Germany for most of the rest of his life. Turgenev died in France in 1883.

LEO TOLSTOY

Count Leo Tolstoy was Russia's leading novelist and moral philosopher. Tolstoy's two great masterpieces of fiction are *War and Peace* (1869) and *Anna Karenina* (1878). *War and Peace* is a love story set in the Napoleonic wars and provides a panoramic view of Russian life. *Anna Karenina* is the story of a woman who gives up everything for her love. Both are novels of great philosophical and psychological depth. Tolstoy described his spiritual crisis and its resolution in *Confessions* (1882). Tolstoy had a productive writing period in his later life, publishing novellas and a final novel, *The Resurrection* (1899). Tolstoy was born in Yasnaya Polyana in 1828 and educated at home by tutors. He served in the Russian army and fought in the Crimea and Caucasus campaigns. He returned to his estate in 1859, married, and taught the children of serfs while he wrote his great novels. Tolstoy retired to his estate and died in Astapovo in 1910.

LOUISA MAY ALCOTT

Louisa May Alcott is one of America's beloved children's writers, novelists, and short-story writers. Alcott began her publishing career writing popular dime novels under pseudonyms to make a living. The publication of *Little Women* in 1868, and its huge popularity, allowed her to pursue serious fiction thereafter. *Little Women* is a fond narrative of family life based partially on her own family. It is a romantic yet realistic novel with strong and memorable characters. Alcott's later novels include *Little Men* (1871) and *Rose in Bloom* (1876), both written for young readers. Her best adult fiction includes *Moods* (1864), a novel of married life, and *Work* (1874), a story based on her financial problems. Alcott was born in Germantown, PA in 1832 and reared in nearby Concord. Her father was the famous transcendentalist thinker Bronson Alcott. She died in 1888.

EMILE ZOLA

Emile Zola, French novelist, wrote finely detailed narratives with a realistic eye. Zola believed objective observation was necessary to maintain the integrity of his work. His first novel, *Therese Raquin* (1867), was written in this dispassionate style. His reputation rests on a mammoth 20-volume novel cycle, called *Les Rougon-Macquart,* narrating the fortunes of a 19th-century family over several generations. Topics in this series often involve the seamy side of life, including prostitution, labor unrest, and alcoholism. Zola was born in Paris in 1840 and raised in Provence. His education was mediocre, and he worked in a publishing house before becoming a journalist. He wrote for several French periodicals on a variety of topics as he honed his new style of writing. His mature novels were very successful and provided Zola with a comfortable life. He died in France in 1902.

ARTHUR RIMBAUD

Arthur Rimbaud, French poet, was a literary figure unlike any other. A revolutionary in every sense, he pioneered the use of free verse in his poetry and lived a life of adventure and daring. At the age of 17, he wrote "The Drunken Boat" (1871), a surreal poem that would remain his greatest work. Rimbaud's "A Season in Hell" (1873) plumbed the depth of his despair, a cry of spiritual longing and the inability to love. His literary career was over at the age of 19, and he experimented with alcohol, drugs, and sensory deprivation. Rimbaud was born in northeastern France in 1854. His family was impoverished, and he left home at age 15 to live on his own. Rimbaud met and fell in love with Paul Verlaine, who served both as a mentor and lover. The relationship was a violent one, and Rimbaud left Paris to wander the world as a merchant, arms dealer, and vagabond. He returned to France and died in Marseille in 1891 at the age of 37.

PAUL VERLAINE

Paul Verlaine, French poet, was the leading light of the Symbolist movement, which stressed the importance of suggestion and shading rather than direct description. Symbolism intuited subtle connections between the spiritual and physical worlds. Verlaine's best work was reflected in his "Song Without Words" (1874) and "Fetes Galantes" (1869). His poetry in later life was influenced by his conversion to Catholicism when he embraced positive values and wrote "Wisdom" (1880), "Love" (1888), and "Happiness" (1891). Paul Verlaine was born in Metz in 1844. Educated in Paris, he joined the radical poets in the salons and cafés of literary Paris. He shocked society when he left his family for 17-year-old Arthur Rimbaud, with whom he carried on a tempestuous and violent affair. Verlaine embraced the Church in his forties, and achieved a peace that had eluded him. He died in Paris in 1896.

HENRIK IBSEN

Henrik Ibsen, Norwegian poet and playwright, is known for his realistic descriptions of modern social problems and psychological dilemmas that haunt his characters. Perhaps his most popular work is *Peer Gynt*, published in 1876. His more mature work is composed of a number of plays written with marked realism. Those include *A Doll's House* (1879), *Hedda Gabler* (1891), *The Wild Duck* (1885), and his final play, *The Master Builder* (1893), perhaps his most autobiographical drama. Henrik Ibsen was born near Oslo in 1828 to a wealthy family. When he was a child, his father's business failed, and he was apprenticed to a pharmacist. Ibsen abandoned his apprenticeship and moved to Oslo to work in the theatre. He became a jack-of-all-trades, managing and directing groups of players. Ibsen died in Oslo in 1906 at the age of 78.

MARK TWAIN

Mark Twain, the pen name of Samuel Langhorne Clemens, was a true American voice in literature. Humorist, novelist, and travel writer, he is best known for *Tom Sawyer* (1876) and *The Adventures of Huckleberry Finn* (1884), beloved novels with memorable characters and undertones of social concern. *Life on the Mississippi* (1883) was an autobiographical account of his days on a riverboat. Twain's acid humor and stories of a fading rural America made him one of the most popular figures of his day. Born in 1835 in Florida, Missouri, Twain, who was self-educated, became a journalist and sometime printer. His literary success made him a popular lecturer in America and Europe. His travels abroad provided him with the material for the satirical *A Connecticut Yankee in King Arthur's*

Court (1889) and *The Innocents Abroad* (1869). His later life was marred by tragedy, including the death of his wife and two daughters, as well as financial difficulty. He died in Connecticut in 1910.

CHARLOTTE PERKINS GILMAN

Charlotte Perkins Gilman was an American writer of short stories, essays, and poetry. She was an early feminist and leader in the women's movement in the early part of the 20th century. She challenged gender stereotypes in her writing. Her most influential work was *The Yellow Wallpaper* (1892), a tale of the abuse of women, medical science, and madness. Other important works include *Women and Economics* (1898) and her utopian novel, *Herland*, published in 1915. Gilman was born in Hartford, Connecticut, in 1860 to a family that included Lyman Beecher and Harriet Beecher Stowe. An unhappy childhood and difficult first marriage contributed to her clinical depression. She divorced her husband and moved to California, where she did her best work. Gilman committed suicide in 1935 after a period of failing health. Her autobiography was published soon after her death.

STEPHEN CRANE

American journalist, short-fiction writer, and novelist, Crane produced a number of memorable works in his 29 years. Best known for his unflinching evocation of a soldier in battle, *The Red Badge of Courage* (1895), Crane ironically never fought in a war. He published a collection of poetry, *The Black Rider and other Lines* (1895), which was a critical success. Crane traveled the world as a journalist, and his experiences provided him with ample material for his fiction.

Crane was born New Jersey in 1871 and became a journalist in New York City. He was what we now term an investigative reporter, writing grim and harshly realistic articles about the poor. Crane eventually settled in Sussex, England, and became an associate of the important literary figures of the day. His short stories are included in many anthologies and are the strength of his writing. He died in England in 1900.

KATE CHOPIN

Kate Chopin was an American novelist and short-fiction writer whose breakthrough work was the novel *The Awakening* (1899). This story of a woman's struggle to attain independence has become a landmark in feminist literature. The book was roundly condemned for its bold use of sexuality, particularly the heroine's illicit affairs. The criticism was so overwhelming it almost ended Chopin's writing career. Her later works are collections of stories of Creole and Cajun life. Kate Chopin was born in St. Louis in 1850. She married and moved to New Orleans in 1870. Chopin continued to live and write in St. Louis until her death in 1904. She is now regarded as an early victim of antifeminist opinion in literary circles. Her inquiries into the nature of female identity are remarkable for the period and prepared the ground for future feminist literature.

THEODORE DREISER

Theodore Dreiser was an American novelist and leader in the literary movement known as Naturalism. Naturalism sought a literary ideal based on an objective, dispassionate description of the world. Dreiser's first novel, *Sister Carrie* (1900), was so controversial the publisher refused to promote it. His magnum opus, *An American Tragedy* (1925), was based on a true story of the day. Dreiser later published three successful novels, *The Financier* (1912), *The Titan* (1914), and a late book, *The Stoic* (1947). Dreiser was born to a poor family in Indiana in 1871. He worked as a journalist for many years as he polished his writing skills. Besides his novels, Dreiser wrote short fiction, plays, and an autobiography. His work is understood to have had a major impact on novel writing in America by its rough portrayal of urban life. Dreiser died in 1945.

ANTON CHEKOV

Anton Chekov, Russian playwright and short-story writer, is regarded as one of the greats in Russian literature. Known for his skillful blend of symbolism and naturalism, Chekov combines comedy, tragedy, and pathos into a heady brew. His greatest short stories include "The Black Monk" (1894), "A Dreary Story" (1889), and "Ward Number Six" (1892). His fame as a dramatist rests on his four later plays, *The Cherry Orchard* (1904), *Uncle Vanya* (1897), *The Three Sisters* (1901), and *The Seagull* (1897). Chekov was born in southern Russia and studied medicine at Moscow University. As a student, he wrote for periodicals to supplement his income. After his early successes, he concentrated on his writing and only occasionally practiced medicine. He suffered from tuberculosis and moved to the Crimea in hopes of a healthier environment. In this he was unsuccessful, and he died in 1904.

HENRY JAMES

American novelist, short-story writer, playwright, and essayist, Henry James is a founder of the modern American novel. His mature fiction includes *The American* (1877), *The Europeans* (1878), *Daisy Miller* (1879), and *Washington Square* (1880). James's middle period features novels of social concern and artists, such as *The Bostonians* (1886). James's mature works use the technique of presenting events through each character's limited perspective, as in *Turn of the Screw* (1898) and *Wings of the Dove* (1902). James was an excellent literary and art critic, writing for a number of newspapers and periodicals. James was born in New York City in 1843 but spent much of his time in Europe. From 1876 until his death, he lived in London, eventually becoming a British subject. Many of his works involve Americans living abroad, particularly in England. James died in London in 1916.

JACK LONDON

Jack London was an American novelist, short-fiction writer, and essayist. London's first collection of short stories, *The Son of the Wolf,* was published in 1900. *The Call of the Wild* (1903), the story of a sled dog that becomes the leader of a wolf pack, was hugely successful, bringing the author both stature and riches. London's other well-known novels include *The Sea Wolf* (1904) and *White Fang* (1906), another tale of survival in the wild. His later works are more ideological, and the best known is *The People of the Abyss* (1903). London was born in Oakland, California, in 1876 into a poverty-stricken home. A vagabond who worked as a gold miner, cannery worker, and seaman, he went to the Klondike on a failed expedition to find gold. He was a passionate socialist, and he spoke and wrote often as an advocate. Destitute and alcoholic, he committed suicide in 1916.

EDITH WHARTON

Born Edith Newbold Jones, Wharton was a prolific American novelist, poet, short-fiction writer, and essayist. She was expert at narrating the foibles of Old New York society, of which she was a member. Wharton's first success was *The House of Mirth* (1905), a novel depicting an individual's struggles against society's mores. Writing in France, she published *Ethan Frome* (1911) and her most popular work, *The Age of Innocence* (1920), which won a Pulitzer Prize for Literature. *The Age of Innocence* chronicles a long and stormy love affair. Wharton was born in New York in 1862 and raised in elite society. Her marriage to Edward Wharton ended after he suffered a number of nervous breakdowns and was caught embezzling her accounts. She divorced Wharton, which presaged her most productive writing period. She moved to France in 1907, and her writing career became the focus of her life. Wharton, much honored and loved, died in 1937.

UPTON SINCLAIR

Upton Sinclair was an American novelist, journalist, and essayist. He was the best known of the muckrakers, a socially-minded band of writers who decried and attacked perceived immoral conduct in business and government. His most popular novel, *The Jungle* (1906), attacked and exposed abuses in the Chicago meat packing industry. *The Jungle* was instrumental in forcing the passage of the Pure Food and Drug Act. Sinclair's later works include *King Coal* (1917) and a novel based on the Sacco-Vanzetti trial, *Boston* (1928). Born in Baltimore in 1878, Sinclair was an ardent socialist who ran (and lost) for the governorship of California in 1934. He remained a muckraker to the end, advocating socialism and attacking social ills. Upton Sinclair died in New Jersey in 1968.

HENRY ADAMS

Adams was an American editor, biographer, and historian famed for his autobiography, *The Education of Henry Adams*, published in 1907. Adams produced two novels, *Democracy, an American Novel* (1880) and *Esther* (1884), both published anonymously. His life's work was the nine-volume *History of the United States of America During the Administrations of Thomas Jefferson and James Madison*, published in 1889–91. Adams was born in 1838 in Boston, the grandson of John Quincy Adams. Educated at Harvard, he chose a profession of scholarship rather than government service. Editor of the *North American Review* for six years, he then accepted an appointment as medieval history professor at Harvard. He remained there until he retired to write full time. Adams died in Washington D.C. in 1918.

GERTRUDE STEIN

Gertrude Stein was an American poet, essayist, novelist, and short-story writer. Her major work is *Three Lives* (1909), a novel of working-class women. Her poetry collection, *Tender Buttons: Objects, Food, Rooms,* published in 1914, was well received. Her autobiography, *The Autobiography of Alice B. Toklas*, published in 1937, has become an icon to millions of individuals. Born in America in 1874, Stein spent most of her childhood in Europe. She studied psychology with William James in Baltimore before moving to Paris for good. With her secretary and partner, Alice B. Toklas, Stein became the center of the Modernist literary scene in Paris and was a close friend of Picasso, Hemingway, and Ford Madox Ford. Stein was a flamboyant figure in Paris, famous for her acid tongue and repartee. Stein died in Paris in 1946.

RABINDRANATH TAGORE

Tagore was an Indian poet, playwright, novelist, short-fiction writer, and songwriter. Best known for his spiritual poetry written in Bengali, his first collection was *The ideal One* (1890). Noted for his lyrical, spiritual poetry, also written in Bengali, Tagore dominated the Indian literary scene for decades. His most popular work, *Song Offerings* (1912), won him a Nobel Prize in literature in 1911. Tagore published a number of poetry anthologies, and his stories of Bengal village life were published as *The Hungry Stones* (1916) and *Broken Ties* (1925). His best novel, *The Home and the World*, (1916), was adapted for film by Satyagit Ray. Tagore was born in Calcutta in 1861 to a wealthy Hindu family. He studied law in London and traveled widely in the West before returning to India. He died in India in 1941.

MARCEL PROUST

Marcel Proust, French novelist, owes his reputation to his epic seven-part masterpiece, *Remembrance of Things Past*, published between 1913 and 1927. This monumental work examines the existential problem of finding meaning and value in the maelstrom of life. Using the device of interior monologue, Proust views the transient nature of life and the flux of consciousness, using observation of minute detail in a manner rarely done with such skill. Proust was forced to publish the first volume himself, but subsequent books were well received. The final three volumes were published after Proust's death. Proust was born in Paris in 1871 and educated at the Lycée Condorcet. As a young man, he was a favorite in the literary salons of Paris, a setting he used repeatedly in his novels. Suffering from chronic asthma and the early death of his mother, Proust withdrew into semi-seclusion, where he devoted himself to his life's work. He died in Paris in 1922.

T. S. ELIOT

Thomas Stearns Eliot—American poet, playwright, and critic—was a major poet of the Modernist school of poetry. Eliot's first success was in 1915 with the publication of "The Love Song of J. Alfred Prufrock," originally appearing in *Poetry*, a small literary magazine. Eliot struggled with his own despair at the futility of life and the spiritual barrenness of modern life. He addressed these themes in "The Waste Land," a powerful and influential work in the history of modern poetry. Eliot wrote several dramas in verse including "Murder in the Cathedral" (1953) and "The Cocktail Party" (1950). Eliot was born in St. Louis in 1888 and educated at Harvard and Oxford University. He moved to London and worked as a banker before becoming an editor at Faber and Faber in 1925. In 1927, he became a British subject and converted to Anglicanism. He was a distinguished figure in literature until his death in 1965.

ROBERT FROST

Robert Frost, American poet, is remembered as a master of the technical aspects of poetry while remaining true to his New England heritage. Frost will always be remembered for his masterful simplicity in such poems as "Stopping By the Woods on a Snowy Evening" (1923) and "The Road Not Taken" (1916). While living in England before World War I, Frost published two collections of poetry. Returning to New England, he published a number of anthologies, including *Complete Poems* (1945), *West Running Brook* (1928), *A Witness Tree* (1942), and *In the Clearing* (1962). Frost was born in California in 1874 and was educated at Dartmouth College and Harvard. He received the Pulitzer Prize four times and capped his career by reading "The Gift Outright" at the inaugural of John Kennedy in 1961. Frost died in 1963.

FRANZ KAFKA

Franz Kafka was a Prague-born and German-writing novelist and short-story writer. Using powerful symbolism and addressing the anxieties and chaos of modern society, Kafka wrote penetrating stories and novels during his lifetime, including the novella *The Metamorphosis* (1915), the short story "In the Penal Colony" (1919), and the collection *A Hunger Artist* (1924). Kafka instructed his executor and literary agent Max Brod to destroy his unpublished manuscripts after his death. Recognizing Kafka's genius, Brod published the works, including the great novels *The Trial* (1925), *The Castle* (1926), and *Amerika* (1927). Kafka was born in Prague to a middle-class Jewish family, with whom he lived most of his life. He attended law school but worked in an insurance firm for many years. His fiction was dark, wounding, and sometimes painful, but always arresting. Kafka died in 1924.

EDNA ST. VINCENT MILLAY

Edna St. Vincent Millay was one of the best-known American poets of the 1920s. Millay won a poetry contest in 1902 with "Renascence," which became her best-known poem. Millay won the Pulitzer Prize for her poem "The Ballad of the Harp-Weaver" in 1923. She published a number of successful collections of poems, including *A Few Twigs from Thistles* (1920), *Fatal Interview* (1931), *Wine From These Grapes* (1934), *Conversation at Midnight* (1937), and *Make the Bright Arrows* (1940), as well as the posthumously published *Collected Poems* (1956). Millay infused traditional sonnets with the voice of an independent, modern woman. Millay was born in Rockland, Maine, in

1892. Educated in liberal arts at Vassar College, she worked as a reporter for *Vanity Fair* magazine in New York. Millay died in 1950 at the apex of her career.

WILLA CATHER

Willa Cather was an American novelist, short-story writer, and essayist. Her breakthrough came with the publication of her second novel, *O Pioneers!*, which narrated the story of an immigrant family's struggle in the new world. *My Antonia*, a story of a woman's struggle and eventual triumph on the prairie, met critical acclaim in 1918. Cather won the Pulitzer Prize in 1922 for *One of Ours*. Cather's later work bemoaned the loss of pioneering spirit in America, which was the theme for *Death Comes for the Archbishop* (1917). She published a successful essay collection, *Not under Forty*, in 1936. Other writing examines the topics of art, loss, and disillusionment, including a novel on the American Civil War, *Sapphira and the Slave Girl* (1940). Cather was born in Virginia in 1873 and moved to the Nebraska frontier as a child. Her experiences in Nebraska furnished much of the material on which she based her work. She died in 1947.

E. E. CUMMINGS

Edward Estlin Cummings, American poet and novelist, was noted for his unique writing style, which used unconventional punctuation and typography, and innovative language and imagery, which made him a leading Modernist voice in poetry. His first book and only novel is *The Enormous Room* (1922). His verse is often light and joyful, but it contains a great depth of irony and complex feeling. His major works include *Tulips and Chimneys* (1923), *50 Poems* (1940), *95 Poems* (1958), and *73 Poems*, published after his death. Cummings also published works of nonfiction and prose.

Cummings was born in 1894, educated at Harvard, and served in France in World War I. He became a popular and important lecturer on the literary scene before his death in 1962.

RAINER MARIA RILKE

Born René Maria Rilke, he was a German poet and a much beloved figure throughout the world, where his work is universally admired. Struggling with themes of life and death, Rilke explored man's relationship to the divine and particularly humanity's perception of the universal. His major works include *The Book of Images* (1906), *Duino Elegies* (1923), *Sonnets to Orpheus* (1923), and *New Plans*, his first volume published in 1908. Rilke is one of the most widely translated poets in the world, some of his translations done by well-known poets, such as Robert Bly and Randall Jarrell. Rilke was born in Prague in 1875. He lived across Europe, with sojourns in Germany, France, and Switzerland. Rilke visited Russia twice, which inspired his first book of poetry. Rilke died in Switzerland in 1926, a giant man of letters.

THOMAS MANN

Thomas Mann, German novelist and essayist, was a writer of great importance in the early 20th century. His work usually focused on art and the struggle of the artist to flourish in European society. This conflict is the theme of the novels *Buddenbrooks* (1903) and *Death in Venice* (1912). Ultimately Mann turned to spirituality in his long allegorical novel *The Magic Mountain,* published in 1924. Later works include *Dr. Faustus* (1947) and *Joseph and His Brothers* (1933–43), a tetralogy of novels about the biblical character. Mann won the Nobel Prize for literature in 1929.

Thomas Mann was born in Germany in 1875 and fled Nazi Germany in the early 1930s after clashing with Hitler's policies. He became a United States citizen in 1944 but remained active in world affairs and visited Europe frequently after the war. He died in Switzerland in 1955.

EZRA POUND

Ezra Pound—American poet, critic, and editor—was a most controversial figure in world literature. He published his most important work of poetry, *The Cantos*, late in his career. His influence as a critic was formidable, and he fostered the work of Robert Frost, Ernest Hemingway, James Joyce, and T. S. Eliot. Pound was an important Imagist, advocating the use of free meter and the extravagant use of image. His first book of verse, *A Lume Spento*, was self-published in Europe.

Pound was born in Idaho in 1885, reared in Pennsylvania, and educated at Hamilton College and the University of Pennsylvania. He moved to Europe after college, where he became an influential critic and editor. Associated with Mussolini and his fascist regime, Pound was arrested for treasonable propaganda. Committed to an asylum in America for mental illness for 12 years, he returned to Italy until his death in 1972.

ERNEST HEMINGWAY

Ernest Hemingway, American novelist and short-story writer, was a Modernist master who became a legendary figure in his own lifetime. He achieved fame with his novels *The Sun Also Rises* (1926) and *A Farewell to Arms* (1929), based on his World War I experiences. Other important works include *For Whom the Bell Tolls* (1940), based on the Spanish Civil War, and *The Old Man and the Sea* (1952), a novel about a Cuban fisherman. Hemingway was awarded the Nobel Prize for Literature in 1954. Hemingway was born in the American Midwest in 1899 and worked as an ambulance driver in World War I. He joined a group of expatriate writers in Paris in the 1920s, a rich literary experience for a young man. Hemingway moved to Cuba in the 1940s and lived there for many years, where he became a local hero. Returning to America, he fell into a period of declining mental health, committing suicide in Idaho in 1961.

WILLIAM FAULKNER

William Faulkner, American novelist and short-story writer, wrote almost solely about Southern history in his fiction. After the publication of his first successful novel, *Sartoris* (1929), Faulkner reeled off a series of impressive novels, including *The Sound And the Fury* (1929), *As I Lay Dying* (1930), *Absalom, Absalom!* (1936), *Sanctuary* (1931), and *Go Down, Moses* (1942). Winner of the Nobel Prize for Literature in 1949, Faulkner also won two Pulitzer prizes. He is remembered as a giant in American literature. Faulkner was born in Mississippi in 1897 and spent most of his life there. His recurring themes include Southern aristocracy's attempt to survive in the modern world, racial inequality in the South, and the burdens of slavery carried by his characters. Much of his work is based on his own family history, both colorful and tragic.

ERICH MARIA REMARQUE

Erich Maria Remarque is the pen name of Erich Paul Remark, German novelist and literary figure. His experiences as a soldier in World War I formed the subject of his first and greatest novel, *All Quiet on the Western Front,* published in 1929. Detailing the experiences of ordinary German soldiers, the book became one of the more important literary works to emerge from the war.

Remarque was born in a small town in northern Germany in 1898. Drafted into the German army, he was gravely wounded and abandoned behind the French lines. He survived to write his fictional history of the conflagration that impacted millions of lives. Remarque never again achieved the fame following his first novel, but he remained active and lived in Europe until his death in 1970 at the age of 72.

JOHN DOS PASSOS

John Dos Passos, American novelist, wrote sobering fiction and prose about the decline of the United States, both spiritually and socially. His literary reputation rests on a trilogy of novels published as *U.S.A.* in 1937. His jaundiced view of America is based on his observations of a country deeply divided by class and coarsened by commercialism. Early novels polished his stream-of-consciousness style he would employ so effectively in *U.S.A.* Dos Passos was born to a wealthy Chicago family in 1896. Educated at Harvard, he worked with Hemingway as an ambulance driver in France in World War I. Dos Passos's essentially negative view of American society is a recurring theme in his literary work. He worked as a journalist most of his life and published several works of biography and history before his death in 1970 at age 74.

HENRY MILLER

Henry Miller—American novelist, short-fiction writer, and essayist—is best known for two books that were banned initially in the United States, *Tropic of Cancer* (1961) and *Tropic of Capricorn* (1962), both of which were published in France first. These two autobiographical novels caused an uproar because of their controversial treatment of sex. The Supreme Court ruled in Miller's favor in 1964, and the books were then legal in America. Miller's later works include *The Rosy Crucifixion*, a trilogy based on Miller's life, along with anthologies of essays and stories. Henry Miller was born in Manhattan, New York, in 1891. He moved to Paris as a young man and celebrated his bohemian lifestyle. His works had a great influence on the Beat Generation of the 1950s. Miller returned to the United States and lived in Big Sur in Pacific Palisades until his death in 1980.

LILLIAN HELLMAN

Lillian Hellman was an American playwright and diarist who burst onto the literary scene in 1934 with *The Children's Hour*, a play about two schoolteachers who are accused of lesbianism. She followed this with *The Little Foxes*, a portrait of a ruthless Southern family. Other notable plays by Hellman include *Watch On The Rhine* (1941) and *Toys In The Attic* (1960). She published several volumes of her autobiography, which were lauded for their eloquence. Lillian Hellman was born in New Orleans in 1905 to a middle-class Jewish family. She grew up in New York and moved to Hollywood to work as a script reader. Blacklisted in the 1950s for her political activism, she fought a long battle to clear her name. Lillian Hellman grew to be a much-loved liberal icon until her death in 1984.

CLIFFORD ODETS

Clifford Odets, American playwright, was an important figure in the theatre of the 1930s. His forte was social protest theatre, in which he became a leader. Odets found his first success in *Waiting for Lefty* (1935) and *Awake and Sing* (1935), both powerful depictions of class struggle. Odets's other notable plays include *Golden Boy* (1937), *The Big Knife* (1949), and *The Country Girl* (1950).

Clifford Odets was born in Philadelphia in 1906 and raised in New York. He began his career as an actor with the Theatre Guild and later became a founding member of the famous Group Theatre. Odets remained active on Broadway as well, working in legitimate theatre. Clifford Odets died in Hollywood in 1963.

ANNA AKHMATOVA

Anna Akhmatova is the pen name of Andreyevna Gorenko, Russian poet, whose work is set against repression in the Soviet Union. She was a leading light of the Acemist school of poetry, which valued accuracy, precision, and realistic clarity as a reaction to Symbolism. A collection of lyrical love poems, *Vecher* (1912), was her first book. Her epic poem "Requiem" (1940) was a response to her husband's execution by the Soviets. Regarded as her masterpiece, "Poem Without A Hero" (1965) narrates the difficulties of an artist working in a repressive regime. Akhmatova was born near Odessa in 1889. Stalinist officials banned her work for almost 20 years, judging it too concerned with love and God. Expelled from the Writer's Union in 1946, she was not published again until the late 1950s. She is now ranked as one of the great poets of the 20th century. She died in the Soviet Union in 1966.

MARGARET MITCHELL

Margaret Mitchell rests her reputation on one book, *Gone with the Wind,* published in 1936. The novel won Mitchell a Pulitzer Prize and was made into one of the most popular films of all time, starring Clark Gable and Vivian Leigh. The book narrates a Southern belle's rise and fall set against the panorama of the plantation South and the American Civil War. The protagonist, Scarlett O'Hara, suffers the end of her Southern society and her values before becoming a resilient and successful survivor. Margaret Mitchell was born in 1900 in Atlanta and lived all of her life there. She attended Smith College in Northampton, Massachusetts, and worked as a journalist in Atlanta. She wrote *Gone with the Wind* over a 10-year period, completing it in 1934. The unprecedented success of the book and film changed her life forever. She spoke, taught, and lectured over the next 10 years until her death in Atlanta in 1949.

JOHN STEINBECK

John Steinbeck, American novelist and short-story writer, wrote with a realistic style about the lives of common people. Steinbeck's most important work describes the plight of itinerant workers set in rural and industrial California. His best-known works include *Of Mice and Men* (1937) and his Pulitzer-Prize-winning novel *The Grapes of Wrath* (1939). The latter evokes the depression-stricken Dust Bowl and a refugee family's travails. Other important books include *Cannery Row* (1945), *East Of Eden* (1952), and his whimsical *Travels with Charley* (1962). Steinbeck won the Nobel Prize for Literature in 1962. John Steinbeck was born in California in 1902. He was educated at Stanford University, where he studied marine biology. Most of his fiction is set in California, and the themes of the sea are evident in his early work. His writing exhibits a lyrical quality combined with a stark realism that was his trademark. Steinbeck died in New York City in 1968.

ROBERT PENN WARREN

Robert Penn Warren was an influential American novelist, poet, and critic. His most famous work is the Pulitzer-Prize-winning novel *All The King's Men*, published in 1946. Based loosely on the life of Huey P. Long, it was adapted into an Oscar-winning motion picture in 1949. Other important fiction includes the novel *World Enough and Time* (1950) and the short story collection *The Circus in the Attic* (1947). Warren published 14 collections of poetry and won the Pulitzer Prize for *Now and Then* (1978). He was an influential literary critic, promoting the New Criticism in important textbooks. Robert Penn Warren was born in Kentucky and attended Vanderbilt University. He taught for many years at Louisiana State University, where he founded the *Southern Review*. He was named Poet Laureate of the United States in 1986. Warren died in 1989.

RICHARD WRIGHT

Richard Wright, American novelist and short-fiction writer, was one of the most influential black voices in American literature. His first book, *Uncle Tom's Children* (1938), included four novellas and won critical acclaim. Wright's publication of the best-selling *Native Son* in 1940 ensured his place in literary history. In addition to *Native Son*, Wright's other important work includes *The Outsider* (1953) and his autobiography, *Black Boy*, published in 1945. Richard Wright was born in rural Mississippi in 1908, the grandson of slaves. Reared in Memphis, largely self-educated, he moved to Chicago at age 19 and entered the Federal Writers' Project. During the Depression, Wright

joined the Communist Party and lived in Mexico before settling in Paris. Richard Wright died in Paris in 1960 at the age of 52.

CARSON MCCULLERS

Carson McCullers, born Lula Carson Smith, American novelist, set her fiction in the small Southern towns she grew up in as a child. Her themes were alienation, loneliness, and spiritual longing. Her best-known novel, *The Member of the Wedding*, narrates the story of a lonely adolescent girl in a Southern town who lives vicariously through her brother. Her literary reputation was established with the appearance of *The Heart Is a Lonely Hunter* in 1940. Other well-known works include *Reflections in a Golden Eye* (1941), *Clock Without Hands* (1961), and a posthumously published story collection, *The Mortgaged Heart* (1971). Carson McCullers was born in Georgia in 1917 and studied music at Julliard before attending Columbia to study writing. She was ill most of her life and a series of crippling strokes began in her twenties. She died in 1967 at age 50.

EUDORA WELTY

Eudora Welty—American novelist, short-fiction writer, critic, and essayist—was one of the great writers of the South. She mastered the Southern vernacular and the culture and customs of the South, and produced an impressive body of work. Her first collection, *A Curtain Of Green* (1941), contained many of her most popular stories. Her novel *The Ponder Heart* (1954) is a classic of absurdist humor. *The Optimist's Daughter* (1972) won her a Pulitzer Prize in 1972. She holds many honors, including the French Legion of Merit and the American Medal of Freedom. Welty was born in Jackson, Mississippi, in 1909, and attended Mississippi State University and the University of Wisconsin. She lived in New York until her father's early death caused her to return to Jackson, where she would live the rest of her life. She was a literary figure of great importance in the South until her death in 2001.

BERTOLT BRECHT

Bertolt Brecht, born Eugene Berthold Friedrich Brecht, was a German playwright and poet whose major contribution to drama was to utilize the stage as a platform for political and social commentary. Brecht believed that the stage was a forum for presenting patterns of human behavior, outlined in his theory of epic theatre. His success dated from the writing of *The Three Penney Opera* in 1928, a work of biting satire coauthored with composer Kurt Weill. Two other plays of interest are *Mother Courage and Her Children* (1941) and *The Life of Galileo* (1943). An anthology of English translations appeared in 1979. Brecht was born in Augsburg, Germany, in 1898. Brecht embraced Marxism and was forced to flee Germany in 1933 by the Nazis. He lived in Europe and the United States for many years until returning to East Germany in 1949. He died there in 1956.

ALBERT CAMUS

Albert Camus—French philosopher, poet, novelist, and playwright—explored the philosophy of the absurd through his work. He examined man's existence in an indifferent universe and stressed the need for humanistic and moral values in this situation. Success came with his novel *The Stranger* (1942) and his essay "The Myth Of Sisyphus" (1942), both arresting explorations of the absurd. Other significant works include the novels *The Plague* (1947) and *The Fall* (1956) and his influential essay "The Rebel" (1951). Camus was born in Algiers in 1913 to a middle-class family. He studied philosophy at the University of Algiers and later worked as a journalist. He was an intellectual leader of the French Resistance under Nazi occupation and served as the editor of the underground paper *Combat*. Camus was awarded the Nobel Prize for Literature in 1957. He died in an automobile accident in 1960.

JORGE LUIS BORGES

Jorge Luis Borges—Argentinean poet, novelist essayist, and short-story writer—combined fantasy, myth, and philosophy in the fabric of daily life. His work is highly original, and his collection of essays, *Other Inquisitions* (1952), explains the writer's philosophy of life and art. Other important works are a book blending poetry and prose, *The Book of Imaginary Beings* (1967), a collection of stories, *The Book of Sand*, and a collection of his poetry in English translation. Born in Argentina in 1899, Borges studied abroad and received his degree from College de Geneva in Switzerland before returning home. During the dictatorship of Juan Perón, Borges was a vocal critic of the government. After the fall of Perón, Borges was appointed director of the National Library of Argentina in Buenos Aires. Borges died in 1986.

JEAN GENET

Jean Genet, French novelist and playwright, is the master of drama and fiction depicting criminal life and antisocial behavior. His absurdist dramas are existentialist nightmares that mix violence and erotic content in a powerful blend. Genet's breakthrough novel was *Our Lady Of The Flowers* (1943), written in prison while serving a life sentence. Sartre and Cocteau successfully argued for Genet's release, and he published his shocking autobiography *The Thief's Journal* in 1949. Genet then turned his attention to drama, writing several successful plays, including *The Maids* (1947), *The Balcony* (1956), and *The Blacks* (1948), all of which were influential in the development of avant-garde theatre. Genet was born in France in 1910, an illegitimate child abandoned by his mother. After spending his youth in unhappy foster homes and orphanages, he joined the Foreign Legion and promptly deserted. Genet died in France in 1986.

TENNESSEE WILLIAMS

Tennessee Williams, born Thomas Lanier Williams II, is regarded as one of the greatest American playwrights of the 20th century. His subject matter was drawn from the earthiest topics and treated with a lyrical touch in a romantic, yet realistic, view of America's South. His rise to fame was meteoric with *The Glass Menagerie* in 1945, followed by his Pulitzer-Prize-winning *A Streetcar Named Desire* in 1947. Other important plays followed, including *Cat on a Hot Tin Roof* in 1955, which earned Williams another Pulitzer, *Suddenly Last Summer* in 1958, *Sweet Bird of Youth* in 1959, and his last hit, *The Night of the Iguana*, in 1961. Williams was born in Mississippi in 1911 and educated at the universities of Washington and Iowa. After his dramatic success had slowed, he published a collection of poetry and his memoirs. Williams is generally regarded, along with Eugene O'Neill and Arthur Miller, as one of the greatest American dramatists. He died in 1983 at the age of 71.

WILLIAM CARLOS WILLIAMS

William Carlos Williams—American poet, novelist and short-story author—found inspiration for his work in the experiences of everyday life. He wrote 45 volumes of prose and poetry, typically American, using his realistic, or Objectivist, style. His best poetry was his five-volume *Paterson* (1946–58), based on the city near his home. His *Pictures From Brueghel* (1962), a three-volume work, won Williams a Pulitzer Prize in 1962. He also published numerous works of short fiction and the Stecher trilogy of novels. His prose includes a book of essays and an autobiography.

William Carlos Williams was born in Rutherford, New Jersey, in 1883 and studied medicine in college. He returned to his birthplace and practiced as a pediatrician for over 50 years while turning out a huge body of innovative and very American work. Williams was unusual in that he literally had two full-time careers his whole adult life. He is now regarded as a leading Modernist writer. He died in New Jersey in 1963.

NORMAN MAILER

Norman Mailer—American novelist, short-story writer, essayist, and journalist—won his initial success with *The Naked and the Dead*, his autobiographical novel of World War II, published in 1948. Blending gritty realism with a unique and arresting writing style, Mailer was granted instant celebrity. His later novels never approached the success of *The Naked and the Dead*, and his reputation today rests largely on his journalism. Mailer won the Pulitzer Prize for *Armies of the Night* and *The Executioner's Song*, both nonfiction books. Norman Mailer was born in New Jersey in 1923 and educated at Harvard University. After his initial success in fiction, he developed his own blend of journalism, political commentary, fictional allusions, and autobiography into a rich style with colorful language. Significant later works include *Ancient Evenings* and *Harlot's Ghost*. He died in 2007.

ARTHUR MILLER

Arthur Miller, American playwright, described the pain of the common man in his stirring dramas. Perhaps his best-known play, *Death Of A Salesman* (1949) earned him a Pulitzer Prize. *The Crucible* (1953), a drama about the Salem witch trials, is regarded as an American classic. Miller was an extremely productive author, penning dramas over six decades. Some of his better early works include *A View From The Bridge* (1955), *The Price* (1968), and *The American Clock* (1980). Notable later works include *The Misfits and Other Stories* (1987) and a novella, *Homely Girl* (1995).

Arthur Miller was born in Harlem in 1915. Educated at the University of Michigan, he began writing plays in the 1940s. Haunted by his father's failure during the depression, Miller returned to the subject of failure in many of his plays. He had an extremely productive career, ending with his death in 2005.

SIMONE DE BEAUVOIR

Simone de Beauvoir—French novelist, philosopher, and memoirist—was a powerful intellectual figure in post-World War II Europe. Perhaps her most important work is *The Second Sex* (1949), a ground-breaking feminist polemic about the secondary status of women in the world. Her best-known novel is *The Mandarins* (1954), which relates her struggles with the repressive regimes of Vichy, followed by Stalinist excesses. De Beauvoir wrote extensively about her life and published five volumes of memoirs that offered a window of history into her time. Born in Montparnasse in Paris in 1908, she met and formed the defining relationship of her life with Jean-Paul Sartre. This was a friendship, a love relationship, and a partnership of philosophy and art. She focused on the themes of individual freedom, particularly between the sexes. She died in Paris in 1986.

J. D. SALINGER

Jerome David Salinger, American novelist and short-fiction writer, is one of the most enigmatic figures in 20th-century literary history. Salinger wrote one novel, *The Catcher In The Rye*, published in 1951, which has been a bible to coming-of-age youth ever since. His hero, Holden Caulfield, seeks meaning in a world he finds contrived and artificial. The book has been required reading in countless college courses over the years. Salinger also wrote several collections of short stories, including *Nine Stories* (1953) and *Franny and Zooey* (1961), which narrate young people's alienation from society. Salinger was born in New York in 1919 and little is known about his early life. After his success in the early 1950s, Salinger became a recluse in New England and withstood all attempts to interview or even meet him. He has published almost nothing since the early 1960s.

RALPH ELLISON

Ralph Ellison, American novelist and essayist, published only one novel in his lifetime. His hugely successful *The Invisible Man*, published in 1952, was a candid and realistic examination of race relations in the United States. The unnamed protagonist, a black man, realizes his color makes him essentially invisible in American society. Winner of The National Book Award in 1952, *The Invisible Man* has become a classic in the study of race relations in modern America. Ellison remained a productive writer, publishing books of essays and short stories. Ralph Ellison was born in Oklahoma and originally trained as a musician. He joined the Federal Writers' Project in 1936 and met and befriended Richard Wright. He lived most of his adult life in New York City, where he held an endowed chair at New York University. Ellison died in New York in 1994.

FRANK O'HARA

Frank O'Hara—American poet, playwright, and art critic—was a leader of a group of poets known as The New York School, which captured the spirit of New York in conventional and conversational verse. Drawing from expressionism and the sounds of jazz and cadences of New York, this school produced poetry that was truly American. O'Hara was known for his improvisational writing such as *Lunch Poems* (1964), *Meditations in an Emergency* (1956), and his tribute to Billie Holiday, "The Day Lady Died" (1955). Frank O'Hara was born in Baltimore in 1926 and raised in Massachusetts. Educated at Harvard and the University of Michigan, he migrated to New York and became editor of *Art News*, where much of his art criticism first appeared. Intimates such as Willem de Kooning and Jackson Pollock provided much of the inspiration for his improvisational work. O'Hara was killed in an accident at Fire Island in 1966, cutting short his career at age 40.

JAMES BALDWIN

James Baldwin—American novelist, playwright, and essayist—became the leading black author of his time. His autobiographical novel *Go Tell It On The Mountain* (1953) is the story of a teenage boy growing up in Harlem. His work almost exclusively deals with intolerance and the struggle for free expression. His own experience of racism in America resulted in his collection of essays, *Notes of a Native Son*, published to critical success in 1955. Several anthologies of his works have been published. James Baldwin was born in Harlem in 1924, the son of a popular clergyman. Depressed by race relations in the United States, Baldwin emigrated to Paris after World War II and remained in France the rest of his life. Baldwin was heavily involved in the Civil Rights movement in America and won praise for his activism. Baldwin died in Saint Paul de Venice in 1987.

SAUL BELLOW

Saul Bellow, Canadian-born American novelist, was noted for the ethical intensity of his work. He depicted the experiences of urban Jews in America in a new voice. Critical and popular success came to Bellow with the publication of *The Adventures Of Augie March* (1953) and *Henderson, the Rain King* (1959). A trio of his best work followed: *Herzog* (1954), winner of the National Book Award, *Mr. Sammler's Planet (*1970), and his Pulitzer-Prize-winning novel, *Humboldt's Gift* (1975). Bellow continued his productivity into the 21st century. Bellow was born in Montreal, Canada, in 1915. He grew up in Chicago, and like many young writers of this period, got his start with the WPA Writers' Project. He grew to be a grand figure in American fiction and is regarded as one of the great modern novelists. Bellow died in 2005.

RAY BRADBURY

Ray Bradbury—American novelist, short-fiction writer, playwright, and poet—is known primarily as a writer of fantasy and science fiction. He is known for weaving social criticism into his work, and shows a constant wariness of the dangers of technology. Bradbury's best works include *Fahrenheit 451* (1953), *The Martian Chronicles* (1950), and *The Illustrated Man* (1951), all best sellers in the then-exploding field of science fiction. Bradbury, a prolific writer, has also published volumes of poetry, children's books, plays, and television and film screenplays. Bradbury was born in 1920 in the Midwest. He was an early contributor to pulp fiction and fantasy magazines. His early success gave him the freedom to experiment with different styles and genres. Bradbury has been a productive author for over 50 years and continues to develop fresh ideas and creative approaches to his craft.

WALLACE STEVENS

Wallace Stevens is one of the great Modernist poets. His verse covers a wide scope of themes but returns continually to the role of poetry in filling the emptiness created by the lack of God. Stevens did not publish his first book until he was 44. Through the 1930s, '40s, and '50s he produced a body of work that includes *The Man With The Blue Guitar* (1937), *Transport to Summer* (1947), and *Parts of a World* (1942), to name only a few. Stevens was ignored during his lifetime for the most part, and only in the last year of his life did he win a Pulitzer Prize and National Book Award.

Born in Reading, Pennsylvania, in 1879, he was educated at Harvard and studied law in New York City. He became an insurance attorney and worked for almost 40 years with The Hartford Accident And Indemnity Company. During this period, he turned out a body of work rarely excelled in modern poetry. Stevens died in 1955.

VLADIMIR NABOKOV

Vladimir Nabokov—Russian-born American novelist, critic, and translator—was a skillful, imaginative, and creative writer who has earned a place in literary history. He published his first few novels under a pseudonym in Berlin. He will always be best known for *Lolita*, his landmark novel published in 1955. This highly controversial novel was about the affair of a middle-aged man and his young stepdaughter. Nabokov wrote other excellent novels, including *Pale Fire* (1962), *Pnin* (1957), and *Ada or Ardor* (1969). He was a translator of talent; his work with Pushkin's *Eugene Onegin* won him plaudits. Nabokov was born in Russia in 1899. He studied literature at Cambridge and then lived in Paris before emigrating to the United States in 1940. He taught at several excellent universities, completing *Lolita* when he was on the faculty at Cornell. He then devoted himself full-time to writing and died in 1977 at the age of 78.

MIGUEL DE CERVANTES

Miguel de Cervantes was an accomplished Spanish novelist, poet, and playwright. A giant in literary history, Cervantes is best known as the author of <u>Don Quixote</u>, an early masterpiece of prose fiction. Many view him as the originator of the novel, and it is agreed that Cervantes demonstrated the possibilities of satirical narrative and fictional realism. His work has inspired novelists for almost 400 years. Born into a poor family outside Madrid, Cervantes became a soldier and was captured and enslaved by Algerian pirates for five years. Ransomed by Trinitarian friars, he worked as a businessman in Andalusia until the success of <u>Don Quixote</u> allowed him the freedom to devote himself to writing. He was productive in later life, writing <u>Exemplary Stories</u>, a work of 12 diverse narratives. He authored at least 30 plays of which about half survive. Cervantes completed an epic romance, <u>The Trials of Persiles and Sigismunda</u>, only three days before his death in 1616.

MOILERE

Jeb-Baptiste Poquelin, known as Moliere, was the greatest playwright of his time. Combining an acute ear for language, sharp character portraits, and the ability to evoke both profound and absurd moods, Moliere delighted his sophisticated Parisian audiences. His most popular plays include <u>La Tartuffe</u>, banned by the Church, <u>The Misanthrope</u>, and <u>The School for Wives</u>. Moliere's unique combinations of talents produced a new type of comedy—the comedy of manners—which brought him both fame and wealth. Moliere was born into a well-to-do Paris family in 1622. He eschewed a promising business career to devote himself to the theatre. He was active as an actor, writer, producer and director, and toured France for ten years. Moliere became a favorite of King

Louis XIV who offered him a theatre in the Louvre. Here he flourished becoming a favorite of French society. Moliere continued his dramatic work in Paris when during a performance of his last play, "The Imaginary Invalid", he collapsed and died in 1673.

JOHAN STRINDBERG

Johan Strindberg was a Swedish novelist, playwright, essayist, and short-fiction writer. His initial success was a novel of bohemian life in Sweden, The Red Room, published in 1879. His writing was noted for blending realism and naturalism together in a unique manner. His best novels include The Father (1887) and Miss Julie (1889). Strindberg later turned to Symbolism mixed with Expressionism for his Ghost Sonata (1908) and The Great Highway (1910), both autobiographical plays. Strindberg was born in Sweden in 1849. An unhappy childhood followed by three failed marriages influenced his work greatly. His public life was full of controversy and he flirted with debilitating mental illness all his life, describing a near-breakdown in Inferno (1897). He died in 1912.

F. SCOTT FITZGERALD

F. Scott Fitzgerald was an American novelist and short-story writer. Fitzgerald has transcended his early reputation as a period novelist, now being viewed as a great modern novelist. He launched his writing career with This Side of Paradise (1920), a novel of the jazz age. His masterpiece, The Great Gatsby (1925), chronicles the life of a bootlegger who reforms. Tender is the Night (1933) is a largely autobiographical novel about a psychiatrist's failing fight to save his wife from mental illness. Fitzgerald was born in St. Paul, Minnesota in 1896. Educated at Princeton University, he became a productive short-story writer after the success of his first novel. His marriage to the flamboyant Zelda Fitzgerald spiraled downward with alcoholism and her increasing mental illness. He worked in Hollywood as a screenwriter before his death in 1940.

HART CRANE

Hart Crane, an American poet, left behind one work on which his reputation rests. "The Bridge," Hart's 18-part epic poem based on the Brooklyn Bridge, celebrates America's muscular industrial strength in a manner that precedes Carl Sandburg. The poem, published in 1930, was a popular and critical success. Combining bold imagery with technical dexterity, the sweeping American themes captured the fancy of the public and critics alike. His complete works including a manuscript found after his death were published in 1966. Crane was born in Ohio in 1899, and was an industrial worker during World War I. Hart suffered from depression his entire life, and committed suicide when returning from a trip to Mexico by jumping off of the ship into the ocean. This bizarre death ended a promising talent in 1932 when Hart was only 32 years old.

NELSON ALGREN

Nelson Algren, born Nelson Ahlgren Abraham, was an American novelist and short-story writer. His work is noted by the stark reality with which he depicts the lives of the poor. Algren is best remembered for his novel The Man With The Golden Arm (1949) which brings the reality of drug addiction to the literary world. The book, which was later adapted into an award-winning film, earned him a National Book Award and gave him a national reputation. Later works include the story collection The Neon Wilderness (1947) and a novel about Bohemian life in New Orleans, entitled A Walk On The Wild Side. Algren was born in 1809 in Detroit and raised in Chicago. Educated at the University of Illinois, he set much of his fiction in the Midwest, where he explored the seamy side of urban life. Algren was always viewed as a radical personality and his work reflects a slice of American urban life largely unnoticed. He died in 1981.

CLEP Practice Test

Questions 1 – 6 pertain to the following passage:

Percy Bysshe Shelley, "Ozymandias"

I met a traveller from an antique land
Who said: "Two vast and trunkless legs of stone
Stand in the desert. Near them on the sand,
Half sunk, a shattered visage lies, whose frown
And wrinkled lip and sneer of cold command
Tell that its sculptor well those passions read
Which yet survive, stamped on these lifeless things,
The hand that mocked them and the heart that fed.
And on the pedestal these words appear:
`My name is Ozymandias, King of Kings:
Look on my works, ye mighty, and despair!'
Nothing beside remains. Round the decay
Of that colossal wreck, boundless and bare,
The lone and level sands stretch far away."

1. What is the rhyme scheme of the first eight lines?

   a. ABACADAC
   b. ABABACDC
   c. ABABABCB
   d. ABADACDC
   e. ABABCBCB

2. What is the central image of the poem?

   a. A collapsed statue in the desert
   b. A wounded king
   c. A face and inscription on a coin
   d. A plaque near a WWII battle site
   e. The Sphinx

3. In what sense are lines 10-11 ironic? Although the inscription was originally intended to boast of a king's power, it appears to later generations as an example of how:

   a. Engineering skills were not as advanced as people believed at the time
   b. A king's power extends only as far as the boundaries of his kingdom
   c. A king can attain immortality through his works
   d. Time and nature will eventually undo the works of even the mighty
   e. The desert is not a suitable climate for a kingdom

4. Read as a symbol, the desert can be seen to represent:

   a. Fertility
   b. The life cycle
   c. The seasons
   d. Life
   e. A wasteland

5. Based on the setting, which of the following do you think best describes Ozymandias?

    a. Roman Emperor
    b. Egyptian Pharaoh
    c. Native American Chief
    d. Dynastic Emperor
    e. English Monarch

6. What poetic form does this poem use?

    a. Italian sonnet
    b. Ballad
    c. Anaphora
    d. Prose poem
    e. Sestina

Questions 7 – 12 pertain to the following passage:

Emily Dickinson, "Success is counted sweetest"

Success is counted sweetest
By those who ne'er succeed.
To comprehend a nectar
Requires sorest need.

Not one of all the purple Host
Who took the Flag today
Can tell the definition
So clear of Victory

As he defeated--dying--
On whose forbidden ear
The distant strains of triumph
Burst agonized and clear!

7. In the final stanza, the imagery suggests a soldier who lies dying on a battlefield. Which of the following interpretations of lines from the poem reinforce this image?

    I. The final line suggests cannon blasts
    II. "Strains of triumph" imply the dying soldier's joy in victory
    III. The words "defeated, dying" in line 9 indicate mortal combat

    a. I only
    b. I and II
    c. II and III
    d. I and III
    e. II only

8. What literary device is employed in lines 3 and 4?

    a. Paradox
    b. Caesura
    c. Metaphor
    d. Dramatic monologue
    e. Anaphora

9. How many stressed syllables are in each line of the first stanza?

a. 1
b. 2
c. 3
d. 4
e. 5

10. By what logical pattern is this poem organized?

a. Main idea, developed with examples
b. Cause and effect
c. Comparison and contrast
d. Chronological order
e. Description

11. Which of the following statements is in keeping with the argument the poem presents?

I. The loser understands success better than the victor
II. It is noble to accept defeat humbly
III. It is best to learn from the mistakes of others

a. I only
b. I and II
c. II and III
d. II only
e. I, II, and III

12. Which of the following represents the first stanza's rhyme scheme?

a. ABCB
b. ABAB
c. ABBB
d. ABCA
e. ABCC

Questions 13 -16 pertain to the following excerpt from Sir Philip Sidney, "An Apology for Poetry"

Therefore compare we the poet with the historian and with the moral philosopher.

. . . .

The philosopher therefore and the historian are they which would win the goal, the one by precept, the other by example; but both not having both, do both halt. For the philosopher, setting down with thorny arguments the bare rule, is so hard of utterance and so misty to be conceived, that one that hath no other guide but him shall wade in him till he be old, before he shall find sufficient cause to be honest. For his knowledge standeth so upon the abstract and general that happy is that man who may understand him, and more happy that can apply what he doth understand. On the other side, the historian, wanting the precept, is so tied, not to what should be but to what is, to the particular truth of things, and not to the general reason of things, that his example draweth no necessary consequence, and therefore a less fruitful doctrine.

Now doth the peerless poet perform both; for whatsoever the philosopher saith should be done, he giveth a perfect picture of it in some one by whom he presupposeth it was done, so as he coupleth the general notion with the particular example. A perfect picture, I say; for he yieldeth to the powers of the mind an image of that whereof the philosopher bestoweth but a wordish description, which doth neither strike, pierce, nor possess the sight of the soul so much as that other doth. For as, in outward things, to a man that had never seen an elephant or a rhinoceros, who should tell him most exquisitely all their shapes, color, bigness, and particular marks; or of a gorgeous palace, an architector, with declaring the full beauties, might well make the hearer able to repeat, as it were by rote, all he had heard, yet should never satisfy his inward conceit with being witness to itself of a true lively knowledge; but the same man, as soon as he might see those beasts well painted, or that house well in model, should straightways grow, without need of any description, to a judicial comprehending of them; so no doubt the philosopher, with his learned definitions, be it of virtues or vices, matters of public policy or private government, replenisheth the memory with many infallible grounds of wisdom, which notwithstanding lie dark before the imaginative and judging power, if they be not illuminated or figured forth by the speaking picture of poesy.

13. What is the author's primary criticism of the philosopher?
   a. The philosopher communicates only general, abstract ideas
   b. The philosopher can make an untrue argument seem true
   c. The philosopher cannot know truth beyond the five senses
   d. The philosopher is difficult to understand
   e. The philosopher cannot attain true wisdom

14. What is the author's primary criticism of the historian?
   a. The historian considers only abstract precepts
   b. The historian may distort events to reflect political preferences
   c. The historian deals only with particular events, not general principles
   d. The historian can see only the past through the lens of the present
   e. The historian is difficult to understand

15. The author praises poets primarily for their ability to:
   a. Preserve the highest values of the past
   b. Write both abstract ideas and particular details
   c. Communicate more clearly than the philosopher
   d. Entertain and instruct
   e. Speak of the present as a historian speaks of the past

16. Which of the following best captures the meaning of the final sentence in the above passage?
   a. A poet can make the philosopher's wisdom appeal to the imagination of the reader
   b. The philosopher's ideas appeal to the imagination of the audience, but not to the intellect
   c. The philosopher is wiser than the poet in matters of public policy and private government
   d. The painter can illuminate the ideas of the philosopher best of all
   e. The imagination is of no use in acquiring wisdom

92

Questions 17 – 21 pertain to the excerpt from Joseph Conrad, Heart of Darkness:

"Going up that river was like traveling back to the earliest beginnings of the world, when vegetation rioted on the earth and the big trees were kings. An empty stream, a great silence, an impenetrable forest. The air was warm, thick, heavy, sluggish. There was no joy in the brilliance of sunshine. The long stretches of the waterway ran on, deserted, into the gloom of overshadowed distances. On silvery sandbanks hippos and alligators sunned themselves side by side. The broadening waters flowed through a mob of wooded islands; you lost your way on that river as you would in a desert, and butted all day long against shoals, trying to find the channel, till you thought yourself bewitched and cut off for ever from everything you had known once--somewhere--far away--in another existence perhaps. There were moments when one's past came back to one, as it will sometimes when you have not a moment to spare to yourself; but it came in the shape of an unrestful and noisy dream, remembered with wonder amongst the overwhelming realities of this strange world of plants, and water, and silence. And this stillness of life did not in the least resemble a peace. It was the stillness of an implacable force brooding over an inscrutable intention. It looked at you with a vengeful aspect. I got used to it afterwards; I did not see it any more; I had no time. I had to keep guessing at the channel; I had to discern, mostly by inspiration, the signs of hidden banks; I watched for sunken stones; I was learning to clap my teeth smartly before my heart flew out, when I shaved by a fluke some infernal sly old snag that would have ripped the life out of the tin-pot steamboat and drowned all the pilgrims; I had to keep a look-out for the signs of dead wood we could cut up in the night for next day's steaming. When you have to attend to things of that sort, to the mere incidents of the surface, the reality--the reality, I tell you--fades. The inner truth is hidden--luckily, luckily. But I felt it all the same; I felt often its mysterious stillness watching me at my monkey tricks, just as it watches you fellows performing on your respective tight-ropes for--what is it? half-a-crown a tumble--"

17. The punctuation marks that open and close this passage indicate that it is taken from:

    a. A novel
    b. Dialogue
    c. The early 1900s
    d. The author's point of view
    e. A soliloquy in a play

18. In the last sentence of this passage, what does the pronoun "it" refer to?

    a. "The inner truth"
    b. "Mysterious stillness"
    c. "Mere incidents of the surface"
    d. "The reality"
    e. "Monkey tricks"

19. When the character in this passage says, "And this stillness of life did not in the least resemble a peace. . . . It looked at you with a vengeful aspect," what literary device is being employed?

a. Metaphor
b. Allusion
c. Personification
d. Metonym
e. Symbolism

20. What is the setting of the story the character is telling?

a. On a river
b. In an aircraft
c. In a horse-drawn carriage
d. On large ocean vessel
e. On the Thames River in London

21. How is this passage organized?

a. Association of ideas
b. Main idea and supporting evidence
c. Chronological order
d. Cause and effect
e. Comparison and contrast

Questions 22 – 26 pertain to the following passage:

Katherine Mansfield, "Mrs. Brill"

The band had been having a rest. Now they started again. And what they played was warm, sunny, yet there was just a faint chill—a something, what was it?—not sadness—no, not sadness—a something that made you want to sing. The tune lifted, lifted, the light shone; and it seemed to Miss Brill that in another moment all of them, all the whole company, would begin singing. The young ones, the laughing ones who were moving together, they would begin, and the men's voices, very resolute and brave, would join them. And then she too, she too, and the others on the benches—they would come in with a kind of accompaniment—something low, that scarcely rose or fell, something so beautiful—moving. . . . And Miss Brill's eyes filled with tears and she looked smiling at all the other members of the company. Yes, we understand, we understand, she thought—though what they understood she didn't know.

Just at that moment a boy and girl came and sat down where the old couple had been. They were beautifully dressed; they were in love. The hero and heroine, of course, just arrived from his father's yacht. And still soundlessly singing, still with that trembling smile, Miss Brill prepared to listen.

"No, not now," said the girl. "Not here, I can't."

"But why? Because of that stupid old thing at the end there?" asked the boy. "Why does she come here at all—who wants her? Why doesn't she keep her silly old mug at home?"

"It's her fu-fur which is so funny," giggled the girl. "It's exactly like a fried whiting."

"Ah, be off with you!" said the boy in an angry whisper. Then: "Tell me, ma petite chere—"

"No, not here," said the girl. "Not yet."

On her way home she usually bought a slice of honeycake at the baker's. It was her Sunday treat. Sometimes there was an almond in her slice, sometimes not. It made a great difference. If there was an almond it was like carrying home a tiny present—a surprise—something that might very well not have been there. She hurried on the almond Sundays and struck the match for the kettle in quite a dashing way.

But to-day she passed the baker's by, climbed the stairs, went into the little dark room—her room like a cupboard—and sat down on the red eiderdown. She sat there for a long time. The box that the fur came out of was on the bed. She unclasped the necklet quickly; quickly, without looking, laid it inside. But when she put the lid on she thought she heard something crying.

22. Who is the "old thing" the boy refers to?
  a. The girl
  b. The band members
  c. Mrs. Brill
  d. The baker
  e. A cat

23. Which of the following statements best characterizes Mrs. Brill at the beginning of the passage?
  a. She feels a connection with the other people on the benches
  b. She feels disoriented
  c. She feels frustrated
  d. She feels hurt
  e. She waits impatiently

24. Which of the following statements best characterizes Mrs. Brill at the end of the passage?
  a. She was furious
  b. She was hurt
  c. She felt nervous and agitated
  d. She felt cheerful
  e. She was short-tempered

25. What is the setting of the first part of this passage?
  a. In a park
  b. On a boat
  c. In a snowstorm
  d. At a movie theater
  e. In a rural area

26. In what point of view is this passage written in?
   a. Third person limited omniscience
   b. First person
   c. Omniscient narrator
   d. Objective narrator
   e. Second person

Questions 27 – 32 pertain to the following passage:

John Donne, "Death be not proud"

Death be not proud, though some have called thee

Mighty and dreadful, for thou art not so;

For those whom thou think'st thou dost overthrow

Die not, poor death, nor yet canst thou kill me.

From rest and sleep, which but thy pictures be,

Much pleasure, then from thee much more must flow,

And soonest our best men with thee do go,

Rest of their bones, and soul's delivery.

Thou art slave to fate, chance, kings, and desperate men,

And dost with poison, war, and sickness dwell,

And poppy, or charms can make us sleep as well,

And better than thy stroke; why swell'st thou then?

One short sleep past, we wake eternally,

And death shall be no more; death, thou shalt die.

27. What form does this poem use?
   a. Villanelle
   b. Sonnet
   c. Epic
   d. Sestina
   e. Haiku

28. To whom is this poem addressed?
   a. To death
   b. To the speaker's lover
   c. To God
   d. To eternity
   e. To the muses

29. When speaking of death, which poetic device does the poet employ?
a. Litany
b. Metaphor
c. Personification
d. Internal rhyme
e. Alliteration

30. Which of the following interpretations best captures the central theme of the poem?
I. We need not fear death
II. Certainty of eternal life takes our fear of death away
III. Death is inevitable and must be faced with humility
a. I only
b. I and II
c. I, II, and III
d. II only
e. III only

31 Which of the following statements captures the logic of lines 5 through 6?
a. Because death is like a "picture" of sleep and rest, which are pleasurable states, death must be even more pleasurable
b. Death is painless, like falling asleep
c. Death is simply a short rest or sleep before reincarnation
d. Death is painful, unlike sleep
e. Death is pleasurable because it is the opposite of sleep

32. What literary device is used in line 6?
a. Alliteration
b. Internal rhyme
c. Symbolism
d. Enjambment
e. Hyperbole

Questions 33 – 38 pertain to the following passage:

Edward Taylor, "Huswifery"

Make me, O Lord, Thy spinning-wheel complete.

Thy holy word my distaff make for me.
Make mine affections Thy swift flyers neat

And make my soul Thy holy spool to be.

My conversation make to be Thy reel

And reel thy yarn thereon spun of Thy wheel.

Make me Thy loom then, knit therein this twine:

And make Thy Holy Spirit, Lord, wind quills:
Then weave the web Thyself. Thy yarn is fine.

Thine ordinances make my fulling-mills.

Then dye the same in heavenly colors choice,

All pinked with varnished flowers of paradise.

Then clothe therewith mine understanding, will,

Affections, judgment, conscience, memory,

My words and actions, that their shine may fill

My ways with glory and Thee glorify.

Then mine apparel shall display before Ye

That I am clothed in holy robes for glory.

33. What is the central metaphor of this poem?
a. A cart
b. A loom
c. A blanket
d. A grain mill
e. A windmill

34. Based on the poem, what is the intended connotation of the term "huswifery"?
a. Being a good husband
b. Being a good wife
c. A wife's doing a husband's job.
d. Sewing garments
e. Breeding and raising livestock

35. Which of the following statements best explains the meaning of the metaphor used in the final stanza?

I. The speaker compares her husband to a robe
II. The speaker compares the Lord to a housewife
III. The speaker wants to the Lord's influence to envelop him like clothes

a. I only
b. I and II
c. II and III
d. II only
e. III only

36. Which of the following best captures the meaning of the metaphor used in line 5?
a. The speaker wants God to speak through him to others
b. The speaker wants to be silenced by his love of God
c. The speaker wants to have a conversation with her husband
d. The speaker wants to learn how to work a loom
e. The speaker wants to converse with his wife

37. What two types of rhyme does the final stanza use?
   a. Masculine and slant rhyme
   b. Slant rhyme and consonant rhyme
   c. Identical rhyme and eye rhyme
   d. Internal rhyme and masculine rhyme
   e. Internal rhyme and eye rhyme

38. Considering the diction of the original version of this poem shown above, when and where do you think this it was written?
   a. 1st Century A.D., Rome
   b. 3rd Century B.C., Greece
   c. 19th Century, America
   d. 14th Century, Italy
   e. 21st Century, England

Questions 39 – 42 pertain to the following passage:

Edgar Allen Poe, "The Poetic Principle"

To recapitulate, then:--I would define, in brief, the Poetry of words as The Rhythmical Creation of Beauty. Its sole arbiter is Taste. With the Intellect or with the Conscience, it has only collateral relations. Unless incidentally, it has no concern whatever with Duty or with Truth.

A few words, however, in explanation. That pleasure which is at once the most pure, the most elevating, and the most intense, is derived, I maintain, from the contemplation of the Beautiful. In the contemplation of Beauty we alone find it possible to attain that pleasurable elevation, or excitement of the soul, which we recognize as the Poetic Sentiment, and which is so easily distinguished from Truth, which is the satisfaction of the Reason, or from passion, which is the excitement of the heart. I make Beauty, therefore--using the word as inclusive of the sublime--I make Beauty the province of the poem, simple because it is an obvious rule of Art that effects should be made to spring as directly as possible from their causes: no one as yet having been weak enough to deny that the peculiar elevation in question is at least most readily attainable in the poem. It by no means follows however, that the incitements of Passion, or the precepts of Duty, or even the Lessons of Truth, may not be introduced into a poem, and with advantage; for they may subserve, incidentally, in various ways, the general purposes of the work:--but the true artist will always contrive to tone them down in proper subjection to that Beauty which is the atmosphere and the real essence of the poem.

39. What is the author's main rhetorical purpose of this passage?
   a. To analyze examples that prove his point
   b. To illustrate his point by analogy
   c. To compare and contrast different types of poetry
   d. To disprove the arguments of those who might disagree with him
   e. To explain the idea that beauty should be the main goal of poetry

40. Which of the following statements seems most compatible with the author's view of poetry?

> I. A poem that morally instructs its readers is always good
> II. Readers react first to a poem's beauty and then to the ideas it expresses
> III. The readers' enjoyment of a poem is contingent on their agreement with its ideas

a. I and II
b. I only
c. II and III
d. II only
e. III only

41. What does the author mean by the statement in paragraph one, "Unless incidentally, it has no concern whatever with Duty or with Truth"?

> I. Abstract ideas such as duty and truth in and of themselves do not make a poem good
> II. Poetry should never contain references to duty or truth
> III. Duty and truth should appear in a poem only if they are incidental to its beauty

a. I only
b. II only
c. III only
d. I and II
e. I and III

42. What is the antecedent for the pronoun "they" in the sentence that reads, ". . . for they may subserve, incidentally, in various ways, the general purposes of the work"?

a. "the incitements of Passion, or the precepts of Duty, or even the Lessons of Truth"
b. "the general purposes of the work"
c. "Beauty"
d. "the Poetic Sentiment"
e. "the real essence of the poem"

Questions 43 – 46 pertain to the following passage:

Lewis Carroll, Alice's Adventures in Wonderland

The Hatter opened his eyes very wide on hearing this; but all he said was, "Why is a raven like a writing-desk?"

"Come, we shall have some fun now!" thought Alice. "I'm glad they've begun asking riddles.--I believe I can guess that," she added aloud.

"Do you mean that you think you can find out the answer to it?" said the March Hare.

"Exactly so," said Alice.

"Then you should say what you mean," the March Hare went on.

"I do," Alice hastily replied; "at least--at least I mean what I say--that's the same thing, you know."

"Not the same thing a bit!" said the Hatter. "You might just as well say that 'I see what I eat' is the same thing as 'I eat what I see'!"

"You might just as well say," added the March Hare, "that 'I like what I get' is the same thing as "I get what I like'!"

"You might just as well say," added the Dormouse, who seemed to be talking in his sleep, "that 'I breathe when I sleep' is the same thing as 'I sleep when I breathe'!"

"It is the same thing with you," said the Hatter, and here the conversation dropped, and the party sat silent for a minute, while Alice thought over all she could remember about ravens and writing-desks, which wasn't much.

43. What is the general emotion this passage seems to invoke?
   a. Frustration and confusion
   b. Joy
   c. Fear
   d. Confidence
   e. Certainty

44. Which of the following terms best characterizes the literary device used in this passage?
   a. Monologue
   b. Stream of consciousness
   c. Flashback
   d. Stock characters
   e. Dialogue

45. How do the other characters attempt to disprove Alice's statement?
   a. By offering contradictory facts
   b. By attacking her character
   c. By presenting false analogies
   d. By appealing to authority
   e. By using a bandwagon appeal

46. Into what genre of literature does this passage best fit?
   a. Fantasy
   b. Mystery
   c. Nonfiction
   d. Drama
   e. Poetry

Questions 47 – 51 pertain to the following passage:

William Shakespeare, Macbeth

To-morrow, and to-morrow, and to-morrow,
Creeps in this petty pace from day to day,
To the last syllable of recorded time;
And all our yesterdays have lighted fools
The way to dusty death. Out, out, brief candle!
Life's but a walking shadow, a poor player,

That struts and frets his hour upon the stage,
And then is heard no more. It is a tale
Told by an idiot, full of sound and fury,
Signifying nothing.

47. Which of the following is NOT a metaphor employed in this excerpt?

a. Life is a candle
b. Life is a bad actor
c. Life is a story told by an idiot
d. Life is one long word with many syllables
e. Life walks along at a petty pace

48. What is the general tone conveyed by this passage?

a. Despair
b. Resolve
c. Fury
d. Humor
e. Inspiration

49. Which of the following statements is most closely in keeping with the sentiment of this passage?

a. Life's hardest lessons are best learned young
b. Life is meaningless.
c. Life is long and unpredictable
d. Character determines fate
e. Nature can be overcome

50. If the phrase "dusty death" suggests the Biblical phrase "from dust to dust," what literary device is being employed?

a. Paradox
b. Imagery
c. Alliteration
d. Allusion
e. Metonym

51. This passage is an excerpt from a play. The lines are delivered by a single actor alone on the stage. This technique is called a(n):

a. Internal monologue
b. Dramatic monologue
c. Stream of consciousness
d. Dialogue
e. Soliloquy

Questions 52 – 55 pertain to the following passage:

Percy Bysshe Shelley, "A Defense of Poetry"

Poetry is the record of the best and happiest moments of the happiest and best minds. We are aware of evanescent visitations of thought and feeling sometimes associated with place or person, sometimes regarding our own mind alone, and always arising unforeseen and departing unbidden, but elevating and delightful beyond all expression: so that even in the desire and the regret they leave, there cannot but be pleasure, participating as it does in the nature of its object. It is as it were the interpretation of a diviner nature through our own; but its footsteps are like those of a wind over the sea, which the coming calm erases, and whose traces remain only as on the wrinkled sand which paves it. These and corresponding conditions of being are experienced principally by those of the most delicate sensibility and the most enlarged imagination; and the state of mind produced by them is at war with every base desire. The enthusiasm of virtue, love, patriotism, and friendship is essentially linked with such emotions; and whilst they last, self appears as what it is, an atom to a universe. Poets are not only subject to these experiences as spirits of the most refined organization, but they can color all that they combine with the evanescent hues of this ethereal world; a word, a trait in the representation of a scene or a passion will touch the enchanted chord, and reanimate, in those who have ever experienced these emotions, the sleeping, the cold, the buried image of the past. Poetry thus makes immortal all that is best and most beautiful in the world; it arrests the vanishing apparitions which haunt the interlunations of life, and veiling them, or in language or in form, sends them forth among mankind, bearing sweet news of kindred joy to those with whom their sisters abide—abide, because there is no portal of expression from the caverns of the spirit which they inhabit into the universe of things. Poetry redeems from decay the visitations of the divinity in man.

52. About our happiest moments, the author of this passage states that their "footsteps are like wind over the sea." In what sense should this simile be taken?

    a.   We risk losing ourselves in the pursuit of happiness, just as a swimmer risks drowning

    b.   Our happiest moments can chill us like wind over a cold sea

    c.   Our happiest moments are often the result of tumultuous times

    d.   Our happiest moments are not permanent and leave very faint traces

    e.   Our happiest moments are as miraculous as a man walking on water

53. Which of the following statements is consistent with the meaning of this quotation, "The enthusiasm of virtue, love, patriotism, and friendship is essentially linked with such emotions; and whilst they last, self appears as what it is, an atom to a universe"?

I. The most powerful emotions are those that make one feel like a small part of a much larger process

II. The danger in too much enthusiasm for strong emotions is a loss of self

III. The self is really only a small part of a larger whole

    a.   I only

    b.   I and II

    c.   II and III

    d.   I and III

    e.   III only

54. Which of the following statements best captures the meaning of this passage as a whole?

    I. Strong emotions should not be experienced in real life, only in poetry
    II. Poetry can capture and preserve fleeting moments of inspiration and beauty
    III. Poets are not obligated to tell the truth

  a. I only
  b. II only
  c. III only
  d. I and II
  e. II and III

55. Which of the following statements would the author of this passage likely agree with?

  a. The poet is most like the philosopher
  b. The poet is most like the lunatic
  c. The poet is most like a medium for the divine
  d. The poet is most like the musician
  e. The poet is most like the painter

Questions 56 – 60 pertain to the following passage:

Henrik Ibsen, A Doll's House

Helmer: This is outrageous! You're just going to walk away from your most sacred duties?

Nora: What do you consider to be my most sacred duties?

Helmer: Do you need me to tell you that? Aren't they your duties to your husband and your children?

Nora: I have other duties just as sacred.

Helmer: No, you do not. What could they be?

Nora: Duties to myself.

Helmer: First and foremost, you're a wife and mother.

Nora: I don't believe that anymore. I believe that first and foremost I'm a human being, just as you are—or, at least, that I have to try to become one. I know very well, Torvald, that most people would agree with you, and that opinions like yours are in books, but I can't be satisfied anymore with what most people say, or with what's in books. I have to think things through for myself and come to understand them.

Helmer: Why can't you understand your place in your own home? Don't you have an infallible guide in matters like that? What about your religion?

Nora: Torvald, I'm afraid I'm not sure what religion is.

Helmer: What are you saying?

104

Nora: All I know is what Pastor Hansen said when I was confirmed. He told us that religion was this, that, and the other thing. When I'm away from all this and on my own, I'll look into that subject too. I'll see if what he said is true or not, or at least whether it's true for me.

Helmer: This is unheard of, coming from a young woman like you! But if religion doesn't guide you, let me appeal to your conscience. I assume you have some moral sense. Or do you have none? Answer me.

Nora: Torvald, that's not an easy question to answer. I really don't know. It's very confusing to me. I only know that you and I look at it in very different ways. I'm learning too that the law isn't at all what I thought it was, and I can't convince myself that the law is right. A woman has no right to spare her old dying father or to save her husband's life? I can't believe that.

Helmer: You talk like a child. You don't understand anything about the world you live in.

Nora: No, I don't. But I'm going to try. I'm going to see if I can figure out who's right, me or the world.

56. Which of the following statements best captures the point Nora is trying to make to Helmer?

I. She has decided to change her life in order to find out who she is
II. She feels that she has been dependent on others' points of view for too long
III. She seeks to learn how to think for herself

a. I only
b. II only
c. III only
d. II and III
e. I, II, and III

57. What is the dominant emotion Nora expresses in this passage?

a. Fear and doubt
b. Resolve and determination
c. Dependence and need for reassurance
d. Pity and compassion
e. Confusion and indecision

58. What can we infer about Helmer and Nora's relationship up to the point of this conversation?

a. He has been too emotionally dependent on her
b. She has been dependent on him
c. They have treated each other as equals
d. Helmer feels that Nora has been too independent
e. They have been too emotionally dependent on each other

59. What sort of appeals does Helmer NOT make to Nora?

a. He appeals to her sense of duty
b. He appeals to her religious values
c. He appeals to her morals
d. He appeals to her fear of being alone
e. He appeals to her desire to be treated as an adult

60. Nora claims she is "a human being—or I must try to become one." In what sense should this statement be taken?

I. She wants to be independent
II. She wants to feel a stronger emotional bond with Helmer
III. She wants to feel a stronger emotional bond with her children

a. I only
b. II and III
c. I, II, and III
d. II only
e. III only

Questions 61 – 65 pertain to the following passage:

Henry James, Washington Square

During a portion of the first half of the present century, and more particularly during the latter part of it, there flourished and practised in the city of New York a physician who enjoyed perhaps an exceptional share of the consideration which, in the United States, has always been bestowed upon distinguished members of the medical profession. This profession in America has constantly been held in honour, and more successfully than elsewhere has put forward a claim to the epithet of "liberal." In a country in which, to play a social part, you must either earn your income or make believe that you earn it, the healing art has appeared in a high degree to combine two recognised sources of credit. It belongs to the realm of the practical, which in the United States is a great recommendation; and it is touched by the light of science--a merit appreciated in a community in which the love of knowledge has not always been accompanied by leisure and opportunity. It was an element in Dr. Sloper's reputation that his learning and his skill were very evenly balanced; he was what you might call a scholarly doctor, and yet there was nothing abstract in his remedies--he always ordered you to take something. Though he was felt to be extremely thorough, he was not uncomfortably theoretic, and if he sometimes explained matters rather more minutely than might seem of use to the patient, he never went so far (like some practitioners one has heard of) as to trust to the explanation alone, but always left behind him an inscrutable prescription. There were some doctors that left the prescription without offering any explanation at all; and he did not belong to that class either, which was, after all, the most vulgar. It will be seen that I am describing a clever man; and this is really the reason why Dr. Sloper had become a local celebrity. At the time at which we are chiefly concerned with him, he was some fifty years of age, and his popularity was at its height. He was very witty, and he passed in the best society of New York for a man of the world--which, indeed, he was, in a very sufficient degree. I hasten to add, to anticipate possible misconception, that he was not the least of a charlatan. He was a thoroughly honest man--honest in a degree of which he had perhaps lacked the opportunity to give the complete measure; and, putting aside the great good-nature of the circle in which he practised, which was rather fond of boasting that it possessed the "brightest" doctor in the country, he daily justified his claim to the talents attributed to him by the popular voice. He was an observer, even a philosopher, and to be bright was so natural to him, and (as the popular voice said) came so easily, that he never aimed at mere effect, and had none of the little tricks and pretensions of second-rate reputations. It must be confessed that fortune had favoured him, and that he had found the path to prosperity very soft to his tread.

61. When does this scene most likely take place in the plot?
   a. The exposition
   b. The rising action
   c. The climax
   d. The falling action
   e. The denouement

62. Given the context of the passage, what is meant by the phrase "He was not the least of a charlatan"?

   I. He was not a magician
   II. He deceived his contemporaries
   III. He was honest

   a. I only
   b. II only
   c. III only
   d. I and II
   e. I and III

63. According to the narrator, for what reasons are doctors highly esteemed in the United States?

   I. They are wealthy, but they earn their wealth
   II. Medicine is a practical field
   III. Doctors are esteemed for their philanthropy

   a. I only
   b. II only
   c. III only
   d. I and II
   e. II and III

64. Based on this passage, what term best describes the narrator?
   a. Objective
   b. Unreliable
   c. Authoritative
   d. First person
   e. Second person

65. What literary device is employed in the line, "He had found the path to prosperity very soft to his tread"?

    a. Metaphor
    b. Simile
    c. Irony
    d. Personification
    e. Hyperbole

Questions 66 – 70 pertain to the following passage:

Matthew Arnold, "The Song of Empedocles"

And you, ye stars,
Who slowly begin to marshal,
As of old, in the fields of heaven,
Your distant, melancholy lines!
Have you, too, survived yourselves?
Are you, too, what I fear to become?
You, too, once lived;
You too moved joyfully
Among august companions,
In an older world, peopled by Gods,
In a mightier order,
The radiant, rejoicing, intelligent Sons of Heaven.
But now, ye kindle
Your lonely, cold-shining lights,
Unwilling lingerers
In the heavenly wilderness,
For a younger, ignoble world;
And renew, by necessity,
Night after night your courses,
In echoing, unneared silence,
Above a race you know not—
Uncaring and undelighted,
Without friend and without home;
Weary like us, though not
Weary with our weariness.

66. What poetic form does this poem use?

    a. Rhymed couplets
    b. Epic
    c. Free verse
    d. Ballad
    e. Sonnet

67. **The poet uses what poetic device when describing the stars as "joyful" or "weary"?**
    a. Personification
    b. Symbolism
    c. Metaphor
    d. Metonym
    e. Synecdoche

68. **Why are the stars weary?**
    I. They miss the older generations of humans who believed them to be gods
    II. They want to expire
    III. They tire of humans creating myths about them
    a. I only
    b. I and II
    c. I and III
    d. II only
    e. III only

69. **Judging from the context of the poem, who might Empedocles have been?**
    I. An ancient writer who wrote about the divinity of the cosmos
    II. A modern writer who spoke out against the pagan beliefs of the ancients
    III. A modern scientist
    a. I only
    b. II only
    c. III only
    d. I and II
    e. II and III

70. **Which of the following would be a plausible conclusion drawn from the poem?**
    I. Modern culture sees the stars through science instead of myth
    II. Modern culture has a poorer set of morals than the ancients
    III. Modern culture does not generally see religious significance in stars
    a. I only
    b. I only
    c. III only
    d. I and II
    e. I and III

Questions 71 – 75 pertain to the following passage:

John Keats, "The Human Seasons"

Four Seasons fill the measure of the year;
There are four seasons in the mind of man:—
He has his lusty Spring, when fancy clear
Takes in all beauty with an easy span:

He has his Summer, when luxuriously
Spring's honey'd cud of youthful thought he loves
To ruminate, and by such dreaming high
Is nearest unto heaven: quiet coves

His soul has in its Autumn, when his wings
He furleth close; contented so to look
On mists in idleness—to let fair things
Pass by unheeded as a threshold brook:

He has his Winter too of pale misfeature,
Or else he would forego his mortal nature.

71. This poem employs an extended metaphor comparing life to the four seasons. Such an extended metaphor is known as which of the following?

    a. Conceit
    b. Symbol
    c. Satire
    d. Apostrophe
    e. Ode

72. One interpretation of this poem is that beautiful things do not seem as important as they used to be. This thought best applies to which season as described in the poem?

    a. Spring
    b. Summer
    c. Autumn
    d. Winter
    e. All four seasons

73. What is the meter of this poem?

    a. Iambic pentameter
    b. Trochaic pentameter
    c. Dactylic tetrameter
    d. Anapestic tetrameter
    e. Iambic trimeter

74. Which statement best describes the main subject of the poem?

    a. The four seasons reflect mankind's fear of death
    b. The four seasons represent the happiness of old age
    c. The four seasons embody the inspiring power of beauty throughout life
    d. The four seasons symbolize reincarnation
    e. The four seasons mirror the stages of life

75. What form does this poem employ?

    a. Sonnet
    b. Villanelle
    c. Haiku
    d. Free verse
    e. Blank verse

Questions 76 – 80 pertain to the following passage:

Jack London, "To Build a Fire"

But all this—the mysterious, far-reaching hair-line trail, the absence of sun from the sky, the tremendous cold, and the strangeness and weirdness of it all—made no

110

impression on the man. It was not because he was long used to it. He was a newcomer in the land, a chechaquo, and this was his first winter. The trouble with him was that he was without imagination. He was quick and alert in the things of life, but only in the things, and not in the significances. Fifty degrees below zero meant eighty-odd degrees of frost. Such fact impressed him as being cold and uncomfortable, and that was all. It did not lead him to meditate upon his frailty as a creature of temperature, and upon man's frailty in general, able only to live within certain narrow limits of heat and cold; and from there on it did not lead him to the conjectural field of immortality and man's place in the universe. Fifty degrees below zero stood for a bite of frost that hurt and that must be guarded against by the use of mittens, ear-flaps, warm moccasins, and thick socks. Fifty degrees below zero was to him just precisely fifty degrees below zero. That there should be anything more to it than that was a thought that never entered his head.

. . . .

At the man's heels trotted a dog, a big native husky, the proper wolf-dog, gray-coated and without any visible or temperamental difference from its brother, the wild wolf. The animal was depressed by the tremendous cold. It knew that it was no time for travelling. Its instinct told it a truer tale than was told to the man by the man's judgment. In reality, it was not merely colder than fifty below zero; it was colder than sixty below, than seventy below. It was seventy-five below zero. Since the freezing-point is thirty-two above zero, it meant that one hundred and seven degrees of frost obtained. The dog did not know anything about thermometers. Possibly in its brain there was no sharp consciousness of a condition of very cold such as was in the man's brain. But the brute had its instinct. It experienced a vague but menacing apprehension that subdued it and made it slink along at the man's heels, and that made it question eagerly every unwonted movement of the man as if expecting him to go into camp or to seek shelter somewhere and build a fire. The dog had learned fire, and it wanted fire, or else to burrow under the snow and cuddle its warmth away from the air.

76. In the story this passage come from, the main character struggles against the cold and eventually freezes to death. Given this information, which of the following devices is the author using in the first paragraph?
   a. First person point of view
   b. Hyperbole
   c. Onomatopoeia
   d. Symbolism
   e. Foreshadowing

77. What is the point of view used in this passage?
   a. First person
   b. First person plural
   c. Unreliable narrator
   d. Third person omniscient
   e. Third person objective

78. Which statement best captures the author's meaning in the statement, "The trouble with him was that he was without imagination"?

    I. The man was not smart
    II. The man did not need imagination because he was rational
    III. The man did not have the foresight to realize that he was putting himself in danger

a. I only
b. II only
c. III only
d. I and II
e. II and III

79. In what sense should the passage be taken when it mentions immortality and man's place in the universe?

a. Humans are frail
b. Humans are stronger than nature
c. Humans will one day attain immortality
d. Humans are smarter than animals
e. Humans have no place in the universe

80. In what way does the narrator say the dog is better off than the man?

a. The dog is better equipped for the cold because of its fur.
b. The dog has a better conscious idea of what the cold means
c. The dog's instinct guides it, while the man's intellect fails him
d. The do understands mankind's place in the universe
e. The dog understands that the temperature is 50 degrees below zero

Answer Key and Explanations

1. B: The rhyme scheme of the first eight lines falls into the following pattern: ABABACDC. The rhyming words are, "land," "stone," "sand," "frown," "command," "read," "things," and "fed."

2. A: A collapsed statue in the desert. The image is explicitly described in lines 2 through 4: "Two vast and trunkless legs of stone / Stand in the desert. Near them on the sand, / Half sunk, a shattered visage lies." None of the other choices reflect the imagery of the poem.

3. D: Is the best interpretation of the ironic meaning of the inscription. Irony is used to describe statements or events with multiple levels of meaning. Specifically, it is defined as a statement in which the apparent meaning of the words contradicts the intended meaning. In this case, the poem describes a collapsed statue with an inscription that reads, "Look upon my works, ye mighty, and despair." The original intended meaning of the words was that one should look upon the majesty of Ozymandias's kingdom and despair because of his power. When read underneath a ruined statue, however, the words take on a different apparent meaning, namely that the reader should look at the kingdom and despair because of the destructive forces of time and nature.

4: E: The symbolic meaning of the desert is best read as a wasteland. A symbol is a specific image in a poem that brings to mind some idea or concept that relates back to the poem's themes. Choice (A), fertility, is not likely since a desert rarely calls fertility to mind. Choice (B), the life cycle, is likewise not commonly associated with the desert. Choice (C), the seasons, does not relate to the poem in any meaningful way. Choice (D), life, is so broad that it could be applied to any symbol and does not yield much insight into the themes of this particular poem. Choice (E), a wasteland, is a connotation (or associated meaning) of the desert that does relate back to the theme of the poem, which has to do with the destructive forces of time and the comparative powerlessness of humans.

5. B: An Egyptian Pharaoh, is the best answer because of the poem's setting among ruins in the desert. Choice (A), a Roman Emperor, may be suggested by collapsed statues, but not by the desert landscape. The desert landscape would not refer to choices (C), (D), or (E)—leaders of Native American, Chinese, or English cultures.

6. A: The poem has fourteen lines, which makes the poem a sonnet. Choice (B), ballad, refers to a type of poem with four-line stanzas and iambic meter. Choice (C), anaphora, is a way of creating emphasis by repeating words at the beginning of each line. Choice (D), prose poem, is a more recent form of poetry that does not have line breaks and resembles paragraphs of prose. Choice (E), sestina, refers to a poem with six-line stanzas in which each line ends with one of the same six words.

7. D: The question provides you with an interpretation of the poem. Your job is to identify any of the following statements that help support or prove that interpretation. Choice (D), interpretations I and III, is the best choice. Interpretation II suggests that the dying soldier was victorious in battle, but line nine, "as he defeated, dying" contradicts this reading. Interpretations I and II both reinforce the reading of the stanza as a scene from a battle.

8: C: A metaphor is an implied comparison between two things. In the first stanza, Dickinson creates an implicit comparison between success and nectar (the sweet fluid produced by plants); since she does not use "like" or "as," this type of comparison is called a metaphor, as opposed to a simile, which does. Choice (A), paradox, which means the poem contains contradictory ideas, may be true of the poem as a whole, but metaphor is the best choice for the specific lines three and four because of the implied comparison Dickinson draws between success and nectar. Choice (B), caesura, refers to a pause within the line, but these lines read without pause. Choice (D), dramatic monologue, is a poetic form written in first person in which the speaker is a character in the poem; however, the speaker of Dickinson's poem does not act as a character in the poem. Choice (E), anaphora, is a rhetorical device using repetition, and this poem does not rely heavily on repetition.

9. C: 3 beats per line, is the best answer. With the syllables stressed, the first stanza reads:

SucCESS is COUNted SWEEtest
By THOSE who NE'ER sucCEED.
To COMPreHEND a NECTar
ReQUIres SORest NEED.

Note that there are three stressed syllables per line. The poem varies this structure in the second stanza, adding a fourth stressed syllable in the first line, but for the most part, Dickinson's poem is written in iambic trimeter. "Iambic" refers to a pattern of syllables in which every other syllable is stressed. "Trimeter" means there are three beats per line.

10. A: Dickinson states the main argument of the poem in the first line and provides examples in the form of metaphors to develop that idea. Choice (B), cause and effect, is not the main logical organization of the poem, as this method usually involves isolating a main cause and explaining the effects that result from it. Choice (C), comparison and contrast, most often involves pointing out the similarities and differences between two things, which this poem does not do at length. Choice (D), chronological order, involves describing an event from its first to last moments. Dickinson's poem focuses on multiple events and does not tell which happened first or last. Choice (E), description, usually examines the details of a single item or event; this poem, however, does not provide a great deal of detail for detail's sake.

11. A: Interpretation I provides the best statement of the poem's main argument. The poem provides metaphors to develop the idea that the loser understands success better than the victor. Interpretation II, which claims that one should accept defeat humbly, is pertinent to the topic of failure and may very well be a logical extension of the poem, but it is not the main concern of the poem itself. Interpretation III, which states that it is best to learn from the mistakes of others, is not especially relevant to the poem and is not the best interpretation of its main argument.

12. A: The poem's rhyme scheme is choice, ABCB. The last words of each line in the first stanza are: "sweetest," "succeed," "nectar," and "need." Only the second and fourth of these words, "succeed" and "need," rhyme with each another.

13. A: "The philosopher only communicates general, abstract ideas," is the best answer. In the passage, the author argues that the philosopher's knowledge "standeth so upon the abstract and general that happy is that man who may understand him." In other words, the philosopher's language is difficult to understand because it is abstract. Choice (B) repeats a common criticism of early Greek philosophers, but it does not reflect the idea stated in this passage. Choice (C) reflects a concern of philosophy—whether knowledge exists that is not filtered through our senses—but it is not the concern of this passage. Choice (D) is, to some extent, correct. However, the question asks you to consider the author's primary criticism, which is better expressed in choice (A). Choice (E) is not implied by the passage.

14. C: The author's criticism of the historian is the inverse of his criticism of the philosopher, "The historian only deals with particular events, not general principles." Choice (B) is not in fitting with the concerns of this passage. Choice (C) is true of the author's criticism of the philosopher but not

114

that of the historian. Choice (D) does not reflect the author's point of view. Choice (E), again, is true of the philosopher but not of the historian.

15. B: The author praises poets for their ability to combine the best characteristics of the historian and the best of the philosopher. Choice (B), which says the poet uses "both abstract ideas and particular details," is the best choice. Choice (A) is something the author might say of the philosopher, but he does not make this statement of the poet. Choice (C) is in one sense true, but it is not the primary point the author makes about the poet. Choice (D) is reminiscent of arguments other philosophers have made about the importance of the poet, but it does not reflect this particular author's point of view. Choice (E) is not in keeping with the argument in this passage.

16. A: It states that the "poet can make the philosopher's wisdom appeal to the imagination of the reader." This statement provides the closest paraphrase of the final sentence from the passage, which states that, the philosopher's wisdom "lie[s] dark before the imaginative and judging power, if [it] be not illuminated or figured forth by the speaking picture of poesy." Choice (B) is not true of the passage; it states the opposite of the passage's main claim. Choice (C) is incorrect because it incorrectly interprets the author's meaning. Choice (D) also incorrectly interprets the author's meaning. Choice (E) contradicts the final statement in the passage.

17. B: The quotation marks that open and close the passage indicate that it is excerpted from dialogue. While choice (A), a novel, may be true, it does not answer the question, as the quotation marks in themselves would not indicate that the passage comes from a novel. Choice (C), the early 1900s, is also true, but likewise has nothing to do with quotation marks. Choice (D), the author's point of view, risks what some literary critics call the "intentional fallacy;" we can never truly know the author's point of view unless we have letters or other types of documentation. Choice (E), soliloquy, which is a type of speech given by a character in a play, is unlikely because the passage contains none of the other typography associated with a play--stage directions, for instance.

18. B: In grammatical terms, the pronoun "it" is singular, and the word it refers to would also have to be singular. This knowledge can help you rule out choices (C) and (E). In best grammatical practice, a singular pronoun should refer back to the nearest singular noun. Choices (A) and (D), then, could both be ruled out because they come before the phrase "mysterious stillness."

19. C: Personification is the best answer. The speaker is attributing human characteristics to an abstract idea. Specifically, the speaker says that the abstraction "stillness of life" looks upon him with "a vengeful aspect" (which means a resentful face). Choice (A), metaphor, is not the best choice because personification is a more precise answer than metaphor. Choice (B), allusion, means that the quotation refers to another work, which it does not. Choice (D), metonym, is not as precise as personification. Choice (E), symbolism, does not apply to this passage because "vengeful aspect" would not be best described as a symbolic image, which refers to an image that that reinforces the themes of the story through some implied meaning.

20. A: Is the best answer because the first sentence of the passage reads, "Going up that river." Choice (B) would be contradicted by the imagery of the passage, which describes the riverbank in close detail. No evidence from the passage can be found that supports choice (C). While choice (D), an ocean vessel, might be a tempting choice, it is unlikely that an ocean vessel would be used for river travel such as is described here. Choice (E) may also be tempting to students who recognize this passage as an excerpt from Joseph Conrad's Heart of Darkness and know that the novel begins on the Thames River, but the question asks about the setting of "the story the speaker is telling," the details of which do not suggest London at all.

21. A: Is the best answer because the only consistent underlying pattern of organization in this passage is association, or the process by which one idea triggers another. Choice (B) may be tempting, since the passage does refer to a main idea, but the passage is not organized by stating the main idea first and presenting supporting evidence. Answer (C), chronological order, is not the strongest choice because the passage seems to recount events and impressions from multiple occasions, and the reader is not told which came first and which after. Choice (D), cause and effect, most often isolates a single cause and looks at its effects one-by-one. This passage, however, does not evidence a pattern of cause and effect. Choice (E), comparison and contrast, looks at the similarities and differences of two things, but this passage does not do so.

22. C: The boy refers to Mrs. Brill as an "old thing." Choice (A) is incorrect because the context of the quotation makes it clear that the boy is speaking to the girl about the "old thing," so he cannot be referring to the girl. Choice (B), the band members, is also improbable. Choice (D) is incorrect because the baker is not present during the scene in the park. Choice (E) is incorrect because at no point is a cat mentioned.

23. A: Mrs. Brill felt connected to the other people on the benches. The narrator describes Mrs. Brill's thoughts, saying, "Yes, we understand, we understand, she thought—though what they understood she didn't know." From this description of Mrs. Brill's thoughts, the reader can sense her feeling of unity with the other people in the park. The other choices are incorrect because the narrator does not indicate any feelings of disorientation, frustration, hurt, or impatience at the beginning of the passage.

24. B: Though the narrator does not explicitly state Mrs. Brill's feelings, the most likely interpretation is choice (B). We can deduce that the boy's harsh words at the park must have hurt her. We know that she skips her usual stop at the baker's, she sits silently for a long time in her chair, and she thinks she hears the sound of something crying inside a box. Each of these details implies that she was hurt by the boy's comment. None of the other interpretations is supported by the passage; it gives no indication that she feels furious, nervous, cheerful, or short-tempered.

25. A: The narrator describes a band and benches, from which we can deduce that Mrs. Brill sits in a park. No evidence from the passage supports the remaining choices.

26. A: The passage refers to Mrs. Brill in the third person, yet the narrator has access to her thoughts. The narrator does not have access to the thoughts of any other characters, which makes third person limited omniscience the best choice for point of view. Choice (B), first person, is incorrect because Mrs. Brill does not narrate the passage from her own perspective, referring to herself as "I." Choice (C) is incorrect because "omniscient narrator" implies that the narrator can read the thoughts of all characters, yet this narrator can read only Mrs. Brill's thoughts. Choice (D) is incorrect because an objective narrator cannot penetrate the thoughts of any of the characters, but the narrator of this story has access to Mrs. Brill's thoughts. Choice (E), second person, is incorrect; if the passage were written in second person, it would refer to the characters as "you."

27. B: Is the best answer because "Death be not proud" is a fourteen-line poem with a strong sense of meter and rhyme, which are characteristics of a sonnet form. Choice (B), villanelle, is incorrect because a villanelle has stanzas with repeating lines at the end of each stanza. Choice (C), epic, is incorrect because an epic is a long work, commonly composed in rhymed heroic couplets. Choice (D), sestina, is incorrect because a sestina has six-line stanzas, and each one repeats the same six words, one at the end of each line. Choice (E), haiku, is not the best choice because it is a short poetic form with three lines and a fixed number of syllables.

28. A: Is the best answer because the poem speaks directly to death; see, for example, the final line: "death, thou shalt die." "Thou" is a pronoun of direct address, and it clearly refers to "death." None of the other answers can be supported with examples from the text.

29. C: Personification is the best answer because the poem talks to death as though it were a human being. Choice (A), litany, is incorrect because the term litany is most often used to refer to poems that resemble lists. Choice (B), metaphor, is not the best answer to the question. Though the poem does contain some implicit comparisons, the main literary device used is personification. Choice (D), internal rhyme, refers to words within a line that rhyme with each other, and the poem does not make extensive use of this technique. Choice (E), alliteration, is used when the poet repeats a consonant sound at the beginning of several words in a line; although the lines in this poem do contain some repeated sounds, choice (E) is not as precise a choice as (C).

30. B: Is the best answer because interpretations I and II both reflect the central idea of the poem. The speaker argues that we shall "wake eternally" from death, and therefore "death shall be no more." Interpretation III claims that death must be faced humbly, a reading that can be contradicted by lines such as "death, thou shalt die," which takes an aggressive stance toward death, the opposite of a humble stance.

31. A: The lines in question read, "From rest and sleep, which but thy pictures be, / Much pleasure, then from thee much more must flow." A paraphrase of these lines might read, "Much pleasure comes from rest and sleep, which are like milder versions of death; therefore, much more pleasure must come from death." While choice (B) sounds like a plausible interpretation, choice (A) better accounts for the reasoning of the poem.

32. A: The line reads "Much pleasure, then from thee much more must flow," and three of the last four words start with the letter "m." The term alliteration describes the repetition of sounds at the beginning of words; therefore, choice (A) is the best answer. Choice (B), internal rhyme, requires two or more words to rhyme within the line. Choice (C), symbolism, refers to a literary device that uses the connotations or associated meanings of an image to help establish the themes of the poem. There is nothing especially symbolic about the imagery in this line. Choice (D), enjambment, is a term used when the line break falls in the middle of a clause or phrase, using no end punctuation, but in this poem, the line break falls on a comma. Choice (E), hyperbole, refers to exaggeration or overstatement, which this line does not contain.

33. B: Because the central metaphor of "Huswifery" is a weaver working a loom, choice (B) is the best answer. Choice (A), a cart, cannot be supported by the poem. Choice (C), a blanket, may be a tempting choice because of the references to threading and weaving, but the first stanza makes it evident that the poem is referring to the parts of a loom. Choices (D) and (E), a grain mill and a windmill, might also be tempting because of their use of the word "mill," which appears in line ten, but no images from the poem suggest either of these metaphors.

34. D: Sewing garments is the best answer. The term itself, "huswifery," refers to the duties of a housewife, but the question asks for the connotation or associated meanings of the word. Choice (A), being a good husband, would contradict the title. Choice (B), being a good wife, is in keeping with the denotation or definition of the title, but the question asks for the best connotation. Choice (C), a wife's doing a husband's job, sounds plausible, but little evidence can be found in the poem to support this reading. Choice (E), breeding and raising livestock, is associated with a related term, "husbandry," but not the term in question.

35. E: Interpretation III best captures the meaning of the metaphor used in the final stanza. Interpretation I may offer a very literal reading of the stanza, but it does not capture the figurative or metaphorical reading. Interpretation II does not reflect the content of the final stanza.

36. A: Line 5 reads, "My conversation make to be Thy reel." A reel is part of the loom the speaker is using as a metaphor throughout the first stanza. Choice (A) is the best interpretation of this line. Choice (B) is inconsistent with the metaphor used in the passage, which refers to conversation, not silence. On a very literal level, choice (C) might work as an interpretation of the line, but the question asks you to interpret the metaphor used in the line. Likewise, choice (E) does not capture the metaphorical sense of line 5. Lastly, many lines in the poem could be presented to contradict choice (D).

37. A: Rearranged to pair the rhyming words together, the final words of the stanza read: "Will" and "fill," "Memory" and "glorify," and "ye" and "glory." Choice (A), masculine and slant rhyme, best reflects the types of rhyme used in this stanza. "Will" and "fill" are masculine rhymes, or rhymes that occur on the final stressed syllable of a line. "Memory" and "glorify" contain some similar vowel sounds, a type of rhyme known as "slant rhyme." Choice (B) is incorrect because the stanza does not contain consonant rhyme, which is a type of rhyme that is created when using words with the same consonants but not the same vowels, for instance, "pan" and "pin." Choice (C) is incorrect because the stanza does not contain identical rhyme (i.e., repeated words) or eye rhyme (i.e., words that look alike but do not sound alike, such as "weight" and "height"). Choice (D) is incorrect because the stanza does not seem to make deliberate use of internal rhyme. Choice (E) is incorrect because the poem does not contain either internal or eye rhyme.

38. C: The question asks you to base your answer on the diction used in the poem. Diction means "word choice." Choice (C) is the best answer. Choices (A) and (B) can be ruled out by the question, which reads, "Considering the diction of the original version of this poem, shown above." This statement would rule out translations, since they would not be the original version of the poem. Historically speaking, it would be impossible to find poems written in the English language from Rome in the 1st Century A.D. or from Greece during the 3rd Century B.C. Choice (D) is easy to eliminate because poems written during the 14th Century in Italy would most likely be written in Italian. This line of reasoning does not rule out choice (E), but it is much more likely that a poem written in the 19th Century would use the traditional diction in Taylor's poem than one written in present-day England.

39. E: Captures the rhetorical purpose of this passage, which is to explain the idea that beauty should be the main goal of poetry. Choice (A) is incorrect because the author does not explore any particular examples. Choice (B) is incorrect because the author does not so much illustrate as explain his reasoning. Choice (C) is incorrect because the passage does not compare and contrast different types of poetry. Lastly, choice (D) is incorrect because nowhere in the passage does the author attempt to disprove the arguments of others.

40. D: Interpretation II reflects the author's thesis that the chief function of poetry is to create something beautiful. The author would likely disagree with interpretation I on the grounds that a morally instructive poem must be beautiful to be good because its beauty is what makes it good, not its moral instruction. Likewise, interpretation III would be contradicted by the author's insistence that a poem must be beautiful above all else.

41. E: Interpretations I and III best capture the sense in which the quotation should be taken. The quotation is arguing that a poem is judged by more than just the presence of ethical actions (i.e., duty) and philosophical statements (i.e., truth); these things are useful in a poem only if they are secondary to its beauty. Interpretation II is misinterpreting or exaggerating the author's meaning.

42. A: "They" is a plural pronoun, and it should replace the nearest plural nouns, which are, "the incitements of Passion, or the precepts of Duty, or even the Lessons of Truth." Choice (B) is incorrect because the phrase "the general purposes of the work" comes after the pronoun "they." Choices (C), (D), and (E) are all singular nouns and should not be replaced by a plural pronoun.

43. A: The constant interruptions and bizarre logic of this passage create a general emotion of frustration and confusion, choice (A). Choices (B) and (C), joy and fear, do not seem to be suggested by the passage. Choices (C) and (D), confidence and certainty, are the opposite of the emotions invoked by the passage.

44. E: Dialogue is the best choice. Choice (A), monologue, refers to a scene in a play in which one character speaks at length. As this scene is from a novel and shows multiple characters speaking to one another, choice (A) is incorrect. Choice (B), stream of consciousness, is a technique an author uses to represent the free association of thoughts as they pass through a character's mind. This passage does not enter at length into any of the characters' thought processes. Choice (C), flashback, is used to describe scenes in a story during which the narrative goes back in time and describes events that take place prior to the main events of the story, but there is no evidence that the narrative is going back in time in this passage. Choice (D), stock characters, is incorrect because the term refers to an author's use of stereotypes or easily recognizable types of people whose characters do not need to be developed over the course of the story. The characters in this passage are entirely unique.

45. C: The characters attempt to disprove Alice's statements by drawing false analogies. In other words, the characters argue that Alice's statement is untrue because other similar statements are untrue; however, the statements they provide are not genuinely similar to Alice's, which makes their reasoning invalid. Choice (A) is incorrect because they do not offer facts so much as propositions. Choice (B) is incorrect because the other characters do not attempt to show that Alice has character flaws that make her unreliable. Choice (D) is incorrect because the characters do not try to disprove her by quoting an authority on the topic. Lastly, choice (E) is incorrect because the characters do not try to convince her that she should act as others act.

46. A: These fantastical characters include talking rabbits and mice, which clue us into the fact that this story fits best into the genre of fantasy. Choice (A) is the best choice. Choice (B) is unlikely because few of the stock characters from a mystery novel are present—the detective and the suspect, for instance. Choice (C) seems unlikely because of the fantastical characters and the highly stylized conversation. Choice (D), drama, can be ruled out because none of the typographical cues of a play are present, such as stage directions. Choice (E), poetry, is incorrect because the passage is much closer in appearance to prose.

47. D: None of the lines compare life to a long word with many syllables. Choice (A) is supported by the line, "Out, out, brief candle!" In this line, life is implicitly compared to a candle. Support for choice (B) can be found in the lines, "but a walking shadow, a poor player, / That struts and frets his hour upon the stage." Choice (C) can be seen in the line "It is a tale / Told by an idiot." Choice (E) is visible in the first two lines of this excerpt: "To-morrow, and to-morrow, and to-morrow, / Creeps in this petty pace from day to day."

48. A: Despair, is in keeping with the tone of this passage. Choice (B), resolve, which generally indicates unwavering commitment to a course of action, is at odds with this passage, which is full of

119

metaphors that show how brief and insignificant life is. Though choice (C), fury, is a word that appears in line 9 of this excerpt, the general tone does not seem to be one of fury so much as despair. Virtually nothing in the passage can support choice (D), humor, given its bleak assessment of life. Choice (E), inspiration, also seems at odds with the passage's grim outlook.

49. B: Only choice (B) can be supported by the passage. No mention is made of learning life's hardest lessons young, choice (A). Choice (C) is directly contradicted by the line, "Out, out, brief candle!" No direct reference is made to the role of character in the poem, so choice (D) does not seem likely. Choice (E) is inconsistent with the passage's tone of despair and futility.

50. D: Allusion is the best choice, as it means an implicit reference to an earlier work, the Bible. Choice (A), paradox, is a term used to discuss assertions that seem to contradict themselves, but little evidence of deliberate self-contradiction is to be found in this short quotation. Choice (B), imagery, is definitely evident in the passage, but the question refers to the use of allusion in the line, making (D) the better choice. Likewise, choice (C), alliteration, is at work in the way the phrase repeats the same consonant sound at the beginning of each word, but the question does not ask about the sound of the line, only its reference to an earlier work. Choice (E), metonym, is a figure of speech that uses a part to represent the whole (e.g., calling a car a "set of wheels"), but the phrase "dusty death" does not use this figure of speech.

51. E: The best choice as the question describes a soliloquy, or a scene from a play delivered by one actor alone on the stage. Choice (A), internal monologue, is incorrect because it is a technique that cannot be used in theater; soliloquy is the main technique plays use to show the thoughts of an actor. Choice (B), dramatic monologue, refers to a poem written in the voice of one of the poem's characters, but the term is not usually used to describe plays. Choice (C), stream of consciousness, is a technique fiction writers employ to enter the thoughts and free-associations of a character, but again, it is not a common technique for a playwright. Choice (D), dialogue, is incorrect because a minimum of two people must be conversing with one another for the passage to be called dialogue.

52. D: Choice (D) best captures the sense in which the simile should be taken. The passage describes the way poetry can preserve the fleeting emotions of the poet, which Shelley implies are faint and impermanent. None of the other choices are logically consistent with the meaning of the passage.

53. D: Interpretations I and III best articulate the meaning of this passage. The author uses a metaphor that compares the self to an atom in the universe. In other words, the self is a small part of a much larger whole. Interpretation II is not in keeping with the meaning of the passage.

54. B: Interpretation II is the only statement that fits the meaning of the passage as a whole. The author argues that poetry preserves the powerful but temporary moments of inspiration that all people experience. Interpretation I is not implied by the passage, nor is interpretation III.

55. C: The final sentence of the passage reads, "Poetry redeems from decay the visitations of the divinity in man." The passage does not explicitly refer to philosophers, lunatics, musicians, or painters.

56. E: All three interpretations are supported by the passage. In the passage, Nora states, "I have to think things through for myself and come to understand them," which supports interpretation I. Interpretation II can be backed up by the quotation, "All I know is what Pastor Hansen said when I was confirmed. He told us religion was this, that, and the other thing." Evidence in support of interpretation III can be found in Nora's statement, "When I'm away from all this and on my own, I'll look into that subject too."

57. B: Nora exhibits much resolve and determination in this passage. Choice (B) is the best choice. Choice (A) is incorrect because any fear or doubt that she expresses is secondary to the great resolve she shows. Choice (C) is incorrect because she has suddenly grown independent. Choice (D) is incorrect because she does not show compassion for Helmer. Choice (E) may seem correct because she does state, "It's very confusing to me," but the question asks for the dominant emotion she shows, and any confusion she feels seems less important than her resolve to come to understand the world on her own terms.

58. B: From this passage, we can infer that Nora has been dependent on Helmer. Choice (A) is incorrect because no evidence in the passage suggests that he has been too emotionally dependent on her. Choice (C) is incorrect because it is unlikely she has been treated as an equal if she insists that he treat her as an equal now. Choices (D) and (E) are contradicted by the passage, which shows that she has felt dependent on him until this moment, but nowhere is it suggested that he has been overly dependent on her.

59. D: Choice (A) is incorrect because he appeals to her sense of duty when he says, "First and foremost, you're a wife and mother." Choice (B) is incorrect because Helmer asks Nora, "What about your religion?" Choice (C) is incorrect because he says, "I assume you have some moral sense. Or do you have none?" Choice (E) is incorrect because he accuses her of talking "like a child."

60. A: Only interpretation I is supported by the passage. Interpretations II and III are incorrect because she is leaving both Helmer and her children.

61. A: Exposition is the best choice. The narrator introduces the characters and establishes the setting in a way that would be unnecessary at any other point of the plot. None of the other choices is correct because by the time of the rising action, the climax, the falling action, and the denouement of a work of fiction, the main character is already well-established and, therefore, would not be introduced.

62. C: Interpretation III is the best choice. The question asks you to determine the meaning of the sentence based on its context, or the meaning of the other words in this sentence and those nearby. The sentence and the one that follows it read, "He was not the least of a charlatan. He was a thoroughly honest man." The context indicates that the word "honest" and the phrase "not the least of a charlatan" are saying the same thing. Interpretation I, he was not a magician, is true on a literal level, but the question asks you to base your answer on context, so interpretation I is incorrect. Interpretation II is easily contradicted by the context of the sentence.

63. D: Interpretations I and II are consistent with the statements the narrator makes at the beginning of the passage. The passage reads, "In a country in which, to play a social part, you must either earn your income or make believe that you earn it, the healing art has appeared in a high degree to combine two recognised sources of credit. It belongs to the realm of the practical, which in the United States is a great recommendation." The first sentence indicates that appearing to earn one's income is valued, and the last sentence states that practical jobs are esteemed in the US. Interpretation III is incorrect because nowhere in the passage is philanthropy mentioned.

64. C: Of these choices, the narrator would best be described as authoritative. Choice (A), objective, is generally used to describe a narrator that sticks to the facts and offers little commentary. Choice (B), unreliable, refers to a narrator who cannot be trusted to tell the truth. Readers familiar with Washington Square may be aware that the narrator is actually a character in the story who tells the story from his own point of view, but the question reads, "Based on this passage," so choice (D), first person, is incorrect because nowhere in this passage does the narrator refer to himself as "I."

121

Choice (E), second person, is incorrect because the narrator does not refer to the characters as "you."

65. A: Metaphor. The passage draws an implicit comparison between wealth and a "path" that is "soft to his tread." Choice (B) is incorrect because the author does not use an explicit comparison word such as "like" or "as." Choice (C), irony, is incorrect because it requires an incongruity between the expected and actual meaning of an event or statement, and this statement does not seem to operate on two contradictory levels the way an ironic statement would. Choice (D) is incorrect because the passage does not give human traits to the concept of prosperity. Choice (E), hyperbole, is incorrect because the statement does not involve significant exaggeration.

66. C: Free verse, because the poem does not rely on a repetitive rhyme scheme or meter. Choice (A) is incorrect because the poem does not consist of pairs of rhymed lines. Choice (B) is incorrect because an epic is a much longer work, often composed in rhymed couplets. Choice (D) is incorrect because the term "ballad" is used to describe a poem divided into four-line stanzas with an ABCB rhyme scheme. Choice (E) is incorrect because a sonnet is a fourteen-line poem.

67. A: Is the best answer because "joyful" and "weary" are human emotions that the poet attributes to the stars using a literary device known as personification. Choice (B) is incorrect because a symbol is usually a concrete image with associated meanings that connect to the themes of the poem, and the terms "joyful" and "weary" are not concrete images. Choice (C) is incorrect because a metaphor makes an implicit comparison. It is true that personification is a type of metaphor, but since you have the choice between the two, personification is the better answer. Choice (D) is incorrect because a metonym is a figure of speech in which one speaks of the part to refer to the whole—e.g., referring to the executive branch of the US government as the White House. Choice (E) is incorrect because synecdoche is a figure of speech very similar to a metonym, but the whole is used to refer to the part. For instance, one might use synecdoche to say, "The town elected a new mayor." The "town" itself did not do anything, only the voting citizens in the town did; the whole, "town," is used to replace the part, "voters."

68. A: Interpretation I is the best choice. The poem says that the stars used to be part of a "mightier order" during a time when they were considered to be the "intelligent Sons of Heaven." Now they are weary because they are "without friend and without home," meaning that humans no longer see stars in the same light because people have changed their view of the cosmos. Interpretation II is not explicitly stated in the poem. Interpretation III is contradicted by the poem.

69. A: Interpretation I is the best choice. Considering the context of the poem and considering the title that reads the "Song of Empedocles," Empedocles is most likely someone who wrote about the divinity of the cosmos. The title suggests that this poem would be in line with the thinking of Empedocles. Interpretation II is unlikely because the poem does not seem to praise people who are critical of the religious beliefs of the past. Interpretation III is unlikely because modern scientists are the ones who stripped the stars of their place in the "mightier order" of the heavens.

70. E: Interpretations I and III are the best choices. Interpretation I and III both capture the poet's argument that the stars have lost their mythological or religious significance. Interpretation II is not the best choice because the poem does not mention morals.

71. A: An extended metaphor is called a conceit. Though the seasonal imagery in the poem could reasonably be identified as symbolic, choice (B) is not as accurate as choice (A) because the question asks for a term that applies to an extended metaphor. Choice (C) is unlikely, as the poem does not use irony to make social commentary. Choice (D), apostrophe, is incorrect because an apostrophe is a poem that directly addresses another person or thing by name. Choice (E) is incorrect because an ode is a structured lyrical poem, but the question asks you what an extended metaphor is called. Furthermore, the poem would be better categorized as a sonnet because of its fourteen-line structure.

72. C: Autumn is the best choice because that stanza contains the line "to let fair things / Pass by unheeded," which means to let beautiful things go without paying much attention to them. Choices (A) and (B) are incorrect because spring and summer are both characterized in the poem as times to revel in the beautiful things the world offers. Choice (D) does not explicitly address the importance of beautiful things. Choice (E) is incorrect.

73. A: The poem is written in iambic pentameter. "Iambic" means that each line follows a pattern of unstressed and stressed syllables. "Pentameter" means there is a total of five stressed syllables per line. The stressed syllables are capitalized below:

> Spring's HONey'd CUD of YOUTHful THOUGHT he LOVES
> To RUMiNATE, and BY such DREAMing HIGH

Choice B, Trochaic pentameter is incorrect because in a "trochaic" meter, the first syllable is stressed, followed by an unstressed syllable, as in the following example: "THROUGH the FORest, THROUGH the UNderGROWTH." Trochaic meter is like iambic meter except backwards. Choice (C), dactylic hexameter, is incorrect because the term "dactyl" refers to a pattern of stresses in which a stressed syllable is followed by two unstressed syllables. "Hexameter" is a term used to describe a line with six feet. Choice (D) is incorrect because in an "anapestic" meter, the first two syllables are unstressed, followed by a stressed syllable. For instance, this Led Zeppelin lyric is written in an anapestic meter: "there's a LAdy whose SURE all that GLITters is GOLD / and she's BUYing a STAIRway to HEAVen. Choice (E), iambic trimeter, is incorrect because it refers to an iambic meter with three stressed syllables, such as in these lines from Theodore Roethke: "we ROMPED unTIL the PANS / slid FROM the KITchen SHELF."

74. E: Is the best answer because the poem uses the four seasons as a conceit to describe the different stages of life. Choice (A) is unlikely because fear of death is not a significant part of the first half of the poem. Choice (B) is incorrect because the poem does not explicitly mention the happiness of old age. Choice (C) is contradicted by the third stanza, which says that autumn is a time to "let fair things pass unheeded." Choice (D) is incorrect because the poem makes no mention of reincarnation.

75. A: Is the best choice because the poem has fourteen lines, making it a sonnet. Choice (B) is incorrect because a villanelle contains three-line stanzas with repeating lines. Choice (C) is incorrect because a haiku is a three-line poem with a fixed syllable count. Choice (D) is incorrect because free verse has no consistent rhythm or rhyme scheme. Choice (E) is incorrect because blank verse has a regular meter without a rhyme scheme.

76. E: Foreshadowing is the best choice. Choice (A), first person point of view, does not answer the question and is incorrect because the story is told from the third person point of view. Choice (B) is incorrect because "hyperbole" generally refers to unrealistic exaggeration, but the imagery in this passage is realistic, even if it does describe extreme conditions. Choice (C), onomatopoeia, is incorrect because the passage contains no words like "cluck" or "quack" that sound like what they describe. Choice (D), symbolism, does not adequately answer the question posed.

77. D: Is the best answer because the narrator can enter the consciousness of both the man and the dog, making it third person omniscient. Choices (A) and (B) can be ruled out because the narrator does not use the pronouns "I" or "we." Choice (C) does not seem likely because the passage gives us no reason to believe that the narrator's account of this information cannot be trusted. Choice (E), third person objective, is incorrect because an objective narrator has no access to the thoughts or impressions of the characters.

78. C: Only interpretation III fits with the meaning of the passage. The narrator's statement that the man lacked imagination means that he did not have the foresight to realize that he was risking his life. Interpretation I is incorrect because the passage reads, "He was quick and alert in the things of life." Interpretation II is incorrect because the passage contradicts this interpretation.

79. A: Offers the best interpretation. The passage refers to immortality and man's place in the universe; the man does not have the imagination to contemplate such issues, and he does not seem to realize the frailty of humans on the planet. Choices (B) and (C) contradict or misinterpret the meaning of the passage. Choice (D) is not really implied by the passage; in fact, the dog's instincts make it seem more intelligent than the man in a certain sense. Choice (E) also misinterprets the passage.

80. C: It can be supported by the following quotation: "[The dog's] instinct told it a truer tale than was told to the man by the man's judgment." Choice (A) may sound possible, but it does not really capture the narrator's main point of comparison. Choice (B) can be contradicted by the following quotation: "In its brain there was no sharp consciousness of a condition of very cold such as was in the man's brain." Choices (D) and (E) can also be contradicted by the preceding quotation.

How to Overcome Test Anxiety

Just the thought of taking a test is enough to make most people a little nervous. A test is an important event that can have a long-term impact on your future, so it's important to take it seriously and it's natural to feel anxious about performing well. But just because anxiety is normal, that doesn't mean that it's helpful in test taking, or that you should simply accept it as part of your life. Anxiety can have a variety of effects. These effects can be mild, like making you feel slightly nervous, or severe, like blocking your ability to focus or remember even a simple detail.

If you experience test anxiety—whether severe or mild—it's important to know how to beat it. To discover this, first you need to understand what causes test anxiety.

Causes of Test Anxiety

While we often think of anxiety as an uncontrollable emotional state, it can actually be caused by simple, practical things. One of the most common causes of test anxiety is that a person does not feel adequately prepared for their test. This feeling can be the result of many different issues such as poor study habits or lack of organization, but the most common culprit is time management. Starting to study too late, failing to organize your study time to cover all of the material, or being distracted while you study will mean that you're not well prepared for the test. This may lead to cramming the night before, which will cause you to be physically and mentally exhausted for the test. Poor time management also contributes to feelings of stress, fear, and hopelessness as you realize you are not well prepared but don't know what to do about it.

Other times, test anxiety is not related to your preparation for the test but comes from unresolved fear. This may be a past failure on a test, or poor performance on tests in general. It may come from comparing yourself to others who seem to be performing better or from the stress of living up to expectations. Anxiety may be driven by fears of the future—how failure on this test would affect your educational and career goals. These fears are often completely irrational, but they can still negatively impact your test performance.

Review Video: <u>3 Reasons You Have Test Anxiety</u>
Visit mometrix.com/academy and enter code: 428468

Elements of Test Anxiety

As mentioned earlier, test anxiety is considered to be an emotional state, but it has physical and mental components as well. Sometimes you may not even realize that you are suffering from test anxiety until you notice the physical symptoms. These can include trembling hands, rapid heartbeat, sweating, nausea, and tense muscles. Extreme anxiety may lead to fainting or vomiting. Obviously, any of these symptoms can have a negative impact on testing. It is important to recognize them as soon as they begin to occur so that you can address the problem before it damages your performance.

Review Video: 3 Ways to Tell You Have Test Anxiety
Visit mometrix.com/academy and enter code: 927847

The mental components of test anxiety include trouble focusing and inability to remember learned information. During a test, your mind is on high alert, which can help you recall information and stay focused for an extended period of time. However, anxiety interferes with your mind's natural processes, causing you to blank out, even on the questions you know well. The strain of testing during anxiety makes it difficult to stay focused, especially on a test that may take several hours. Extreme anxiety can take a huge mental toll, making it difficult not only to recall test information but even to understand the test questions or pull your thoughts together.

Review Video: How Test Anxiety Affects Memory
Visit mometrix.com/academy and enter code: 609003

Effects of Test Anxiety

Test anxiety is like a disease—if left untreated, it will get progressively worse. Anxiety leads to poor performance, and this reinforces the feelings of fear and failure, which in turn lead to poor performances on subsequent tests. It can grow from a mild nervousness to a crippling condition. If allowed to progress, test anxiety can have a big impact on your schooling, and consequently on your future.

Test anxiety can spread to other parts of your life. Anxiety on tests can become anxiety in any stressful situation, and blanking on a test can turn into panicking in a job situation. But fortunately, you don't have to let anxiety rule your testing and determine your grades. There are a number of relatively simple steps you can take to move past anxiety and function normally on a test and in the rest of life.

Review Video: How Test Anxiety Impacts Your Grades
Visit mometrix.com/academy and enter code: 939819

Physical Steps for Beating Test Anxiety

While test anxiety is a serious problem, the good news is that it can be overcome. It doesn't have to control your ability to think and remember information. While it may take time, you can begin taking steps today to beat anxiety.

Just as your first hint that you may be struggling with anxiety comes from the physical symptoms, the first step to treating it is also physical. Rest is crucial for having a clear, strong mind. If you are tired, it is much easier to give in to anxiety. But if you establish good sleep habits, your body and mind will be ready to perform optimally, without the strain of exhaustion. Additionally, sleeping well helps you to retain information better, so you're more likely to recall the answers when you see the test questions.

Getting good sleep means more than going to bed on time. It's important to allow your brain time to relax. Take study breaks from time to time so it doesn't get overworked, and don't study right before bed. Take time to rest your mind before trying to rest your body, or you may find it difficult to fall asleep.

Review Video: The Importance of Sleep for Your Brain
Visit mometrix.com/academy and enter code: 319338

Along with sleep, other aspects of physical health are important in preparing for a test. Good nutrition is vital for good brain function. Sugary foods and drinks may give a burst of energy but this burst is followed by a crash, both physically and emotionally. Instead, fuel your body with protein and vitamin-rich foods.

Also, drink plenty of water. Dehydration can lead to headaches and exhaustion, especially if your brain is already under stress from the rigors of the test. Particularly if your test is a long one, drink water during the breaks. And if possible, take an energy-boosting snack to eat between sections.

Review Video: How Diet Can Affect your Mood
Visit mometrix.com/academy and enter code: 624317

Along with sleep and diet, a third important part of physical health is exercise. Maintaining a steady workout schedule is helpful, but even taking 5-minute study breaks to walk can help get your blood pumping faster and clear your head. Exercise also releases endorphins, which contribute to a positive feeling and can help combat test anxiety.

When you nurture your physical health, you are also contributing to your mental health. If your body is healthy, your mind is much more likely to be healthy as well. So take time to rest, nourish your body with healthy food and water, and get moving as much as possible. Taking these physical steps will make you stronger and more able to take the mental steps necessary to overcome test anxiety.

Review Video: How to Stay Healthy and Prevent Test Anxiety
Visit mometrix.com/academy and enter code: 877894

Mental Steps for Beating Test Anxiety

Working on the mental side of test anxiety can be more challenging, but as with the physical side, there are clear steps you can take to overcome it. As mentioned earlier, test anxiety often stems from lack of preparation, so the obvious solution is to prepare for the test. Effective studying may be the most important weapon you have for beating test anxiety, but you can and should employ several other mental tools to combat fear.

First, boost your confidence by reminding yourself of past success—tests or projects that you aced. If you're putting as much effort into preparing for this test as you did for those, there's no reason you should expect to fail here. Work hard to prepare; then trust your preparation.

Second, surround yourself with encouraging people. It can be helpful to find a study group, but be sure that the people you're around will encourage a positive attitude. If you spend time with others who are anxious or cynical, this will only contribute to your own anxiety. Look for others who are motivated to study hard from a desire to succeed, not from a fear of failure.

Third, reward yourself. A test is physically and mentally tiring, even without anxiety, and it can be helpful to have something to look forward to. Plan an activity following the test, regardless of the outcome, such as going to a movie or getting ice cream.

When you are taking the test, if you find yourself beginning to feel anxious, remind yourself that you know the material. Visualize successfully completing the test. Then take a few deep, relaxing breaths and return to it. Work through the questions carefully but with confidence, knowing that you are capable of succeeding.

Developing a healthy mental approach to test taking will also aid in other areas of life. Test anxiety affects more than just the actual test—it can be damaging to your mental health and even contribute to depression. It's important to beat test anxiety before it becomes a problem for more than testing.

Review Video: Test Anxiety and Depression
Visit mometrix.com/academy and enter code: 904704

Study Strategy

Being prepared for the test is necessary to combat anxiety, but what does being prepared look like? You may study for hours on end and still not feel prepared. What you need is a strategy for test prep. The next few pages outline our recommended steps to help you plan out and conquer the challenge of preparation.

STEP 1: SCOPE OUT THE TEST

Learn everything you can about the format (multiple choice, essay, etc.) and what will be on the test. Gather any study materials, course outlines, or sample exams that may be available. Not only will this help you to prepare, but knowing what to expect can help to alleviate test anxiety.

STEP 2: MAP OUT THE MATERIAL

Look through the textbook or study guide and make note of how many chapters or sections it has. Then divide these over the time you have. For example, if a book has 15 chapters and you have five days to study, you need to cover three chapters each day. Even better, if you have the time, leave an extra day at the end for overall review after you have gone through the material in depth.

If time is limited, you may need to prioritize the material. Look through it and make note of which sections you think you already have a good grasp on, and which need review. While you are studying, skim quickly through the familiar sections and take more time on the challenging parts. Write out your plan so you don't get lost as you go. Having a written plan also helps you feel more in control of the study, so anxiety is less likely to arise from feeling overwhelmed at the amount to cover.

STEP 3: GATHER YOUR TOOLS

Decide what study method works best for you. Do you prefer to highlight in the book as you study and then go back over the highlighted portions? Or do you type out notes of the important information? Or is it helpful to make flashcards that you can carry with you? Assemble the pens, index cards, highlighters, post-it notes, and any other materials you may need so you won't be distracted by getting up to find things while you study.

If you're having a hard time retaining the information or organizing your notes, experiment with different methods. For example, try color-coding by subject with colored pens, highlighters, or post-it notes. If you learn better by hearing, try recording yourself reading your notes so you can listen while in the car, working out, or simply sitting at your desk. Ask a friend to quiz you from your flashcards, or try teaching someone the material to solidify it in your mind.

STEP 4: CREATE YOUR ENVIRONMENT

It's important to avoid distractions while you study. This includes both the obvious distractions like visitors and the subtle distractions like an uncomfortable chair (or a too-comfortable couch that makes you want to fall asleep). Set up the best study environment possible: good lighting and a comfortable work area. If background music helps you focus, you may want to turn it on, but otherwise keep the room quiet. If you are using a computer to take notes, be sure you don't have any other windows open, especially applications like social media, games, or anything else that could distract you. Silence your phone and turn off notifications. Be sure to keep water close by so you stay hydrated while you study (but avoid unhealthy drinks and snacks).

Also, take into account the best time of day to study. Are you freshest first thing in the morning? Try to set aside some time then to work through the material. Is your mind clearer in the afternoon or evening? Schedule your study session then. Another method is to study at the same time of day that you will take the test, so that your brain gets used to working on the material at that time and will be ready to focus at test time.

STEP 5: STUDY!

Once you have done all the study preparation, it's time to settle into the actual studying. Sit down, take a few moments to settle your mind so you can focus, and begin to follow your study plan. Don't give in to distractions or let yourself procrastinate. This is your time to prepare so you'll be ready to fearlessly approach the test. Make the most of the time and stay focused.

Of course, you don't want to burn out. If you study too long you may find that you're not retaining the information very well. Take regular study breaks. For example, taking five minutes out of every hour to walk briskly, breathing deeply and swinging your arms, can help your mind stay fresh.

As you get to the end of each chapter or section, it's a good idea to do a quick review. Remind yourself of what you learned and work on any difficult parts. When you feel that you've mastered the material, move on to the next part. At the end of your study session, briefly skim through your notes again.

But while review is helpful, cramming last minute is NOT. If at all possible, work ahead so that you won't need to fit all your study into the last day. Cramming overloads your brain with more information than it can process and retain, and your tired mind may struggle to recall even previously learned information when it is overwhelmed with last-minute study. Also, the urgent nature of cramming and the stress placed on your brain contribute to anxiety. You'll be more likely to go to the test feeling unprepared and having trouble thinking clearly.

So don't cram, and don't stay up late before the test, even just to review your notes at a leisurely pace. Your brain needs rest more than it needs to go over the information again. In fact, plan to finish your studies by noon or early afternoon the day before the test. Give your brain the rest of the day to relax or focus on other things, and get a good night's sleep. Then you will be fresh for the test and better able to recall what you've studied.

STEP 6: TAKE A PRACTICE TEST

Many courses offer sample tests, either online or in the study materials. This is an excellent resource to check whether you have mastered the material, as well as to prepare for the test format and environment.

Check the test format ahead of time: the number of questions, the type (multiple choice, free response, etc.), and the time limit. Then create a plan for working through them. For example, if you have 30 minutes to take a 60-question test, your limit is 30 seconds per question. Spend less time on the questions you know well so that you can take more time on the difficult ones.

If you have time to take several practice tests, take the first one open book, with no time limit. Work through the questions at your own pace and make sure you fully understand them. Gradually work up to taking a test under test conditions: sit at a desk with all study materials put away and set a timer. Pace yourself to make sure you finish the test with time to spare and go back to check your answers if you have time.

After each test, check your answers. On the questions you missed, be sure you understand why you missed them. Did you misread the question (tests can use tricky wording)? Did you forget the information? Or was it something you hadn't learned? Go back and study any shaky areas that the practice tests reveal.

Taking these tests not only helps with your grade, but also aids in combating test anxiety. If you're already used to the test conditions, you're less likely to worry about it, and working through tests until you're scoring well gives you a confidence boost. Go through the practice tests until you feel comfortable, and then you can go into the test knowing that you're ready for it.

Test Tips

On test day, you should be confident, knowing that you've prepared well and are ready to answer the questions. But aside from preparation, there are several test day strategies you can employ to maximize your performance.

First, as stated before, get a good night's sleep the night before the test (and for several nights before that, if possible). Go into the test with a fresh, alert mind rather than staying up late to study.

Try not to change too much about your normal routine on the day of the test. It's important to eat a nutritious breakfast, but if you normally don't eat breakfast at all, consider eating just a protein bar. If you're a coffee drinker, go ahead and have your normal coffee. Just make sure you time it so that the caffeine doesn't wear off right in the middle of your test. Avoid sugary beverages, and drink enough water to stay hydrated but not so much that you need a restroom break 10 minutes into the test. If your test isn't first thing in the morning, consider going for a walk or doing a light workout before the test to get your blood flowing.

Allow yourself enough time to get ready, and leave for the test with plenty of time to spare so you won't have the anxiety of scrambling to arrive in time. Another reason to be early is to select a good seat. It's helpful to sit away from doors and windows, which can be distracting. Find a good seat, get out your supplies, and settle your mind before the test begins.

When the test begins, start by going over the instructions carefully, even if you already know what to expect. Make sure you avoid any careless mistakes by following the directions.

Then begin working through the questions, pacing yourself as you've practiced. If you're not sure on an answer, don't spend too much time on it, and don't let it shake your confidence. Either skip it and come back later, or eliminate as many wrong answers as possible and guess among the remaining ones. Don't dwell on these questions as you continue—put them out of your mind and focus on what lies ahead.

Be sure to read all of the answer choices, even if you're sure the first one is the right answer. Sometimes you'll find a better one if you keep reading. But don't second-guess yourself if you do immediately know the answer. Your gut instinct is usually right. Don't let test anxiety rob you of the information you know.

If you have time at the end of the test (and if the test format allows), go back and review your answers. Be cautious about changing any, since your first instinct tends to be correct, but make sure you didn't misread any of the questions or accidentally mark the wrong answer choice. Look over any you skipped and make an educated guess.

At the end, leave the test feeling confident. You've done your best, so don't waste time worrying about your performance or wishing you could change anything. Instead, celebrate the successful

completion of this test. And finally, use this test to learn how to deal with anxiety even better next time.

Important Qualification

Not all anxiety is created equal. If your test anxiety is causing major issues in your life beyond the classroom or testing center, or if you are experiencing troubling physical symptoms related to your anxiety, it may be a sign of a serious physiological or psychological condition. If this sounds like your situation, we strongly encourage you to seek professional help.

Thank You

We at Mometrix would like to extend our heartfelt thanks to you, our friend and patron, for allowing us to play a part in your journey. It is a privilege to serve people from all walks of life who are unified in their commitment to building the best future they can for themselves.

The preparation you devote to these important testing milestones may be the most valuable educational opportunity you have for making a real difference in your life. We encourage you to put your heart into it—that feeling of succeeding, overcoming, and yes, conquering will be well worth the hours you've invested.

We want to hear your story, your struggles and your successes, and if you see any opportunities for us to improve our materials so we can help others even more effectively in the future, please share that with us as well. **The team at Mometrix would be absolutely thrilled to hear from you!** So please, send us an email (support@mometrix.com) and let's stay in touch.

> **If you'd like some additional help, check out these other resources we offer for your exam:**
> **http://MometrixFlashcards.com/CLEP**

Additional Bonus Material

Due to our efforts to try to keep this book to a manageable length, we've created a link that will give you access to all of your additional bonus material.

Please visit http://www.mometrix.com/bonus948/clepailit to access the information.